AMERICA'S NEW WORKING CLASS

KATHLEEN R. ARNOLD

AMERICA'S
NEW WORKING CLASS

RACE, GENDER, AND ETHNICITY
IN A BIOPOLITICAL AGE

THE PENNSYLVANIA STATE UNIVERSITY PRESS
UNIVERSITY PARK, PENNSYLVANIA

Library of Congress Cataloging-in Publication Data

Arnold, Kathleen R., 1966–
America's new working class : race, gender, and ethnicity in a biopolitical age /
Kathleen R. Arnold.
p.   cm.
Includes bibliographical references and index.
ISBN 978-0-271-03276-4 (cloth : alk. paper)
1. Working class—United States.
2. Unskilled labor—United States.
3. Working poor—United States.
4. Political culture—United States.
5. Social conflict—United States.
6. Globalization—Economic aspects—United States.
I. Title.
II. Title: Race, gender, and ethnicity in a biopolitical age.

HD8072.5.A757 2008
305.5'620973—dc22
2007019591

The Pennsylvania State University Press
is a member of the
Association of American University Presses.

It is the policy of
The Pennsylvania State University Press
to use acid-free paper. This book is printed on Natures Natural,
containing 50% post-consumer waste, and meets the
minimum requirements of American
National Standard for Information Sciences—
Permanence of Paper for Printed
Library Material, ANSI Z39.48–1992.

CONTENTS

FOR HANNAH WITH ALL MY LOVE

ACKNOWLEDGMENTS

First, I would like to acknowledge *Theory and Event* for allowing me to reprint a version of "Asceticism in Contemporary Political Theory: Marx, Weber, Nietzsche, and Beyond," *Theory and Event* 8, no. 2 (2005); and Polity for allowing me to reprint a version of "Domestic War: Locke's Concept of Prerogative and Implications for U.S. 'Wars' Today," *Polity*, January 2007.

It is difficult to thank everyone who has spoken to me about this book—from interlocutors at conferences to colleagues at my former and current universities, not to mention students who have challenged my ideas or passed on interesting articles to me—so please let this serve as a general acknowledgment of the wealth of opportunities I have had to have my work discussed and examined thoughtfully. In particular, I would like to thank Karen Zivi, with whom I exchanged ideas at the beginning of this project, as well as Thad Williamson, Christopher Sturr, Tommie Shelby, Joshua Dienstag, Karuna Mantena, and Verity Smith—all good friends from the Social Studies Program (or thereabouts) at Harvard. Verity Smith was an especially important reader, critic, and friend, and I thank her for her comments and time. Older friends such as Nick Xenos, Kimberly Sims, Kevin Cameron, Antonio Vazquez y Arroyo, and Eugene Sheppard were also great sounding boards for my initial ideas. In particular, Nick encouraged me a great deal in working on the chapters on asceticism and prerogative power.

More recently, I would like to thank Steven Amberg and Daniel Engster at the University of Texas, San Anonio, for extensive comments and conversations about these ideas. They not only helped me with my work but facilitated my integration into academic life in San Antonio. I am also grateful to audiences, discussants, and chairs at the American Political Theory conferences and the Western Political Science Association and American Political Science Association meetings.

Sandy Thatcher has been a wonderful editor with whom to work—his comments and suggestions were incredibly useful, and I thank him for his enthusiasm for this project. My anonymous reviewers were also constructive in the best possible ways. Finally, I would like to acknowledge the support of my parents and close friends. My sister, Michelle, has also been an incredible source of strength for me over the years—both as a fellow academic and as a friend. She has been an invaluable listener, regardless of the subject, and an irreplaceable part of my life. I am very luicky to have her as a sister. Last, Marcus Pepper has introduced me to a whole new life and perspective in Texas—the viewpoint of a small farmer, a contractor who works with immigrants, and someone who grew up on the border. I dedicate this book to our daughter Hannah.

INTRODUCTION: GLOBALIZATION,
PREROGATIVE POWER, AND THE NEW WORKING CLASS

In this book, explore the relationship of the state to global capital by looking at the new working class. In the early twenty-first century, the question of the survival of the nation-state has been central. In the literature on the globalization of the economy, it is often argued that the nation-state's authority is inevitably (and rightly) being challenged and undermined by multinational corporations and some transnational bodies.[1] The increased presence of foreign workers in many Western countries is viewed as challenging nation-states to create alternatives to citizenship—alternatives that end up looking very similar to traditional forms of citizenship but without the boundaries of the past, thus opening up a new era of "post-national citizenship."[2] As the United States, the United Kingdom, and Germany (among others) have all discovered, guest workers do not often leave a country; in staying they are disproving

---

1. Friedrich Hayek's work has been influential among neoliberals who assess the global economy in this way. Thomas Friedman's *The Lexus and the Olive Tree* is one of many examples of these sorts of arguments. See Chiaki Nishiyama and Kurt R. Leube, eds., *The Essence of Hayek* (Stanford: Hoover Institution Press, 1984); Friedman, *The Lexus and the Olive Tree* (New York: Anchor Books, 2000).

2. See, for example, Yasemin Soysal, *Limits of Citizenship: Migrants and Postnational Membership in Europe* (Chicago: University of Chicago Press, 1994).

the "sojourner theory"[3] and ostensibly undermining national sovereignty and border controls. According to this story, the globalization of the economy will follow its inner logic, leaving a minimal and substantively empty role for the nation-state (e.g., administering voting, organizing the military and police, and addressing the few needs that the market cannot satisfy). Capital and people will flow across borders freely, naturally distributing wealth and labor where needed. The disappearance of the boundaries and strictures of the nation-state, not to mention ethnic nationalism, is not only highly desirable but also inevitable. Put more simply, deregulation is said to equal freedom, and the traditional role of the nation-state, with its accompanying problems of ethnic nationalism, is a hindrance to this freedom.

Critics of the nation-state, who were most prominent in the 1990s, also believe that the nation-state is an obstacle to freedom, albeit democratic rather than economic freedom. Their texts, which focus on the illiberal aspects of the power of the nation-state and nationalism—aspects that not only curtail freedom but also uproot people more permanently than ever before—do not see the nation-state or nationalism disappearing any time soon. These criticisms thus seem increasingly irrelevant as we enter a more global world;[4] nonetheless, in response, many of these thinkers have begun to theorize a politics of cosmopolitanism.[5] In this view, the problems of the nation-state remain but are complicated by increasing economic globalization. Cosmopolitanism addresses the need for a corresponding political program to attend to the changes that economic globalization has brought. However, despite this adaptation, had it not been for the events of September 11, 2001, and the ensuing events

3. Edna Bonacich calls sojourners "fortune seeking," stating that "many groups, commonly called sojourners, migrate long distances to seek their fortune, with the ultimate intention of improving their position in their homeland." Bonacich, "A Theory of Ethnic Antagonism: The Split Labor Market," *American Sociological Review* 37 (1972): 551. See Alejandro Portes and Rubén Rumbaut's critique of this theory in *Immigrant America* (Berkeley and Los Angeles: University of California Press, 1996), 76.

4. Michael Hardt and Antonio Negri suggest as much in *Empire* (Cambridge, Mass.: Harvard University Press, 2000), part 2.

5. See David Held, "Democracy and Globalization," in *Re-imagining Political Community*, ed. Daniele Archibrugi, David Held, and Martin Köhler (Stanford: Stanford University Press, 1998); Bonnie Honig, *Democracy and the Foreigner* (Princeton: Princeton University Press, 2001); Pheng Cheah and Bruce Robbins, eds., *Cosmopolitics: Thinking and Feeling Beyond the Nation* (Minneapolis: University of Minnesota Press, 1998); Martha Nussbaum et al., *For Love of Country: Debating the Limits of Patriotism* (Boston: Beacon Press, 1996); Nicholas Xenos, "A Patria to Die For," paper presented at the annual meeting of the International Studies Association, Toronto, April 1997; and Verity Smith, "Shaking the State: Of Sovereigns, Subjects, and the Concept of Constitutionalism," Ph.D. diss. (in progress).

leading up to the Iraq War, the literature critiquing the nation-state and nationalism might have all but disappeared.[6]

In this book, I propose that the nation-state's power is indeed changing and that the nation-state (particularly the United States) is both fighting its own obsolescence and promoting economic globalization. Thus, while neoliberals would have us believe that economic and political deregulation is the most advantageous route for us all, allowing greater freedoms, they also paradoxically demand total faith in the state and its decision making in the war against terrorism (most recently in the Iraq bombardment and war of 2003), signaling an absence of freedom. This paradox suggests strongly that prerogative power—state action outside of the law, "that which marks the state as a state"[7]—is being strengthened while democratic power (discussed below) is on the decline. Hence, the case of the United States weakens the argument that the nation-state is disappearing; rather, it is democratic values and practices that appear to be more endangered now than ever before. This position is possible if the process of economic globalization is viewed not as a tendency to erase the boundaries of the nation-state but rather as a tendency to reconfigure and obscure the hegemony of more privileged nations over less privileged ones. The United States can be then viewed as strengthening its own position even with blurrier boundaries. Indeed, the globalization of the economy not only requires a stronger state but also allows for more intensive economic exploitation than in the past fifty years as well as greater disenfranchisement. In this way, sovereign power and the contingency of global capital are mutually reinforcing.[8] I will examine these ideas by exploring the changing workforce and nature of work in the United States in the present day.[9]

It is widely recognized that blue-collar work has changed in the United States, along with the workforce performing these jobs. As a result of

6. Alternatively, any study of nationalism would have been limited to ethnic conflict and thereby marginalized.

7. Wendy Brown, *States of Injury: Power and Freedom in Late Modernity* (Princeton: Princeton University Press, 1995), 176.

8. Regarding this relationship, see Sheldon Wolin, "Democracy and the Welfare State: The Political and Theoretical Connections Between Staatsräson and Wohlfahrsstaatsräson," in *The Presence of the Past: Essays on the State and the Constitution* (Baltimore: Johns Hopkins University Press, 1989); Leo Panitch, "The New Imperial State," *New Left Review* 2 (March–April 2000): 5–20.

9. Saskia Sassen's work has suggested these power dynamics; yet I believe that her political conclusions could be explored in more depth and that they recognize the exploitive nature of work. See Sassen, *Globalization and Its Discontents: Essays on the New Mobility of People and Money* (New York: New Press, 1998).

changes in the demand for labor in the United States, blue-collar work now largely means service work, agricultural work, and unskilled manufacturing. Significantly, this employment is more labor intensive (for example, handwork over using machinery in garment production; physical labor over use of machinery in agriculture) as well as more dangerous than in the recent past (as a result of deregulation, the proliferation of sweatshops and illegal factories, and the nature of some work, especially agricultural work).[10] Most of the individuals performing this work are not unionized and are subject to low-wage strategies that include temporary or contract jobs, no benefits, and irregular hours. In fact, the conditions that Marx described in the mid 1800s—disenfranchisement of workers, inability to unionize, subsistence-level wages without benefits, long hours, dangerous conditions—now exist because of deregulation, the globalization of the economy, *and* the regular exercise of prerogative power (the legitimate suspension of the law).

Marx's ideas have often been discredited in the United States because workers were eventually allowed to vote, unionize, and assert their civil rights and were gradually paid decent wages, with benefits and guaranteed job stability. Workers' political enfranchisement thus (theoretically) undermined the possibility of their economic exploitation. When Marx was writing, workers were politically disenfranchised, were forbidden to unionize, had few political rights, and were paid subsistence-level or even lower wages. Thus, economic exploitation was necessarily tied to political disenfranchisement as well as to political domination. Furthermore, workers toiled in dangerous conditions that often led to their physical deterioration. The conditions that Marx described, which were once viewed as obsolete, exist again today and are being legitimated and encouraged by the state.

This connection between the state and global capital seems counterintuitive in an increasingly deregulated economy. The dismantling of the welfare state and transition to workfare, the elimination of affirmative

---

10. Alvaro Bedoya states that the United States has the most labor-intensive agricultural sector of any Western nation; Bedoya, "Captive Labor," *Dollars and Sense* 249 (September–October 2003): 30–34. See also Sassen's arguments regarding the development of new industries as traditional manufacturing slowly disappears; Sassen, *Globalization and Its Discontents*. See, as well, Human Rights Watch, "Migrant Domestic Workers Face Abuse in the U.S.," http://hrw.org/English/docs/2001/06/14/usdom176_txt.htm; "Human Rights Watch Welcomes U.S. Government Meat and Poultry Study," http://hrw.org/English/docs/2005/02/03/usdom10117_txt.htm; "Abusive Child Labor Found in U.S. Agriculture," http://hrw.org/English/docs/2000/06/20/usdom580_txt.thm; and National Catholic Rural Life Conference, "U.S. Agricultural Workers," http://www.ncrlc.com/AgriculturalWorkers.html.

action in hiring,[11] and the promotion of worker flexibility (meaning that jobs are nonunion, temporary, without benefits, and so on) are all examples of what would appear to be the state's yielding power to the economy. Mobility of capital, increasingly deregulated workspaces, and the promotion of low-wage strategies (which, the argument goes, provide for full employment and reduce welfare expenditures) are also examples of what appears to be the growing absence—or even impotence—of the state. In one sense, this absence is real: working conditions are now more "casual" or informal, variously involving temporary contracts, long hours, casual factories, and industrial homework.[12] Market-driven decisions ostensibly preclude the state's presence. But in another sense, the state has merely been playing a different role—and an increasingly economic one—since the end of the Cold War.[13] As Saskia Sassen argues, the state is still indispensable for guaranteeing contracts, providing military support, and protecting capital investments.[14] It is also an active agent in choosing low-wage strategies, promoting worker flexibility (and the corresponding decline of unions), and ensuring that there is a supply of low-wage workers. I will be analyzing these last elements in terms of prerogative power as it has manifested itself significantly in the suspension of law in U.S. wars on terror, drugs, and narco-terrorism. That is, the individuals being targeted in these wars are significant elements of a new, more flexible labor pool. Exploitation, I will argue, cannot be simply economic; it necessarily involves asymmetries of political power such that workers are treated as less than citizens.

Nevertheless, the relation between the state and global capital is obscured in several ways, as is the possibility of exploitation (both political and economic). First, as mentioned above, it would seem that if workers are politically enfranchised, then they cannot be exploited on the job. If they are full citizens in a democratic country—so goes the reasoning—then they have voluntarily chosen their workplace, wages, and conditions. Furthermore, even as changes are made in the global economy that affect us all—such as the loss of health insurance and the growth of temporary

---

11. Regarding affirmative action, see Jacqueline Jones, *American Work: Four Centuries of Black and White Labor* (New York: W. W. Norton, 1998).

12. Granted that each state in the United States has different employment policies, as Steven Amberg argues in his work. Nevertheless, I believe that while neoliberal policies are neither absolute nor all-pervasive, they are certainly predominant today and worth exploring for that reason.

13. See Cheryl Shanks, *Immigration and Politics of American Sovereignty, 1890–1990* (Ann Arbor: University of Michigan Press, 2001).

14. See Sassen, *Globalization and Its Discontents*.

or contract work—it appears that these changes are part of a collective decision to adopt low-wage strategies, thus ensuring full employment. Consequently, the argument goes, the United States is more fiscally responsible in adopting low-wage policies and in calling for more worker flexibility in comparison to the European welfare states with their high rates of unemployment.[15]

However, the groups that are most affected by the dismantling of the American welfare state, the promotion of workfare, and low-wage policies are the most disenfranchised groups. For various reasons the new working class is largely disenfranchised, be it historically (women, African Americans, poorer immigrants of color), de facto (the very poor and homeless), or because those who are affected are unauthorized immigrants, for example. In other words, the changing demographics of the workforce constitute a group's transformation from one that has historically been enfranchised to one that has been historically disenfranchised or has never been enfranchised (for example, immigrants). In this situation, partial or total disenfranchisement and economic exploitation become mutually reinforcing. Furthermore, the old "labor aristocracy" has suffered unemployment, lower wages, lower skilled jobs, and increased relative powerlessness. This "old" working class is also increasingly being affected by the loss of a social safety net and by a less stable job market. Although I focus much more on the new working class than on the increasingly disenfranchised "old" working class, the shifting power dynamics apply to all, albeit in different ways. In the context of low-wage strategies and demands for worker flexibility, one group has chosen the austerity plan and another group is suffering its effects.

Another obfuscating factor is the idea that the traditional working class has disappeared along with traditional manufacturing jobs. Forgotten is that the "old" working class has not disappeared—rather, it has shifted to service work, in which labor relations are more flexible. Furthermore, the new working class is not recognized as such because the feminization and racialization of labor on the one hand and the growing participation of poorer immigrants on the other are conventionally viewed as distinct processes. The media, academics, and policymakers treat welfare and workfare recipients, poor immigrants, and poor inner-city, American-born minorities as radically different groups. These same groups are

15. See William Julius Wilson, *When Work Disappears* (New York: Vintage Books, 1997), 149–60; Joseph M. Schwartz, "Democracy Against the Free Market: The Enron Crisis and the Politics of Global Deregulation," *Connecticut Law Review* 35, no. 3 (April 7, 2003): 1111, 1114, 1118, 1121, 1122.

also often viewed as marginal, criminal, or irrational and parasitical and thus the *opposite* of the paradigm of the working class in, say, the 1950s and 1960s. Welfare mothers are treated as parasitical on the state, inner-city residents are often labeled the "underclass"—thus excluding any recognition that they work—and immigrants are viewed contradictorily as stealing jobs, as embodying the Protestant ethic, and as leeching off of the welfare state. All of these groups are perceived as posing problems, but separate ones. Yet at the same time, these groups are often blamed for creating poor work conditions, depressing wages, *and* exploiting the welfare system.

For example, part of the blame for these changes in the conditions and availability of jobs has been placed on immigrants and policymakers; both are accused of encouraging more relaxed employment laws for foreigners and guest workers. Clearly, immigrant labor in the United States is viewed as conceptually different from American-born labor. For immigrant workers the ongoing debate about their presence and the rhetoric of parasitism (for example, immigrants not only take our jobs and welfare but also send all their earnings back to their native countries) together block any real recognition of exploitative work conditions and wages in the mainstream press and political rhetoric. When exploitation is recognized—as in the case of illegal Thai workers locked up in a makeshift factory[16]—it is presented as anomalous and shocking.

At the same time, for American-born workers, the disappearance of a significant number of skilled manufacturing jobs, the shift from formal work conditions to more informal and deregulated ones, declining union membership, lower wages, the loss of benefits, and the increase in contract or temporary work all serve to mask any exploitation "on the job." Both images of American-born workers represent a signal change in low-tier work: it is no longer secure, stable, or mainstream. For this reason, exploitation does not appear to be possible; rather, it seems that low-tier jobs are disappearing. Similarly, the feminization of labor hides the fact that work itself has changed; rather, it seems that women are taking jobs away from men and that gender relations have been altered rather than labor relations.

Furthermore, the emphasis on workfare illuminates the relationship between welfare recipients, poor workers, and immigrant workers. This is why, instead of conceptually separating immigrant workers from

---

16. See George White, "Workers Held in Near-Slavery, Officials Say," *Los Angeles Times*, August 3, 1995, 1. There are, of course, numerous cases of late modern enslavement.

American-born workers who would fill the same jobs, or the working poor from welfare recipients, I will be arguing that these groups have much in common that these conventional distinctions do not account for. Indeed, the distinction between receiving welfare and working a low-skilled or unskilled job in the inner city can only be arbitrary; the fact is that many individuals pass from one to the other depending on their resources, transportation, and job opportunities as well as the state of the economy. To ignore the linkages between and disciplinary effects on *all* low-tier workers—whether those workers are new immigrants or part of the old labor aristocracy—is also problematic. However, these distinctions do serve an ideological purpose; in each case, exploitation (political and economic) is hidden behind seemingly moral—and, I will discuss below, ascetic—arguments.

When these groups are analyzed together, a different perspective emerges. The working poor often share the same neighborhoods, but they overlap in various other ways as well, including these: they intermarry; they pass from welfare to low-paid jobs and back again; and they are closely related in their integration into the workforce. An influx of relatively poor immigrants beginning in the 1960s allowed for the feminization of labor and at the same time generated an exploitable class of workers. Meanwhile, civil rights legislation facilitated the increased entry of African Americans into the workforce beginning in the 1970s, and this has led to the feminization of African American labor as well as to racial prejudice and more sporadic employment for poorer African American men.[17] Additionally, the decline in manufacturing has decreased the power of the old working class and increasingly made it part of the flexible labor force. Significantly, all of the above groups are now competing for the same types of jobs with similar conditions. Nonetheless, these groups have come to be conceptually separated, and this has allowed political and economic exploitation to remain hidden behind the stereotypes attached to each group. When groups are viewed as discrete units in this way, economic processes can be depoliticized. More disturbingly, workers often internalize these distinctions, turning on one another instead of challenging employers, neoliberal policies and policymakers as well as the old, damaging divisions between skilled and unskilled, productive and reproductive, legal and illegal.

Indeed, these divisions illuminate racial and gender bias and exploitation. First, the immigrants who are most often exploited are women and

17. See Jones, *American Work*.

of color. Second, the same is true for American-born workers, who are subject to racial comparisons. This pits the "groups" against one another, setting off what Edna Bonacich has referred to as the split-market theory of ethnic antagonism, which also applies to gender and prison labor.[18] A split market serves to conceal economic exploitation so that it appears as problems of lax immigration laws, racial conflict, or the breakdown of gender relations among certain groups. Examples include the perception that inner-city turmoil is the inevitable tribal conflict between racial groups; the association of single motherhood with African American pathology, which results in their being blamed for the dissolution of the nuclear family; the "natural" inclination of poor whites to express racial hatred; and comparisons between immigrants and African Americans that portray the former as hard workers and the latter as lacking a work ethic. Samuel Huntington's recent article about Mexican immigrants not assimilating, not having a work ethic, and generally not being loyal to the United States is further evidence of this antagonism.[19] The focus is persistently on differences among these groups, and it is often contended that these differences are inherent or biological.

When we apply Bonacich's notion of ethnic and gender antagonism to current conditions, we find that indeed, gender relations have been altered in African American and immigrant communities and that different low-wage groups often do view one another with hostility and suspicion.[20] Less obvious are the gender, ethnic, and racial antagonisms expressed by those policymakers and academics who makes these comparisons or who resort to stereotypes when formulating policies such as the dismantling of welfare and affirmative action. I contend that academic and political elites are antagonistic toward these racial groups and resentful of single mothers on welfare and that economic elites are hostile toward the poor. In fact, the greater participation of poorer immigrants in global forms of blue-collar work has facilitated the reemergence of biological racism and the promotion of a paradigm of femininity among poor women workers that has docility and submissiveness at its core. The elites' antagonism often goes unrecognized; yet at the same time, the various manifestations of antagonism among these groups are construed as social problems and in this way are depoliticized and removed from an economic context.

18. Bonacich, "A Theory of Ethnic Antagonism," 547–59.
19. Samuel Huntington, "The Hispanic Challenge," *Foreign Policy* (March–April 2004): 30–45, http://www.foreignpolicy.com.
20. See, for example, Wilson, *When Work Disappears.*

Clearly, then, labor exploitation is openly practiced, with consequences that make the "new working class" (semiskilled or unskilled labor made up of women, African Americans, immigrants, and the former labor aristocracy) politically vulnerable. They are underpaid, and furthermore, immigrants can be subject to deportation or placed in holding cells indefinitely. Poor American-born minority workers are also vulnerable: they must compete against immigrants for jobs that are neither well paid nor stable, and as a consequence they become increasingly disenfranchised.[21] Indeed, the political element of this relationship is crucial to any analysis of exploitation.

The economic exploitation of immigrants is not so very different from what is faced by American-born workers; so it is wrong to argue that a focus on the former must be at the expense of the latter or that the two groups are conceptually different. This exploitation does, however, demonstrate the complex interweaving of global processes, the corresponding increase in administrative functions and prerogative power, and exploitation in a capitalist economy. But at the same time, a crucial part of this argument rests on the relationship between the needs of a global economy and those of prerogative power; this is why I focus much more on minorities, women, and immigrants than on poor white workers, even though the broader dynamics of exploitation (and even racial hierarchies) affect all low-tier workers. That is, as many workers become disenfranchised (if they are not already), they are subject to prerogative power rather than democratic processes. On the one hand, deregulation and a more global economy mark the absence of government regulation in determining the work contract. Workplaces become more deregulated even while jobs in a global economy become physically more demanding. With the decrease in unionization, hours and job security become irregular and unstable. On the other hand, the government ensures that there is an available supply of low-wage workers through workfare programs, guest-worker policies, requirements for worker flexibility, and low-wage strategies. It is significant that the particular groups that make up the new working class are all groups that are policed more often than the average citizen: through immigration surveillance, racial profiling of poor neighborhoods, and the state's monitoring of welfare and workfare recipients. The United States' vague and endless "wars"—the War on Terror, the War on Drugs, the war on narco-terrorism—and the criminalization of

21. See Kathleen Arnold, *Homelessness, Citizenship, and Identity* (Albany: SUNY Press, 2004); Wilson, *When Work Disappears.*

the homeless[22] articulate with the control of poor workers on the job. It is a crucial point that the targets of these wars are not merely the victims of bad laws whose conditions could be ameliorated by reform. More and more, the individuals who make up the new working class are being conceptualized and treated as less–than human based on their historical treatment by liberal institutions. In this context, I will be examining how an ascetic belief system (that is, beliefs based on the Protestant work ethic) obscures and facilitates economic and political exploitation, making it possible to treat some individuals as biological or "bare life," in Giorgio Agamben's terms, rather than as citizens or possible citizens.[23]

The concept of bare life is an appropriate conceptual apparatus for this subject because it captures the dynamics of economic globalization, the increasing emphasis on material well-being in contemporary logic, and the status of those who are subject to prerogative power. By bare life, Agamben means biological life that is not abandoned by the state but that does serve as a negative identity against which citizenship is formulated. I will be using the citizenship–bare life distinction as a historically situated epistemological category rather than an ahistorical, ontological one.[24] The notion of bare life is an extension of Michel Foucault's concept of bio-power—that is, the increasing politicization of biological matters in the modern state. Bare life is a more appropriate term than "enemy" (alone) when analyzing the low-tier labor force, whose members are subject to harsh working conditions and are policed through the War on Drugs, the War on Terror, and the criminalization of poverty more generally. The term bare life, rather than enemy, captures the power dynamics of these "wars" that are waged domestically against individuals who have been criminalized as a result of their status rather than their conduct. However, Agamben believes that bare life is the link between democracy and sovereignty, whereas I will be suggesting that bare life—as he has

22. The criminalization of the homeless became worse across the board—state by state in the United States, and in other industrialized nations—in the 1990s, when the War on Drugs and the War on Terror (which, it must be remembered, began before September 11, 2001) were also in full swing.

23. Giorgio Agamben's most important elucidation of this concept is in *Homo Sacer: Sovereign Power and Bare Life,* trans. Daniel Heller-Roazen (Stanford: Stanford University Press, 1998).

24. See Antonio Vázquez-Arroyo, "Agamben, Derrida, and the Genres of Political Theory," *Theory and Event* 8, no. 1 (2005): 11; Andrew Norris, "The Exemplary Exception—Philosophical and Political Decisions in Giorgio Agamben's *Homo Sacer," Radical Philosophy* 142 (May–June 2003).

conceived of it—is more to be found in the linkage between liberalism and sovereignty.[25]

Moreover, Agamben's concept of bare life should be viewed falling on a continuum; for example, the political status of concentration camp internees is not equal to that of agricultural workers in the United States. The notion of bare life expresses the political status of the new working class, a group that is disenfranchised (de facto or de jure) and that is conceived of in biological rather than human terms—for example, in terms of race, ethnicity, and gender rather than as a citizen; or as subhuman in the case of the homeless. This concept also captures the power dynamic exercised on bare life: prerogative power. Agamben does not use this term; he does, however, state that sovereign power is most political when exercised through the suspension of law—and this is prerogative power. An individual who is bare life is subject to prerogative power whether that power is exercised positively (for example, through a presidential pardon or the benevolence of a welfare worker) or negatively (as with the detainees at Guantánamo Bay in 2005).

As stated above, this notion is developed as an extension of Foucault's theory of biopower, which can be defined succinctly as the growing concern of politics with biological matters.[26] As Foucault notes, modern power is characterized in part by its concern with biological existence; this is evidenced by the introduction of the census, population control, and matters of public health on the one side, and by genocide, state racism, and sexism[27] on the other.[28] To put it differently, the state cares about the biological well-being of the populace and institutes mechanisms of control to aid public health—that is, it concerns itself with promoting life—but it also treats certain groups as absolutely biological (and there-fore not human) and as threats to the citizenry. At this point it is not identity that matters but the reduction of a human to biological status; in other words, anyone can become bare life.

Agamben's notion of bare life is a radical extension of the concept of biopower for at least two reasons. *First*, Foucault conceived of state sovereignty as separate from disciplinary power and biopower, whereas Agamben suggests that sovereignty is deployed through these other two

---

25. See Agamben, *Homo Sacer*, 6, 9; *State of Exception*, trans. Kevin Attell (Chicago: University of Chicago Press, 2003), 5.

26. Michel Foucault, *The History of Sexuality, Volume I: An Introduction*, trans. Robert Hurley (New York: Vintage Books, 1980).

27. Foucault (ibid., 104) calls this the "hysterization of women's bodies."

28. Ibid., 134–44.

power dynamics.[29] While Agamben is right to worry about a unitary conception of power,[30] the examples discussed above are evidence that "placing biological life at the center of its calculations, the modern State therefore does nothing other than bring to light the secret tie uniting power and bare life."[31] Thus, power is certainly not total but does have totalizing tendencies that must be critically investigated. I, however, supplement Agamben's more unitary notion of sovereign power by drawing from Foucault's important contention that late modern power is dispersed, both legal and extralegal, and local. *Second*, while Foucault focused on the prison as an example of modern power, Agamben maintains that it is the concentration camp that is the most absolute biopolitical space. Bringing together Foucault's observations on biopower with Hannah Arendt's studies of totalitarianism,[32] Agamben connects absolute power with contemporary political forms by suggesting that Nazism was merely an extreme form of modern and (especially) late modern sovereignty rather than a historical curiosity or anomaly.

He explains that antecedent to modern power and liberalism, a separation was maintained between *oikos* (the household) and the political. The political was viewed as a transcendence of the biological and natural. *Oikos* represented subsistence living and animal need. As Aristotle states, "it is evident . . . that mastery and political [rule] are not the same thing. . . . Household management is monarchy . . . while political rule is over free and equal persons."[33] In Agamben's terms, bare life would be located in *oikos,* in contradistinction to the status of the citizen. Aristotle's conception of *oikos* was similar to Locke's (but not Hobbes's) notion of the State of Nature: familial relations with the father as head of the household, a subsistence economy, and mere living. However, one realm implied the other; that is, Western politics constituted itself through the exclusion of bare life.[34] If premodern politics founded the separation between man and animal (as in animal need), modern politics was established through the growing union of the two. In this way, bare life

29. See Agamben, *Homo Sacer,* 6.

30. Ibid., 6–7.

31. Ibid., 6.

32. Ibid., 3; see also Hannah Arendt, *The Origins of Totalitarianism* (New York: Harcourt Brace Jovanovich, 1979), chap. 9.

33. Aristotle, *The Politics,* trans. Carnes Lord (Chicago: University of Chicago Press, 1984), 43.

34. See both Pasquale Pasquino and Richard Tuck on the relation between the State of Nature and the constitution of political power in Locke: Pasquino, "Locke on King's Prerogative," *Political Theory* 26 (April 1998): 198–208; Tuck, *The Rights of War and Peace* (New York: Oxford University Press, 1999).

perhaps remained in the State of Nature (as liberal writers implied certain individuals did who were lacking rationality) but was not "natural" per se. Thus, modern politics does not signal a rupture from the past but rather the "the growing inclusion of man's natural life in the mechanisms and calculations of power."[35] To put it differently, bare life was the exception that has since become the rule.[36]

Bare life constitutes the political by means of exclusion; it is life abandoned by the law: "*Not simple natural life, but life exposed to death (bare life or sacred life) is the originary political element.*"[37] The sacred realm in premodern times represented a "zone of indistinction" between the political and the natural. Sacred man could be murdered but this act was not considered sacrifice or homicide:[38] "Life that cannot be sacrificed and yet may be killed is sacred life."[39] The significance of this, Agamben goes on to show, is that sovereign power has been conceived of in terms of bare life as abandonment or suspension of life itself. This is a highly ambivalent status: "The ban is the force of simultaneous attraction and repulsion that ties together the two poles of the sovereign exception: bare life and power, *homo sacer* and sovereign."[40]

For this reason, he argues that sovereign power now concerns itself with power over life. Instead of indicating that human dignity has been given meaning or that modern power is significantly more humane, this demonstrates "the absolute and inhuman character of sovereignty."[41] Political power is thus most fully realized "when it [that power] is permitted to kill without committing homicide and without celebrating a sacrifice, and sacred life—that is, life that may be killed but not sacrificed—is the life that has been captured in this sphere."[42] In premodern politics this significance was largely confined to specific figures such as a monarch, sacred individuals, or exiles; political power has since been reconfigured in such a way that bare life has become less the exception and more the rule.

The concept of bare life began to take on greater political significance as a result of two developments. *First,* the sacred body—the political body—shifted from the king to the people with the development of liberal

35. Agamben, *Homo Sacer,* 119.
36. Ibid., 9.
37. Ibid., 88, emphasis in original.
38. Ibid., 71, 72.
39. Ibid., 82.
40. Ibid., 110
41. Ibid., 101.
42. Ibid., 83.

democracies.[43] *Second*, capitalism as it developed began to demonstrate the power of political techniques (disciplinary power[44]) to create "bestialized" individuals (or "docile bodies"), who then became the working class;[45] meanwhile, the meaning of politics began to change, increasingly involving itself in biological matters, not only as an extension of scientific reason and techniques but also because sovereign power in preliberal and liberal thought included the zone of indistinction (the State of Nature), which made bare life possible both as a crucial element of political theory and as a justification for sovereign power.

Agamben's most significant example of bare life is the political status of Nazi concentration camp internees. By arguing that workers are treated as bare life in the United States, I am by no means equating their status with that of Holocaust victims; rather, I am suggesting that the power dynamics of the late modern nation-state, in combination with the demands of global capital, have brought about a situation where the law is used to suspend the law. The result is a realm of political undecidability.[46] At best, this places workers in a politically vulnerable position; at worst, it means they can be deported, imprisoned for crimes once considered misdemeanors, detained in holding cells without legal representation, or (in the case of the homeless) arrested for occupying public space. These conditions do not make them criminals with full legal rights and protections but rather stateless, even if this statelessness is more temporary than that of other groups. Clearly, there is a continuum between the status of enemy combatants at Guantánamo Bay and that of individuals imprisoned or detained through the War on Terror, the War on Drugs, and the criminalization of poverty.[47] In other words, these examples are not conceptually distinct but rather can be placed on a continuum. However, relative to the detainees at Guantánamo Bay, the political status of poor

43. See ibid., 122.

44. See Foucault, *Discipline and Punish*, trans. Alan Sheridan (New York: Vintage Books, 1979).

45. Agamben, *Homo Sacer*, 3.

46. See Agamben's discussion of the suspension of law in liberal democracies in *State of Exception*.

47. In making this argument, I am disagreeing with Arendt's distinction between the stateless and prisoners. Her contention is that the stateless do not have the "right to have rights" because their status is absolutely ambivalent, given the centrality of the nation-state in any human rights claims. Prisoners, in contrast, ironically do have rights by virtue of their internment by the juridical order. I would argue that the treatment of the poor and some minorities in police surveillance, searches, prison sentencing, and many other areas brings some prisoners (or potential prisoners) closer to the status of the stateless than to that of citizens. See Arendt, *The Origins of Totalitarianism*, 296.

workers is much more ambivalent, evidenced by various examples of resistance even when the law is de facto suspended. American ascetic values, developed from the Protestant work ethic, are the ideational justification for treating some individuals as bare life and for denigrating what is viewed as reproductive work (such as service, agricultural, domestic, and informal work). Indeed, service work and the other low-tier, "flexible" jobs of a more globalized labor market reinforce the splits between productive and reproductive work, males and females, citizens and less-than-citizens, and thereby obscure today's superexploitation of the lowest-tier jobs.[48]

Ascetic beliefs based on the Protestant ethic as analyzed by Max Weber have determined how we define work in the United States as well as who constitutes a working class. Today, the predominant types of low-tier work available in the United States are not considered blue-collar work by those ascetic standards. This is because service, low-skill, and agricultural work and the places where such work is performed (in the home, in casual factories or sweatshops, or in remote areas of the United States in the case of agricultural workers) are associated with subsistence economies and the private sphere. Accordingly, this work is devalued and those who perform it are not recognized as working class. At the same time, the groups who now fill these positions have been conceived of politically, economically, and historically primarily in terms of their identity (biopolitical status)—as blacks, women, poor whites ("white trash"), or immigrants (poor immigrants, of color)—rather than as workers. These identities, which are rooted in biological classifications, demonstrate the increasing importance of biopower in liberal democracies. Add to this cluster of groups those workers who were once unionized and employed in full-time, stable jobs; their transition to nonunion, flexible work conditions signifies their declining political status and increasing criminalization. Clearly, what the elites count as work is economically mainstream, officially recognized, and legally sanctioned. In a more global economy it is difficult to comprehend that employment and the working class have changed rather than disappeared. Nonetheless, it is important to acknowledge

48. By connecting bare life to exploitation, I do not wish to conflate the two. As Andrew Norris has pointed out, the Muselmänner in Agamben's account are engaged in useless work. Nevertheless, bringing forth Foucault's notion of disciplinary power as a supplement to Agamben's analysis, I believe that one can understand how superexploitation articulates with the treatment of the new working class as bare life. As Agamben states in relation to Foucault, "the development and triumph of capitalism would not have been possible, from this perspective, without the disciplinary control achieved by the new bio-power, which, through a series of appropriate technologies, so to speak, created the 'docile bodies' that it needed." *Homo Sacer*, 3.

these transitions if we are to better understand the economic and political position of these workers.[49]

Ascetic beliefs were intended for all as they developed in the United States. Thus they now constitute an organizing ethos of contemporary politics and the economy; they are not merely a private or individual ethos. Ascetic beliefs continue to inform how economic and political power are wielded, yet a double standard has evolved: hard work, long hours, and toil for low pay are really only expected of the poor. Meanwhile, the middle classes and the wealthy view their spending and investments as signs of election to grace by God. This double standard does more than mark a cultural divide; it also reveals how it is justified that certain groups are subjected to arbitrary power.[50] To put it in Marxist terms, the values of the Protestant ethic continue to be the ideological justification for the exploitation—both political and economic—of low-tier workers today.

Among other examples I will examine in this book, the fact that guest workers (and many other low-tier workers) cannot unionize, that immigrants are monitored by the Bureau of Citizenship and Immigration Services (BCIS), that inner-city workers are racially profiled, and, more generally, that there is less public space for the poor, are all symptoms of a systematic suspension of the law. Indeed, the calls for increased security resulting from the events of September 11, 2001, combined with the general instability that economic globalization has created for *all* workers, have strengthened the prerogative elements of the state even while devaluing democratic practices. This is why immigrant unions and community organization efforts are viewed as separatist and disloyal, why African Americans' efforts to protest poor working conditions are perceived as a sign of laziness,[51] and why dissent against the war on terrorism—internationally and domestically—is considered traitorous. The sharp increase in free-speech zones and exclusion zones over the past six years is evidence of decreased tolerance for dissent—

49. Hardt and Negri contend that the old distinctions among productive, reproductive, and unproductive labor have now disappeared. It is crucial to my own analysis that this is not true discursively and that it is precisely these distinctions (and the ascetic values based on the Protestant ethic) which have led to the devaluation of jobs—a devaluation that now holds sway in the low-tier job market. See Hardt and Negri's last chapter in *Empire*.

50. Similarly, the austerity of neoliberal policies is more of a reality for low-tier workers; trade subsidies, corporate bailouts, and other forms of protectionism are still predominant at the elite level.

51. On this point, see Wilson, *When Work Disappears;* Jones, *American Work*.

particularly left-wing dissent.[52] In this way the instability, insecurity, and anxiety generated by global terrorism and a globalized economy have fortified the arbitrary—prerogative—elements of the state. One contingency feeds the other.

In Chapter 1, I explore the history of certain key ascetic arguments in liberal thought and modern philosophy in order to deduce the role they have played not only as the "spirit of capitalism" (Weber's term) but also as the guiding ethos of modern politics, particularly in the United States. In interrogating the ostensible moral basis of asceticism, I suggest that Carl Schmitt's notion of "political theology"—the intermixing of ethical or religious, political, and economic concerns—is an apt term for modern ideational structures. In this way, ascetic values are not especially moral or humane but do, however, illuminate the divide between productive labor and subsistence economies, between civilization and barbarity, and between those who occupy civil society and those who occupy the State of Nature. These divisions are clearly political and economic. Furthermore, a double standard operates in such a way that one group is subject to the rule of law and the other has the power to suspend it. Weber, Marx, and Friedrich Nietzsche have all theorized on the origins and meaning of asceticism in modernity; by comparing their theories we can elucidate the complex mechanisms by which ascetic values are tied to the regular exercise of prerogative power domestically.

This argument challenges the conventional separation of welfare— and its related attributes or forms—and warfare.[53] This distinction is posited as one between a liberal, democratic state that functions according to the rule of law and a state that operates in the international realm, can declare war, and deals with foreign nationals. The divide between the two functions of a modern nation-state can be attributed to the idea that a liberal democracy can only be deemed so if it is free from arbitrary power. This reasoning, I contend, is faulty: liberal theorists never intended

---

52. See American Civil Liberties Union (ACLU), "Free Speech," http://www.aclu.org/FreeSpeech/FreeSpeech.cfm?ID=13699&c=86; Julie Hilden, "Constitutionality of Free Speech Zones," CNN, http://www.cnn.com/2004/LAW/08/04/hilden.freespeech; Jim Hightower, "Bush Zones Go National," *The Nation*, July 29, 2004, http://www.thenation.com/doc.mhtml?i=20040816&s=hightower. The ACLU has investigated these zones and found patterns of systematic discrimination, in that such zones punish the content of protesters' messages and cordon off left-wing or antigovernment protesters from other protesters.

53. On this distinction, see, for example, Mary Kaldor, "Reconceptualizing Organized Violence," in *Re-imagining Political Community*, ed. Daniele Archibugi, David Held, and Martin Köhler (Stanford: Stanford University Press, 1998); Carole Pateman, *The Disorder of Women* (Stanford: Stanford University Press, 1992); Wolin, "Democracy and the Welfare State."

to do away with prerogative power but rather the arbitrary power of a king. Prerogative power was conceived of in a liberal democracy, notably in Locke's writings, as being deployed legitimately in the domestic realm *if* it was for the common good and exercised rationally.[54] As discussed above, contemporary examples of prerogative include the increased surveillance of immigrants through the Patriot Act and the indefinite detention of prisoners at Guantánamo Bay. This argument also challenges the moral basis of welfare, workfare, and treatment of the poor more generally. Family caps, workfare, antiabortion legislation, the promotion of heterosexual, two-parent families, and the decreasing well-being of welfare and workfare recipients are evidence that what is at stake is not improving the lot of the poor but controlling and "re-engineering" them. I maintain that the ascetic beliefs applied through these policies constitute a mechanism of domination and are being used to justify coercion. Finally, I explore how ascetic values have an elective affinity with biological categories such as race and gender in such a way that vices and excess are associated with poor women, minorities, and immigrants. Poor men are also subject to ascetic judgments and policies and are often blamed for not fulfilling their predestined role as independent wage earners.[55] Ascetic values are thus tied to biopolitical considerations. Alternatively, consumer spending, stock-market speculation, and capital investments are all linked to civic duty and patriotism. In all of these manifestations, ascetic values provide a nexus between economic exploitation and the deployment of prerogative power even while obscuring these relations.

In Chapter 2, I critically examine this component of state power and how it relates to bureaucratic and administrative processes. The term prerogative power is not altogether familiar; and when it is used, it is usually lumped together with sovereign power. However, it is a very important application of sovereign power that, while it has been conceived of as anomalous when deployed domestically, is increasing in regularity and strength at that level. Liberal governance signifies the *rule* of law; prerogative power is the *suspension* of law.[56] The former is rational in the Weberian sense; the latter is arbitrary. Prerogative is exercised in times of emergency or during a war; alternatively, it is deployed when the laws

54. See Carl Friedrich, *Tradition and Authority* (New York: Praeger, 1972), on the relation between rationality and authority. Friedrich challenges the conventional separation of the two.

55. See Kurt Borchard's arguments that homeless men suffer the effects of the Protestant work ethic more than other groups; *The Word on the Street: Homeless Men in Las Vegas* (Reno: University of Nevada Press, 2005), introduction and chap. 1.

56. See Brown, *States of Injury*, 176.

are outdated or do not adequately account for a particular situation. The subject (in the philosophical sense) of liberal governance is a citizen or a citizen-subject, whereas the subject of prerogative power is "bare life" (Agamben's term) or an "enemy" (in Schmitt's formulation). The politicization of bare life is not altogether new, but in modernity it is no longer the exception; rather, it is the exception that has become the rule.[57]

In much of contemporary political theory analyzing the United States, the government is conceived of as being wholly liberal. As a consequence, capitalism is viewed as having an elective affinity with liberal values, yet there is no recognition of a closer relationship. Political theorists leave the analysis of foreign-policy decisions to those who study security or international relations; or alternatively, they analyze exercises of political sovereignty in liberal democratic terms (for example, the idea that the war in Vietnam should have been stopped because it was incongruous with democratic values). In this way, the study of sovereignty—more specifically, prerogative power—has been conceptualized as something entirely different from liberal or democratic power *or* as entirely the same as liberal power and values. When sovereignty is studied, it is often framed in terms of Machiavelli and Hobbes and is frequently used as either a critique of liberalism (as with Strauss, Schmitt, and others) or for the purposes of international relations theory. In fact, what needs to be asked is how prerogative power operates in liberal capitalist states (particularly the United States) and how and why it is deployed domestically and not just on foreign soil.[58] For this reason, John Locke's ideas on liberal democracy and prerogative are central to my investigations.

It is important to ask what democratic power can mean as the seeming opposite of this conceptual pair: prerogative power versus democratic power. Democratic power involves at least two crucial elements. Eschewing the binary between democracy as only agonism, protest politics, tension, and always outside institutions (hence, it must be "fugitive")[59] *and* the idea that democracy is always institutional and systematic, I argue that democratic actions and processes must retain elements of both. The first type of argument often tacitly assumes that there is an "outside" to power; the limitations of the second type have been described by authors since the 1800s. First, democratic power is strongest when secondary associations

---

57. See Walter Benjamin, "Critique of Violence," in *Reflections*, ed. Peter Demetz, trans. Edmund Jephcott (New York: Schocken, 1986), 277–300; Agamben, *Homo Sacer*, 55.

58. See Pasquino, "Locke on King's Prerogative."

59. Wolin's famous term.

are encouraged to exist and flourish, not just as social clubs or spheres of influence but as checks on governmental power. Nevertheless, these civic groups cannot be classified as democratic if their means or ends are undemocratic (as is the case with white supremacist and vigilante groups).[60] Furthermore, these secondary associations are most salubrious for a modern democracy when they remain contingent and temporary rather than embodying the *ressentiment* of a permanent minority. Dissent should be not only tolerated but also openly encouraged and respected. However, as Sheldon Wolin states, democracy "involves more than participation in political processes: it is a way of constituting power. Democracy is committed to the claim that experience with, and access to, power is essential to the development of the capacities of ordinary persons because power is crucial to human dignity and realization. Power is not merely something to be shared, but something to be used collaboratively in order to initiate, to invent, to bring about."[61] Nonetheless, against Wolin, this constitution can include institution building or actions within given institutions and processes—innovation arises from existent conditions rather than any mythical "outside." Given the dynamics I will be elaborating in this book, it is difficult to argue that truly democratic power is being deployed today in the United States except in isolated pockets. Democratic *conditions* certainly exist, but as de Tocqueville presciently remarked, the same conditions also make totalitarianism possible.

In Chapter 3, I review notions of economic exploitation that pertain to our particular historical context, linking this concept to the exercise of prerogative power and ascetic values and to the processes of economic globalization in the United States. First I explore why or how Marxist thought—in particular the idea of exploitation—has largely been pushed aside in academic and popular thought since the end of the Cold War. I maintain that as people declare that communism is dead, Marx's ideas now represent a "return of the repressed . . . not as false consciousness but alterity repressed by the metaphysics of presence in its specifically modern form: to wit, the metaphysics of subjective self-reflection," as Samuel Weber aptly states.[62] If Marxism is a specter that continues to haunt us, as Jacques Derrida claims in *Specters of Marx,* then the notion that capitalism and neoliberalism have replaced Marxism once and for all can be problematized: "The return of the ghost—the specter *as* revenant—

---

60. See Wolin, "What Revolutionary Action Means Today," in *Dimensions of Radical Democracy,* ed. Chantal Mouffe (New York: Verso, 1992), 240–52.

61. Wolin, "Democracy and the Welfare State," 154.

62. Samuel Weber, "Piecework," *Strategies* 9 (1994): 9–10.

describes the impossibility of neatly separating life from death, same from other, presence from absence, past from future."[63] The denial that exploitation is taking place involves more than a brokering of power or economic interest; it can also be explained by a temporal amnesia during which the past and future are overwhelmed by the present. In this way our ideational structures—namely, asceticism and neoliberalism—negate the validity of challenges to their foundations. Beyond these two rubrics, however, lies the notion of bare or biological life, which is at the root of ascetic ideas and allows issues of race, ethnicity, and gender to obscure economic exploitation.

Exploitation is also hard to discern due to the globalization of the economy and thus the temporary nature of jobs and the possibility that businesses will relocate overseas. That is, it seems that jobs are disappearing rather than exploitation occurring. To argue that exploitation is indeed happening, I begin with Tommie Shelby's "naturalistic" theory of exploitation and build on the power dynamics he suggests by referring to Foucault; at the same time, I historicize Shelby's theory. As Shelby remarks, what is crucial to understanding exploitation is not physical coercion or even involuntary participation in an exploitative activity. Rather, it is power differentials that determine whether a situation is potentially exploitative. For this reason, I investigate not only how subjects are economically exploited but also how they become the objects of prerogative power, and hence, how state interests are inextricably tied to economic interests—especially in times of neoliberal political domination. Exploitation at such times is both economic *and* political—for example, poorer groups serve as normative models against which citizenship is constructed.[64] In keeping with Marxist theories of racism and sexism, I also examine materialist bases for prejudice that are reinforced in academic work, the media, and popular culture.

In Chapter 4, I explore these changes in terms of race and gender, arguing that women and minority groups fit the dictates of biopower and thus give meaning and substance to who is treated as bare life (the subject of prerogative power). Departing from Agamben, I contend that racism, sexism, and ethnic hatred (among other things) are precisely ideo-

63. Ibid., 8.
64. One could also construe this difference as being that certain groups (the poor, women, racial minorities) represent the biological or animal on behalf of us all. This distinction is suggested by Agamben in *The Open*, trans. Kevin Attell (Stanford: Stanford University Press, 2004). I thank Verity Smith for this insight; Smith, private correspondence, June 12, 2004.

logical effects of biopower that must be examined in tandem with analyses of power and sovereignty. The political and economic conditions of these groups have important similarities and illuminate the growth of prerogative power and the effects of economic globalization. First, I trace the history of immigration to the United States beginning with the 1965 Immigration and Nationality Act, which has led to the greater participation of immigrants in the low-tier labor force. Second, I investigate the greater racialization of working-class jobs since the (relative) desegregation of the job market in the 1970s and the effect that economic globalization has had on poorer African Americans since the 1980s. Third, I look at the feminization of labor, which is tied to the first two processes. Backlashes against immigration, the increasing popularity of pseudoscientific racism against African Americans, and the paradigm of the ideal female worker (docile and politically and economically vulnerable) are connected in several ways. In the first place, each of these historical developments is inextricably linked to the others. The racialization of labor and the greater participation of immigrants in low-tier work allowed for a change in the workforce performing blue-collar work; at the same time, it facilitated the transformation to a more global economy. Meanwhile, the feminization of labor is a result of the increased presence of poorer, low-skilled immigrants and rising prejudice against African American males. To put it differently, each of these groups (albeit there is considerable overlap among them) is competing for the same types of work in a globalized economy; this only ensures that wages remain low and that processes of deregulation, worker "flexibility," and capital mobility can continue to develop unchallenged.

Rather than recognize the difficulties that poor workers face, the media as well as politicians and prominent academics have pointed to racial conflict (as with the Los Angeles Riots of 1992) and the decline of marriage in inner cities as occurring *naturally* (as a result of either tribalism or the inherent immorality of certain groups). These examples allow comparisons to be made between immigrant and American-born minority communities regarding patriotism, the work ethic, and commitments to family values. Often as well, they facilitate comparisons between male and female workers. Recent arguments that Mexican immigrants lack a work ethic and any loyalty to the United States[65] may appear to contradict the much more prevalent claims that immigrants are far better workers than African Americans,[66] but both sets of contentions issue

---

65. See Huntington, "The Hispanic Challenge."

from ethnic, gender, and class antagonisms—that is, the antagonism that European (that is, white) Americans feel toward all minorities, the tension between the poor and the middle-class and wealthy (exacerbated by the instability that economic globalization fuels at all levels), and resentments generated by the feminization of labor. All of these antagonisms are inverted in such a way that middle-class and elite observers lament the deterioration of family values in African American communities; yet the same observers ignore the fact that divorce rates and the incidence of single motherhood are high across the board.[67] At the same time, the Los Angeles Riots and other racial incidents are viewed as inevitable tribal conflicts among certain groups; yet the antagonism that is reflected in biological racism against African Americans and Latinos by Anglos is never exposed. Moreover, the economic reasons for ethnic or racial conflict and for marital decline among dominant groups are almost never investigated in any sustained fashion.[68] The constant discussions about which groups have better morals and work ethics mask the elites' antagonism toward these groups, as well as the economic conditions that foster tensions.

In this way, ascetic values obfuscate exploitation as well as the antagonism of political and economic elites toward the most oppressed and exploited groups. More disturbingly, these reactions to the poor (be they immigrant, African American, white males, or females of any group) are based on biological conceptions that place individuals below the level of citizen and consign them to subhumanity. This reflects a profound cultural division; furthermore, it brings to strong light the powerful consequences of these groups' political and economic status. It is in this chapter that I connect the deployment of prerogative power, justified and facilitated by ascetic ideas, to economic and political exploitation. A close examination of the recent history of these three groups shows how all of these are linked in ways that are not conventionally recognized.

66. This includes a range of sources. See Jim Naureckas, "Racism Resurgent: How Media Let *The Bell Curve*'s Pseudo-Science Define the Agenda on Race," http://www.fair.org/ extra/ 9501/bell.html; Joseph Barnes, "Book Review: *The End of Racism* by Dinesh D'Souza," *ZMagazine*, http://www.zmag.org/zmag/articles/dec95reviews.htm; Adam Miller, "Professors of Hate," *Rolling Stone* 693 (1994); Charles Lane, "The Tainted Sources of 'The Bell Curve,'" *New York Review of Books* 41, no. 20 (1994).

67. See Wilson, introduction to *When Work Disappears*; Frances Fox Piven, "Poorhouse Politics," *The Progressive* 59, no. 2 (1995): 22–24; Deborah Connolly, *Homeless Mothers: Face to Face with Women and Poverty* (Minneapolis: University of Minnesota Press, 2000).

68. Except, perhaps, by authors such as Francis Fukuyama, who invokes sexism, homophobia, and cultural racism to make his points about moral lapses of the majority.

In Chapter 5, I discuss possible ways to address the increasingly impersonal and diffuse processes and deployments of economic and political power. There are certainly examples of grassroots activity (ranging from the World Trade Organization protests to the unionization efforts of Justice for Janitors to recent mass protests on behalf of immigrants in the spring of 2006) that allow us to hope for a transformation of power structures, both economic and political. In fact this constant grassroots activity by workers (be they immigrants or American born), by immigrant groups such as MECHA, La Raza, and AIWA, and by protesters against the WTO and other global institutions is evidence that *apathy* is not the problem (never mind that mainstream political theorists seem to focus constantly on that issue in their citizenship studies). The problem, rather, is that these activities are being devalued, criminalized, or condemned instead of being seen for what they are—the agonistic activities that a vibrant democracy needs. This is why it matters so much how institutions respond to protests and grassroots organizations. Alternatively, Bonnie Honig argues that groups of individuals need to *take* power; they must not simply wait around for it to be granted.[69] The problem is that spaces of prerogative power are effectively stateless, which makes "taking" a risky proposition.. As Patchen Markell remarked recently, what may be at stake in this sort of situation is "the erosion of the contexts in which events call for responses and, thus, in which it makes sense to act at all."[70] For this reason, governance must do more than provide for democratic dissent, unionization, and other organizing activities; it must also reconfigure sovereignty so that it is more diffuse, democratic, and local, and so that it can serve as a check—rather than a partner—on the more destructive aspects of global capitalism.[71]

In response to the questions I pose in this book, I draw from Simone de Beauvoir's notion of mutual love, arguing that short-term commitments (such as guest-worker programs), exploitation, and de facto or de jure disenfranchisement will only ensure that democratic power (manifested as protests or unionizing) remains weak and ineffective. In contrast, authentic love—which is merely a theoretical construct for the purposes of my argument rather than a politicized emotion—holds the binaries of

---

69. Bonnie Honig, *Democracy and the Foreigner* (Princeton: Princeton University Press, 2001).

70. Patchen Markell, "The Rule of the People: Arendt, *Archê*, and Democracy," *American Political Science Review* 100, no. 1 (2006): 2.

71. See Smith, "Shaking the State: Of Sovereigns, Subjects, and the Concept of Constitutionalism," (Ph.D. diss., University of California, San Diego, in progress 2006), on whether and how sovereign power can be divided.

productive–reproductive work, citizen–non-citizen, and biological–human in healthy, dialectical tension, thus removing the hierarchy in each pair. Beauvoir's concept of authentic love remains true to the Heidegerrean framework on which Agamben relies and allows for a fuller elucidation of how the suspension of these binaries will open them to a more democratic potential.[72] Conceiving of democracy in terms of this existentialist perspective contests any unitary conception of sovereignty and necessarily demands responsibility and accountability in the use of prerogative power. Furthermore, it emphasizes that what has been taken to be exceptional, deviant, or anomalous in contemporary politics is in fact symptomatic of the problems of modern citizenship.

In sum, in this book I explore how prerogative power in the United States is deployed domestically and consistently (rather than as an exception); and how, given the changes that economic globalization has brought, this power has enabled the state to fight its own obsolescence while allowing for the disenfranchisement and greater exploitation of some workers. In this project, I examine how ascetic ideas in liberal and modern philosophy not only justify and function as catalysts for the deployment of prerogative power, but also serve to obscure its exercise domestically. The contemporary manifestation of ascetic values is neoliberal discourse and policies that allow for greater freedom and mobility of capital and enterprise. Supposedly, this results in a freer and more flexible workforce that is much less likely to be exploited politically and economically. But what in fact happens is the opposite: in this age of economic globalization, these different variables are working together to exploit the new working class politically and economically and are veiling state power in a capitalist ethos in which the ascetic spirit subsumes the political.

All of the arguments in this book owe a great intellectual debt to the work of Saskia Sassen, William Julius Wilson, Wendy Brown, Sheldon Wolin, Michel Foucault, and Giorgio Agamben. I hope to investigate not just the economic consequences of globalization but also the political, connecting the literature on nationalism and statelessness to materialist critiques of capitalism. And in the process, I will be exploring how the racialization and feminization of labor and the increased use of immigrant labor are crucial to these power dynamics.

---

72. On Agamben's notion of potentiality, see his *Potentialities*, ed. and trans. Daniel Heller-Roazen (Stanford: Stanford University Press, 1999). See also Brian Dillon, "Book Review: *Potentialities*," *SubStance* 30, nos. 1 and 2 (2001): 254–58; and Colin McQuillan, "The Political Life in Giorgio Agamben," *Kritkos* 2 (2005).

ASCETICISM, BIOPOWER, AND THE POOR

In this chapter, I investigate ascetic ideas in the United States as they are applied by neoliberals and "new Democrats" to welfare and workfare policies as well as low-wage policies.[1] These ideas are reflected, for example, in the Personal Responsibility and Work Opportunity Reconciliation Act, resultant workfare policies, and demands for worker flexibility in low-tier employment. This discourse became especially prevalent in the 1990s, in the form of arguments calling for welfare cutbacks, an end to affirmative action (in other words, the blame for inequality, unemployment, and perceptions of racism was shifted to the victimized groups),[2] and the backlash against immigration that led in 1996 to changes in immigration policy. Ascetic ideas are increasingly being emphasized in order to justify deregulation, worker flexibility, and the dismantling of the welfare state. In creating a "freer" market and ostensibly reducing government intervention in hiring practices, labor regulations, and work conditions, the government comes

1. For a closer examination of actual practices regarding welfare and workfare in relation to ascetic ideas and Foucault's theories, see Barbara Cruikshank, *The Will to Empower: Democratic Citizens and Other Subjects* (Ithaca: Cornell University Press, 2004); and Leonard Feldman, *Citizens Without Power: Homelessness, Democracy, and Exclusion* (Ithaca: Cornell University Press, 2002).

2. See Dinesh D'Souza, *The End of Racism; Principles for a Multiracial Society* (New York: Free Press, 1995); Richard Herrnstein and Charles Murray, *The Bell Curve: Intelligence and Class Structure in American Life* (New York: Free Press, 1994).

across as not only neutral but absent. In such a climate, ascetic practices ostensibly "release" the individual from state assistance (in the case of welfare recipients) or state intervention (in the case of poor workers). These changes are justified by the argument that it is not hypocritical or unreasonable to demand ascetic practices from workfare recipients and poor workers because we all acknowledge and practice this belief system. This explains why people are outraged by the high salaries of CEOs just as much as they are irritated by the idea of poor single mothers on welfare. The implementation of increasingly moralistic policies for the working poor and welfare recipients is then justified by the notion that "we" all adhere to the same values. In all this, the assumption is made that some individuals have achieved self-mastery whereas others need to be guided. The aim of asceticism in liberal capitalism is for the individual to be morally responsible, economically independent, and hard working; in this way, ascetic ideas suggest an absence of the state and state power.

The link between capitalism and asceticism is, of course, not new and can be traced to the ascetic morals that Max Weber described in *The Protestant Ethic and the Spirit of Capitalism*. In his account, the Protestant ethic took hold in Western nations to varying degrees, influencing our behavior and contributing to the notion that a hard-working, self-disciplined individual of moral integrity is the paradigm of capitalist behavior and success. According to Weber, these values are internalized and not forced upon us by the state; even his idea of an "iron cage" that forces us all to labor endlessly in employment that we haven't necessarily chosen is more the result of an "invisible hand" than state legislation. In this way, he conceptually distinguishes between the rationalization of everyday life, including bureaucracy, and ascetic ethics, and his analysis of the modern, sovereign state which has a monopoly on the means of legitimate violence. In this vein, contemporary arguments about welfare and the poor also often view welfare and warfare as absolutely separate, with welfare occupying a moral, democratic, and therefore noncoercive sphere (here, welfare does not mean cash payments but rather moral requirements and rules imposed on welfare/workfare recipients).[3] An ascetic ethos is also framed both as a personal choice and as morally important to society; individuals who purportedly do not have a work ethic—such as the homeless, welfare mothers, and unauthorized immigrants—are thought to negatively affect others by usurping resources, occupying public space, and serving as

---

3. This is particularly salient in welfare-to-workfare programs as family values, individual responsibility, and abstinence (be it reproductive or other) are emphasized.

negative role models. It is up to these individuals to change their behavior and become productive members of society.

In this way, two key issues affecting the poor—welfare-to-workfare programs, and policies impacting on poor workers such as low-wage policies and "right to work" laws—are depoliticized. Consequently, the promotion of family values in welfare programs is not viewed as politically coercive because these values are thought to involve individual behavior. At the same time, the exhortation to accept low-wage policies as fiscally responsible shifts the burden from the state to the individual. In a climate like this, the state seems absent and ascetic values seem humane—a form of tough love or collective austerity. Nevertheless, I will argue that ascetic principles based on the Protestant ethic not only are inextricably linked to the state and prerogative (legitimate, arbitrary[4]) power but also are applied coercively and disingenuously to the poor. This both produces and reflects a double standard, which is reflected in the state's treatment of the poor.

While it is true that the government has absented itself from regulating work conditions and job stability, it is present and active in *choosing* and enforcing low-wage policies. Furthermore, it takes measures to ensure that inner-city residents stay within the confines of their neighborhoods,[5] it criminalizes poverty and homelessness through antibegging and antiloitering ordinances,[6] it enacts welfare and workfare guidelines that demand ascetic behavior in exchange for benefits, and it monitors immigrants and guest workers through the BCIS (Bureau of Citizenship and Immigration [formerly INS]). To put it more concisely, aid and recompensatory measures may have been scaled back, but not policing, surveillance, and "wars" (on terror and drugs). As one clear consequence, the poor have far more contact with government authorities than middle-class and wealthy individuals and the asceticism demanded of them is imposed rather than chosen.[7] Furthermore, the coincidence of race, gender, and disenfranchisement (be it actual or historical) is not incidental: all of these factors fit the norms of biopower, to which asceticism is particularly suited.

4. *Arbitrary* does not mean irrational; rather, it relates to the suspension of law. Thus, arbitrary power is irrational in the Weberian sense but not as the word is commonly defined.
5. See Zygmunt Bauman, *Globalization* (New York: Columbia University Press, 1998), 20–22; Mike Davis, *City of Quartz* (New York: Vintage Books, 1992); William Julius Wilson, *When Work Disappears* (New York: Vintage Books, 1997) 3, 4, 23, 24; Jacqueline Jones, *American Work: Four Centuries of Black and White Labor* (New York: W. W. Norton, 1998), 370.
6. See Bauman, *Globalization*, 5, 97; Kathleen Arnold, *Homelessness, Citizenship, and Identity* (Albany: SUNY Press, 2004), chaps. 3 and 4.
7. See, for example, John Gilliom, *Overseers of the Poor: Surveillance, Resistance, and the Limits of Privacy* (Chicago: University of Chicago Press, 2001).

Modern power's concern with the biological is aptly captured by Michel Foucault's notion of biopower, in which "biological existence" is "reflected in political existence."[8] Hence, "[modern] power is situated and exercised at the level of life, the species, the race, and the large-scale phenomena of population."[9] Historically, the exclusion of women and racial minorities was based on their identities as biological rather than human beings. Their enfranchisement did not obliterate these categories; it merely neutralized and displaced them. As Foucault remarks, the emergence of biopower signaled an increased concern with women's sexuality, with women as reproducers, and with the hysterization of women's bodies.[10] Similarly, racial categories and racism were logical outcomes of a growing interest in the population as a species.[11] Foucault's notion of biopower captures the racist and gendered aspects of ascetic policies toward the poor, even as ascetic language has been framed as all-inclusive. What this means is that biological categories are *immediately* political and constitutive of sovereign concerns instead of being incidental criteria on which political inclusion and exclusion happen to be based.[12]

In our present historical context, asceticism has an elective affinity with the differentiation of gender and its intersection with poverty and race in shaping political identity in liberal capitalist society. Values associated with poverty are thus marked as feminine and racial; those associated with wealth are linked to mainstream men and some women. Those who are economically independent and who participate in the labor market are viewed as rational and fit for citizenship; at the same time, individuals who are perceived biologically retain this biological status at the political–economic level, experiencing varying degrees of political exclusion and, at worst, representing bare or biological life. Ascetic values

---

8. Michel Foucault, *The History of Sexuality, Volume I: An Introduction*, trans. Robert Hurley (New York: Vintage Books, 1980), 142.

9. Ibid., 137.

10. Ibid., 146, 147, 153–55. This concern is evident in the cases that are dismantling *Roe v. Wade*, for example, and in state concerns regarding mothers who are HIV infected. See Karen Zivi's work on this subject; for example, "Contesting Motherhood in the Age of AIDS: Material Ideology in the Dabate over Mandatory HIV Testing," *Feminist Studies* 31, no. 2 (2005): 347–74.

11. See Foucault, *The History of Sexuality*, 149, 150. Racial categories persist in the seemingly innocuous census statistics as well as in the more obviously pernicious racial profiling of immigrants and American-born citizens. Although Foucault would object to my pairing of biopower with asceticism, I will argue below that the two are inextricably linked (see Foucault, 141).

12. See Giorgio Agamben, *Homo Sacer: Sovereign Power and Bare Life*, trans. Daniel Heller-Roazen (Stanford: Stanford University Press, 1998).

in early liberal writings were not aimed at any group in particular but at the entire population; since then, however, ascetic policies have intersected with race, gender, and class in such a way that there are now varying levels of political inclusion. This exclusion is harshest when individuals are treated as "bare life" (Giorgio Agamben's term)—that is, when they are subject to prerogative power.

In light of these power dynamics, I explore notions of asceticism in political theory in relation to contemporary welfare prescriptions and low-wage policies[13] in the United States. I interrogate the idea that there is a double standard operating in ascetic demands and normative values and analyze how this double standard is deployed in terms of biopower and disciplinary power. Furthermore, I argue that welfare "solutions" and the more general policing of the poor not only are lacking in compassion but also signal the deployment of prerogative power domestically—significantly, at the bureaucratic level. Prerogative power is "legitimate arbitrary power"[14] that indicates the suspension of law and that can be deployed systematically, rationally, and domestically. In this context, recent cutbacks in welfare and aid programs, combined with flexible work conditions, are not an abandonment of the poor by the government; they are in fact evidence of a change in power relations, the result of a strengthening of ascetic standards such that the greater use of prerogative power domestically is justified.

This argument challenges two widely held assumptions: that prerogative power is only exercised in the international realm; and that because it is characterized by arbitrary decision making and the suspension of the law, bureaucracy and its modalities *preclude* the existence of prerogative power.[15] In fact, prerogative power has always been exercised domestically just as much as internationally, and bureaucracy facilitates the exercise of it in the modern state.

Connected to this, I will also demonstrate that the conventional theoretical separation of warfare and welfare is misguided. That is, I will be

13. To be more specific, I am discussing guest workers, those on workfare, and unskilled or low-skilled laborers.

14. Wendy Brown, *States of Injury: Power and Freedom in Late Modernity* (Princeton: Princeton University Press, 1995), 176.

15. A discussion of these assumptions can be found in Mary Kaldor, "Reconceptualizing Organized Violence," in *Re-imagining Political Community*, ed. Daniele Archibugi, David Held, and Martin Köhler (Stanford: Stanford University Press, 1998), 92–96; Carole Pateman, *The Disorder of Women* (Stanford: Stanford University Press, 1992); Sheldon Wolin, "Democracy and the Welfare State: The Political and Theoretical Connections Between Staatsräson and Wohlfahrsstaatsräson," in *The Presence of the Past: Essays on the State and the Constitution* (Baltimore: Johns Hopkins University Press, 1989).

linking ascetic principles to the development of the state and prerogative power in contradistinction to the conventional linkages among asceticism, welfare, and democracy. My argument will follow Agamben in challenging Foucault's notion that sovereignty, on the one hand, and disciplinary and biopower, on the other, are distinct exercises of power.[16] To this end, I will be critiquing the gendered ideology and racialized public policies (manifested in welfare/workfare policies, low-wage strategies, the War on Terror, and the War on Drugs) that place poor women, immigrants, and minorities in a politically and economically vulnerable position. I will first discuss recent welfare cuts in the context of economic globalization, as well as the alternative to welfare: low paid, unskilled or semiskilled, temporary work. This section is meant to introduce the dynamics of the problems that will be explored in more detail in Chapters 3 and 4. Then I will investigate arguments relating to asceticism in modernity as found in Nietzsche, Marx, Weber, and (later) Foucault and Agamben. In particular, I will critically examine how groups whose political status is defined biologically fit into what Sheldon Wolin calls "the Economic Polity," within which capitalist values inform criteria for citizenship. Finally, I will discuss what citizenship means in this context as well as the political status of poor women, minorities, and immigrants, which I contend has relevance for everyone in the United States.

Welfare, Work, and the Economy

In the late 1990s and early part of this century, income polarity is said to be the same as it was during the Great Depression.[17] This signals profound changes in the economy as it becomes increasingly deregulated and globalized. A supposedly freer market is being accompanied by increasingly unfree labor conditions whether in workfare, guest-worker

16. Although Foucault hints that this is possible and Agamben argues that Foucault's later work indeed implies this possibility. Agamben, *Homo Sacer,* 5, 6.

17. Even if one argues that this statement is a gross exaggeration, it is widely agreed that real wages have not increased since the Reagan years. See Robert Pollin, "Anatomy of Clintonomics," *New Left Review* 3 (May–June 2000): 35, 39, 42; Robert Brenner, "The Boom and the Bubble," *New Left Review* 6 (November–December 2000): 12, 30, 31, 37; James R. St. George, "No Trickling Down in Massachusetts," *Boston Globe,* January 19, 1999, A11; Carolyn Shaw Bell, "The Rich vs. the Poor," *Boston Globe,* July 27, 1999, D4; John Kenneth Galbraith, "The Unfinished Business of the Century," *Boston Globe,* July 12, 1999; Laura Meckler, "White House Cites Economy in Welfare Dip," *Boston Globe,* May 10, 1997, A1.

programs, free zones, or the low-tier labor market in general. The discourse and policies of neoliberalism, including free-market conditions, capital mobility, and deregulation, are masking the increasingly harsh demands being placed on workers and their greater surveillance by the state. This is only logical, in that the increased calls for and enactments of a free market are tied to ascetic notions of austerity, fiscal responsibility, and the avoidance of excess (for example, through bloated government, especially the welfare state). Thus, the well-known claim that capital has become increasingly mobile while people are decreasingly mobile is true not only internationally but also domestically. The free market has merely deepened the hypocrisy of asceticism—it has not liberated anyone.

Changes at the elite level include the increased mobility of capital ("hypermobility" in Saskia Sassen's words); new methods of managing finance such as "securitization," which allows for capital to circulate more rapidly;[18] and the growth of the service industry in both high- and low-end jobs. The greater trend toward export manufacturing in particular has led to a general downgrading of manufacturing and, consequently, the increased "informalization" of manufacturing jobs.[19] In contrast to the wave of industrialization after World War II that served to build a middle class, the new dynamics of globalization, a service economy, and export manufacturing have led to increasing inequalities in wealth.[20]

The corresponding changes in the job market have led to a split between high-end, high-profile positions (for example, financial consultants and analysts) and low-end, informal employment. This split is reflected both in wages and in what is socially and culturally valued as work. Trends in lower-end employment include the following: the increasingly informal character of work, the feminization of labor, the greater use of immigrant labor, lower wages, less unionization, and the downgrading of manufacturing.[21] Moreover, changes in the labor pool have resulted in less security for those who were once part of the labor aristocracy. For example, service employment now predominates in the labor market, and this sort of employment is often part-time, low waged, and on contract,

18. "Securitization is the transformation of hitherto 'unliquid capital' into tradeable instruments, a process that took off dramatically in the 1980s." Saskia Sassen, *Globalization and Its Discontents: Essays on the New Mobility of People and Money* (New York: New Press, 1998), xxxv n4.

19. Ibid., 88, 120.

20. Ibid., 149.

21. Ibid., 91, 111, 112, 146, 158, 161, 163. See Wilson, *When Work Disappears*, 27, 28; Michelle Conlin and Aaron Bernstein, "Working . . . and Poor," *Business Week*, May 31, 2004, 58–65.

besides providing no benefits. Owing to the unstable nature of these jobs, "involuntary part-time employment has grown significantly over the past decade."[22] In these circumstances, the contributions of workers are often undervalued as well as obscured by the discourses of flexibility, deregulation, and freedom, which together imply that workers are somehow freer than in the past.[23] It is predicted that the demand for this type of labor will only expand. Indeed, low-wage, flexible labor conditions are viewed as absolutely crucial to U.S. competitiveness in the world economy.

Furthermore, the informalization of many jobs has led to the proliferation of industrial homework as well as the growth of sweatshops. Because these jobs are temporary and part-time, and also because these workers are isolated from one another if they work in the home, there are numerous barriers to unionization. These jobs are increasingly being filled by immigrant labor in the United States, and by women regardless of their geographical location. In fact, it is often argued that these groups are *responsible* for sweatshops and other forms of "illegal" or informal work, as if the demand would not exist otherwise. In fact, finance and industry well understand the benefits of low-wage, nonunion, immigrant labor.[24] Not the least, this type of labor generates a disciplinary effect among all workers, whatever their race or gender: flexible labor becomes the norm; and work is typed as reproductive (for example, service work normally associated with the serving classes) rather than productive (for example, manufacturing, which is normally associated with white men) and thereby devalued.

As Sassen notes, the connection between globalization and the feminization of labor has not been made in the scholarly literature even though there seems to be a strong correlation between the two.[25] Campaigns to deregulate the economy and to turn what were once secure, full-time jobs with benefits into insecure, part-time ones without benefits articulate with the cultural, political, and economic place that women have traditionally occupied. What is significant for my argument is that these conditions and types of work become "female typed" and thus devalued. Sassen contends that the greater availability of low-wage work has empowered

22. Sassen, *Globalization and Its Discontents*, 146.
23. See Bauman, *Globalization*, and Jones, *American Work*, among others, on the irony of these discourses.
24. See Sassen, *Globalization and Its Discontents*, 154, 158, 161, 163; Bonnie Honig, *Democracy and the Foreigner* (Princeton: Princeton University Press, 2001), 82; Edna Bonacich, "A Theory of Ethnic Antagonism: The Split Labor Market," *American Sociological Review* 37 (October 1972): 547–59.
25. Sassen, *Globalization and Its Discontents*, 91, 131. On this subject, see also Wilson, *When Work Disappears*, as well as the collection of essays in Sonia Shah, ed., *Dragon Ladies: Asian American Feminists Breathe Fire* (Boston: South End Press, 1997).

women, especially immigrant women; yet it could also be argued that greater informalization (for example, casual factories and industrial homework) and the feminization of the labor market have led to the greater exploitation of women. At the very least, positive changes are quite clearly being accompanied by negative ones. This is why Gayatri Chakravorty Spivak remarks that "now women all over the world are absorbing many of the costs of management, of health care, of workplace safety and the like by working at home"; indeed, she calls the feminization of labor "pimping."[26] The move from welfare to workfare, which pressures poor women to leave welfare and work low-paid jobs, is linked to this global trend; so are those structures which create a silence of "the subaltern" whether this subaltern resides in a "developed" or "underdeveloped" region of the world.[27]

As William Julius Wilson and others have argued, the effects of poverty in times of deregulation do not bode well for the future.[28] Wilson, like Sassen, has noted that full-time, stable jobs have effectively disappeared and that real wages have declined. Wages are further divided along gender and racial lines, benefiting women[29] (although I will problematize this "benefit") and worsening conditions for African American males.[30] The employment that is available now does not offer the same benefits as in the past, nor is it secure or steady. Immigrants in particular are vulnerable not only to vigilante groups and BCIS surveillance but also often to the whims of their employers. For these reasons, welfare, which has historically been under the poverty line, brings more income stability than many of the new types of jobs.[31] It seems that poor women are much better off than poor men, in that they receive welfare more often and fill the new service jobs produced by the global economy; overall, though, the political and economic consequences of structural changes in the economy arising from neoliberal policies and deregulation are negative.[32]

26. Gayatri Chakravorty Spivak, "Cultural Talks in the Hot Peace: Revisiting the 'Global Village,'" in Cosmopolitics: Thinking and Feeling Beyond the Nation, ed. Pheng Cheah and Bruce Robbins (Minneapolis: University of Minnesota Press, 1998), 336, 342.

27. See Spivak, "Cultural Talks in the Hot Peace"—for example, the fact that home workers are not unionized.

28. Wilson, When Work Disappears, 25, 26, 28, 29, 53, 54, 151–54, 177, 207, 232, 235.

29. Ibid., 27, 28, 117, 118, 122, 123, 126, 143, 144, 154.

30. See ibid., chap. 5.

31. Ibid., 79–86.

32. Although there is considerable geographic variance in the adoption of neoliberal policies. Nevertheless, I believe that the power dynamics are relatively similar across the board: work and the working class have largely changed, and workers are now more vulnerable both politically and economically.

The benefits of a "freer" economy accrue to political and economic elites; meanwhile, demands to embrace austerity and to break the "culture of dependency," and charges of reverse exploitation (as in "immigrants are *stealing* jobs"), have led to the simultaneous denigration and exploitation of the poor. What Joe Schwartz has rightly called a "risk economy" tends to place the burden of risk on the poor.[33]

In general, groups that are most at risk of being poor in this economy are often those that have historically been disenfranchised, receive unequal pay for the same work, and suffer other types of discrimination. This is particularly true of women and especially women of color, despite the seeming benefits of the feminization of labor. The feminization of labor (and its racialization) is a dubious benefit because in essence, the new paradigm of a job for poor, uneducated, low-skilled individuals is short-term, low-paid, potentially dangerous, and nonunion. With the intersection of race, the odds are even worse for low-wage workers. For example, African Americans and immigrants are paid less than European Americans; they also face discrimination in employment and housing.[34] Again, these conditions and norms produce a disciplinary effect, with an impact on all low-tier workers regardless or gender or race. Meanwhile, changes in welfare policies lead to a strengthening of moral demands at the same time that safety nets are being removed. In the name of responsibility and autonomy, women who transition to workfare lose their medical benefits, any income for day care, and any long-term economic stability by accepting these positions. Whatever the appearance of greater autonomy and self-mastery as single mothers make the transition from welfare to workfare, ascetic values are being imposed on welfare recipients and workfare participants alike. The leviathan of neoliberal policies leads to cuts in entitlement programs at the same time that conservative values—individual responsibility, morality, and family values—are emphasized.[35]

In the first place, a great deal of money is being poured into programs promoting marriage, two-parent families, and "family values"; at the same time, welfare payments have been scaled back and family caps imposed, and workers are expected to pay for their welfare benefits through workfare. President Bill Clinton's welfare reform—the Personal Responsibility and Work Opportunity Reconciliation of 1996—was passed

33. See Joseph M. Schwartz, "Democracy Against the Free Market: The Enron Crisis and the Politics of Global Deregulation," *Connecticut Law Review* 35, no. 3 (April 7, 2003).

34. See Wilson, *When Work Disappears.*

35. See David Garland, *The Culture of Control* (Chicago: University of Chicago Press, 2001), on this paradoxical relationship.

in conjunction with the Illegal Immigration Reform and Immigrant Responsibility Act of 1996. Changes included a two-year limit on receiving welfare; family "caps" in various states that limited the number of children a woman could have and still receive welfare; and stricter eligibility requirements. All of these revisions have a "moral" component to them (for example, the fact sheet for Temporary Assistance for Needy Families [TANF] states that the purposes of TANF are: "to reduce dependency by promoting job preparation, work and marriage; to prevent out-of-wedlock pregnancies; and to encourage the formation and maintenance of two-parent families").[36] Both family caps and workfare are aimed at changing behavior[37] and sending a moral message: "The government will not subsidize irresponsible behavior."[38] The most prevalent terms used in this debate are *irresponsibility*, *dependency*, and *illegitimacy*; the underlying assumption is that single mothers on welfare have children merely to increase their cash entitlements. Tightened eligibility has even been extended to food stamps and, furthermore, has hurt qualified adults and children.[39] Ironically, the constant push for "family values" and the endorsement of marriage on the one hand, and family caps on the other, have resulted in many poor women feeling pressured into staying with an abusive husband on behalf of their children or into having an abortion.[40] Yet many have continued to have children despite the monetary disincentive to do so.[41] Clearly, the safety net is becoming increasingly unstable for women at the same time they are facing multiple pressures to (purportedly) become more moral, self-denying, and disciplined. Welfare-to-work policies

36. Welfare Fact Sheet: "Temporary Assistance for Needy Families," U.S. Department of Health and Human Services, http://www.acf.hhs.gov/programs/ofa, 2.

37. See Rebekah J. Smith, "Family Caps in Welfare Reform: Their Coercive Effects and Damaging Consequences," *Harvard Journal of Law and Gender* 29 (2006): 151–201; David Kopel, "Family Cap Urged on Welfare Reform," Independence Institute, http://www.dave-kopel.net; Jennifer McNulty, "Economist Says 'Family Cap' Welfare Policies May Not Work," *Currents*, publication of the University of California, Santa Cruz, October 20, 1997; Barbara Vobejda and Judith Havermann, "Doing the Math on the Welfare 'Family Cap,'" *Washington Post*, March 30, 1997, A1.

38. Kopel, "Family Cap Urged on Welfare Reform."

39. See Shawn Fremstad, "Immigrants and Welfare Reauthorization," LII/ Legal Information Institute, http://www.cbpp.org/pubs/welfare.htm; Patrica A. King and Cynthia Phillips, "Welfare Reform," U.S. Conference of U.S. Catholic Bishops—Social Development and World Peace," http://www.usccb.org/sdwp/national/welfare.htm; "Some Jobless Adults Face Food Stamp Cutoff," *Boston Globe*, February 23, 1997, A9; Editors, "An Anemic Food Stamp Program," *Boston Globe*, August 5, 1999, A24.

40. See Deborah Connolly, *Homeless Mothers: Face to Face with Women and Poverty* (Minneapolis: University of Minnesota Press, 2000), 60–65, 96–104; Smith, "Family Caps."

41. See Vobejda and Havemann, "Doing the Math"; McNulty, "Economist Says . . .'"

do not guarantee poor women's increasing economic autonomy, though they do encourage the growth of what amounts to an industrial reserve army.

The shorter amount of time that a family can receive welfare also carries a moral message: welfare programs do not solve the problem of poverty, but individual responsibility and hard work do. One precludes the other. However, it has been shown that workfare is not replacing welfare in any meaningful way—former recipients often lose benefits and day care and earn less money. The point of workfare seems in fact to be that the poor need to learn how to work long hours, practice thrift, and live with the instability of the labor market.[42] The imposition of ascetic values is less a solution to the problem of poverty than it is a form of tough love for wayward children. It is a baptism by fire, and the salvation to be reached takes the form not of wealth but rather of self-discipline and self-mastery. As Zygmunt Bauman notes, those who profit from the global economy "resent the much publicized 'public costs' of keeping the vagabonds [i.e., the inner-city poor] alive."[43] Workfare ostensibly solves this problem.

The ascetic framing of those issues not only obscures structural issues but also creates and determines marginalized subjectivities based on ascetic double standards. For example, a single mother of color who is poor is considered irresponsible, lazy, and parasitic, and this leaves her open to ascetic demands placed on her by workfare employers, welfare workers, and housing authorities in exchange for aid or work. Yet a single European American woman who has a child on her own is viewed as strong, liberated, and a feminist and is treated as autonomous and responsible. A laid-off executive is eligible to receive unemployment benefits while an unemployed contract worker in a casual factory is not. It seems that one must *earn* the right to these things. That is, ascetic values are not applied equally to all but acquire different meanings depending on one's economic and political status.

As a result of this double standard, there appears to be a "moral" impetus to push people off of welfare at all costs. Similarly, the Illegal Immigration Reform and Immigrant Responsibility Act of 1996 addressed moral concerns about poor immigrants. Since August 22, 1996, new immigrants have been denied most federal means-tested programs for five years.

---

42. See Connolly, *Homeless Mothers:* 24; LII/Legal Information Institute, "Wex: Welfare; Welfare Law: An Overview," http://www.law.cornell.edu/wex; Center on Budget and Policy Priorities, "Assessing TANF 10 Years Later," http://www.cbpp.org/pubs/welfare.htm.

43. Bauman, *Globalization*, 96.

After five years, individuals will still be ineligible for programs if the combination of their income and that of the person who sponsored their entry into the country does not meet the income eligibility requirements (this procedure is called "deeming").[44] Cutting immigrants off welfare highlights the limits of citizenship as well as the stereotypes about female immigrants, who are broadly perceived as having too many children, abusing the welfare and health-care systems, and even posing a danger to the nation's survival given their (allegedly) high fertility rates.[45] Although these policies are seemingly targeted at men as well, the onus of reproductive decisions and material well-being falls on the women be they immigrants or native born.

President Bush, encouraged by the lower numbers on welfare rolls, decided to tighten welfare eligibility even more. On February 8, 2006, once the Clinton plan had expired, he reauthorized the plan.[46] Bush strengthened the emphasis on family values—for example, by including a "strong pitch for marriage." As with the Clinton plan, states receive bonuses for shorter welfare rolls, and benefits are still denied to legal immigrants for five years (with some caveats). States have been given more flexibility in assessing their caseloads; at the same time, though, welfare recipients are required to work more hours than under the Clinton plan, and wages are still locally determined, ranging from minimum wage to below minimum wage.[47] While states have lowered their welfare rolls, there is little evidence that workfare recipients have secured steady, well-paid work.[48]

44. See National Alliance to End Homelessness (NAEH), "Changes in Laws Relating to Immigration: Impact on Homeless Assistance Providers," http://www.naeh.org/pub/immigration/imig2.htm.

45. See Antonio McDaniel, "Fertility and Racial Stratification," *Population and Development Review* 2, Supplement: Fertility in the United States: New Patterns, New Theories (1996): 134–50. McDaniel argues that European American fertility rates are viewed as the norm and all other fertility patterns as deviations; moral judgments then follow. See also Leo R. Chavez, "A Glass Half Empty: Latina Reproduction and Public Discourse," *Human Organization* 63 (Summer 2004).

46. See U.S. Department of Health and Human Services, Administration of Children and Families, "Fact Sheet: Welfare Reform: Deficit Reduction Act of 2005," http://www.acf.hhs.gov/programs/ofa/regfact.htm; "Welfare Reform Reauthorized," http://www.acf.hhs.gov/opa/spotlight/welfarereauthorized.htm; Office of Press Secretary, "President Signs S. 1932, Deficit Reduction Act of 2005," http://www.whitehouse.gov/news/releases/2006/02.

47. See Michele Keller, "Bush Proposal Would Pay Workfare Recipients Less Than Minimum Wage," National Organization for Women, http://www.now.org/issues/economic/030702workfare.html; Ray Goforth, "Workfare in the USA: America's New (non-union) Subminimum Wage Underclass," *Washington Free Press*, http://www.washingto freepress org/29/First.html.

48. Laura Meckler, "Bush Outlines Welfare Plans," *Boston Globe,* February 26, 2002. See also "Working on the Margins," *Boston Globe,* March 10, 2002, D6.

These policy changes are determined more by an ascetic belief system than by empirical findings that the simultaneous scaling back of cash aid and the greater imposition of moral requirements and counseling have improved the overall welfare of the poor. In fact, this punitive model and the public opinion that supports it are based on hoary stereotypes. For example, three ideas have been predominant over the past few decades: that there is a culture of dependency which leads to years of welfare use and abuse; that minorities make up the bulk of single mothers on welfare; and that many welfare recipients are "cheats." Yet 50 percent of people on welfare are on it for less than a year, 70 percent for less than two years.[49] And a twenty-year study found that in any given year, a significant percentage of women on welfare were also working.[50]

Moreover, less than half of all welfare recipients are African American, yet the conventional image of the welfare client is that of a poor, abusive mother of color squandering taxpayers' money.[51] This demonstrates how ascetic values have been racialized and feminized.[52] Linda Faye Williams points out that the chief beneficiaries of all types of welfare are white; she adds that the view that African American women are unfairly receiving welfare benefits obscures the fact that many African Americans provide unremunerated work, are blocked from racist unions, and face numerous barriers to receiving the welfare benefits for which they are eligible.[53] In addition, although out-of-wedlock births have increased in all economic classes by about eight times the rate in the 1940s,"[54] the nonmarital birth rates of black women have not changed in two decades.[55] Most of the single mothers who are raising children are neither teenagers nor minorities, and welfare was not found to be a significant factor in the recent increases in numbers of children born outside of marriage.[56] Nonetheless, Aid to Families with Dependent Children (AFDC) has been eliminated as a response to these alleged problems, and caps have been established a

49. Frances Fox Piven, "Poorhouse Politics," *The Progressive* 59, no. 2 (1995): 22–24.
50. Derrick Z. Jackson, citing Kathleen Mullan Harris in "The Real World for Welfare Mothers," *Boston Globe*, April 9, 1997, A19.
51. See Connolly, *Homeless Mothers*, 162–64.
52. On this point, see Wilson, *When Work Disappears*.
53. Linda Faye Williams, *The Constraint of Race* (University Park: Penn State University Press, 2003), 150–73.
54. Elizabeth Mehren, "So Who *Are* Those Unwed Mothers?" *Los Angeles Times*, October 30, 1995, E1.
55. Piven, "Poorhouse Politics," 23; Wilson, *When Work Disappears*, 87, 88.
56. Mehren, "So Who *Are* Those Unwed Mothers?" E1.

reaction to what is perceived to be "irresponsible reproduction."[57] Additionally, the new welfare rules have been combined with a presumption of criminality or "cheating" on the applicants' part,[58] and this has led to increased screening of applicants, including fingerprinting. All of these rules and the treatment meted out to welfare recipients has led many to accept low-wage jobs or workfare positions. In both cases (workfare or welfare), ascetic values determine both eligibility and whether an individual is a "success." These policies and discourses not only marginalize poor women further by fostering damaging images and stereotypes but also invite welfare workers, employers, the media, and the public to scrutinize and judge these women's lives.

In fact, these programs should be viewed in the same terms as parole—the recipient is not merely a client, an individual whose transaction with a bureaucracy has a beginning and end. Rather, like parole, welfare entails strict adherence to rules (including the monitoring of one's sexual activities and limits to the number of children one can have), close scrutiny of what are normally considered private details, and harsh penalties for noncompliance. For parolees, the threat is a return to prison; for noncompliant welfare or workfare recipients, the threats involve one's very existence: homelessness, malnourishment, and a deeper descent into poverty.[59] As Sheldon Wolin states: "The state is, therefore, allowed to deal arbitrarily with all welfare recipients, not by lynching them but by redefining the conditions and categories of their existence";[60] "thus, marginality is a means of expanding a particular kind of state power, one less hedged by ordinary rules (due process), one freer to respond in accordance with the 'objective situation.'"[61] In other words, what appear to be the most bureaucratically organized and rule-bound programs are also the most arbitrary and punitive; as I will argue below, prerogative is enabled by the rule of law rather than precluded by it.

Clearly, the word "reform" is disingenuous when applied to the welfare changes of 1996; instead of improving the situation of the poor, reform "is punishment of individuals or restriction of their rights in order to improve their characters or behaviors, as in 'reform school.' This type of

57. See Smith, "Family Caps in Welfare Reform," 154.

58. See Michael Patrick MacDonald, *All Souls: A Family Story from Southie* (Boston: Beacon Press, 1999), for an account of having to look poor for social workers.

59. On "penal welfarism," or the connection between the welfare state and criminal justice, see Garland, *Culture of Control*.

60. Wolin, "Democracy and the Welfare State," 159.

61. Ibid., 160–61.

welfare reform has a long tradition" in both the United States and the United Kingdom.[62] As many authors have demonstrated, the notion that poverty or joblessness is a result of personal failings is particularly American, even as some European countries have shared the values of the Protestant work ethic to a lesser extent. This explains why our policies are far more punitive and individually oriented than in other liberal capitalist countries (although England comes close).[63]

As Sheila D. Collins and Gertrude Schaffner Goldberg discuss, the history of welfare or poor relief in the United States has had the following undemocratic characteristics:[64] outdoor relief is limited or denied (this is still true—many cities ban individual food donations and regulate outdoor bread lines);[65] work is provided under coercive conditions (workfare today is not voluntary, wages are below minimum wage, benefits are not provided, and workfare wages can be garnished to pay back welfare); there is an assumption that paupers are irresponsible and individually flawed (this assumption is still evident in the ascetic prescriptions of TANF and nearly all other welfare programs); the notion that the provision of aid is a causal factor in the demand for it (this is evident today in talks about welfare dependency and cheating); authorities have required relatives who are often also poor to aid their poor relations (this is still true, particularly with entrance to a homeless shelter—the individual must prove that he or she has exhausted the list of relatives with whom to stay before entering the shelter);[66] aid is not viewed as an entitlement in the United States (and never has been, and furthermore, this is truer today than it was in the early part of the twentieth century); welfare relief varies from state to state; (and always has); despite Supreme Court rulings that strike down residency requirements as limiting freedom of travel, local authorities deny or limit assistance to newcomers (and always have), be they citizens or immigrants;[67] and, finally, welfare has "denied recipients

---

62. Sheila D. Collins and Gertrude Schaffner Goldberg, *Washington's New Poor Law* (New York: Apex Press, Council on International and Public Affairs, 2001), 6.

63. See Wilson, *When Work Disappears.*

64. Collins and Goldberg, *Washington's New Poor Law,* 9. The characteristics listed in this paragraph are Collins and Goldberg's; the parenthetical comments are mine.

65. For example, San Francisco has arrested individuals for feeding the homeless. In many other cities, outdoor bread lines have been hotly contested.

66. As a housing advocate in Boston's shelter system, I was required to go through a list of relatives and friends with whom shelter residents could stay. Among other problems this causes, staying with a relative or friend can endanger the terms of that person's lease.

67. See Sanford F. Schram, "Introduction," in *Welfare Reform: A Race to the Bottom?* ed. Schram and Samuel H. Beer (Washington, D.C.: Woodrow Wilson Center Press, n.d.). Recent changes in TANF requirements (2006) may allow American-born recipients to move

political and civil rights in return for a meager dole"[68] (this is still true de facto if not de jure). These broad characteristics of welfare throughout U.S. history highlight not only the punitive character of the welfare system[69] but also the coercive nature of workfare. The crucial assumptions behind workfare programs are two: participants must be forced to work; and they have no motivation to do so and thus must be guided, shaped, and disciplined. This is why they are denied choices that ordinary workers would ideally have, such as what hours to work, what they will be paid, and where their wages will go.

It needs to be emphasized that workfare is dependent *not* on job creation but rather on a flexible labor market:

> Contemporary workfare policies rarely involve job creation on any significant scale, along the lines of the old-fashioned public-works programs; they are more concerned with deterring welfare claims and necessitating the acceptance of low-paid, unstable jobs in the context of increasingly "flexible" labor markets. Stripped down to its labor-regulatory essence, workfare is not about creating jobs for people that don't have them; it is about creating workers for jobs that nobody wants. In a Foucauldian sense, it is seeking to make "docile bodies" for the new economy: flexible, self-reliant, and self-disciplining.[70]

Welfare and workfare indicate bare survival—recipients are not meant to rise even to lower-middle-class status. As Piven and Cloward note:

> In New York City, some 45,000 people, mainly women, sweep the streets and clean the subways and the parks. They do the work once done by unionized municipal employees. But instead of a paycheck and a living wage, they get a welfare check that leaves them far below the poverty level, and they have none of the benefits and protections of unionized workers. Perhaps just as bad, they have become public spectacles of abject and degraded labor—of slave labor, many of them say.[71]

---

from state to state without cessation of welfare; however, it is unclear whether this will be implemented efficiently.

68. Collins and Goldberg, *Washington's New Poor Law,* 9.
69. See, for example, Garland, *Culture of Control.*
70. Jamie Peck, *Workfare States* (New York: Guilford Press, 2001), 6.
71. Richard Cloward and Frances Fox Piven in Peck, *Workfare States,* ix.

The word slavery is an exaggeration but it is not incidental: workers in Marx's analysis were also "free" to sell their labor and participate in a "free" market; but their limited choices, de facto political disenfranchisement, lack of collective bargaining or representation (i.e., unions), and inhuman work conditions indicated a profound asymmetry of political power. These dynamics, which are present today just as in Marx's time, challenge any claims about "freedom." Today, workfare and welfare programs have taken away many of the rights (not necessarily in the legal sense but broadly conceived) that ordinary citizens enjoy, including the rights to privacy and individual moral choice as well as the right to determine work conditions.

Furthermore, if the new working class (low-tier workers) is viewed as part of the inner city, as composed of both formal citizens and migrants, it must be recognized that this same group is not only subject to welfare and workfare surveillance and control, but also to the War on Drugs, racial profiling, the War on Terror, immigration controls, and the resurgence of racial prejudice and sexism. As I will elucidate below and in the next chapter, this set of power dynamics indicates a far more complex and intricate system of controls—one that in effect suspends the law through bureaucratic mechanisms in a systematic fashion (systematic meaning that the impact is long-lasting and that this population is treated consistently as a biological threat to national security).[72] Unlike the conditions at Guantánamo Bay (not to idealize conditions there), the ideational system that creates ethnic, racial, and gender antagonisms obscures these power dynamics and often inverts them, positing these groups as the true usurpers or exploiters (of "us": the welfare system, taxpayers' dollars, our moral sensibility, and so on).

All of these policies disproportionately affect low-tier workers and the very poor;[73] combined with workfare, guest-worker policies, and the War on Drugs, they also strengthen sovereignty domestically and allow for political and economic exploitation. To put it differently, laws that permit greater latitude in exercising prerogative power should be viewed in conjunction with economic policies aimed at the poor, be they American born or immigrant. Similar to workfare policies and low-wage strategies, the U.S. guest-worker program combines these two elements: "flexible"

72. See Arnold, *Homelessness, Citizenship, and Identity* , Chapter 4.
73. See, for example, David L. Marcus, "Three Times and Out," *Boston Globe*, October 14, 1998, A1; Nancy Gertner and Daniel Kanstroom, "The Recent Spotlight on the INS Failed to Reveal Its Dark Side," *Boston Globe*, May 21, 2000, E1, E3.

work conditions; and heavy surveillance and political control, accompanied by the political powerlessness of workers. One of the more prominent sectors of the guest-worker program is agriculture; the United States has the most physically intensive agricultural system in the West, while at the same time, agricultural jobs have been rated by various authorities as the most and second most dangerous jobs in America.[74] Because many of these workers are on agricultural visas, they are monitored by the BCIS as well as by local police forces, employers, and citizens' watch groups. Guest workers are tied to one employer, must be on site twenty-fours hours a day, seven days a week, are provided housing that lacks both refrigeration and sewage, often live in tents or other makeshift housing, and have no access to doctors, electricity, or outside help. As of this writing, guest workers cannot strike, change employers, or bargain for wages.[75] If they are fired from their positions, they have less than a week to leave the country and no legal recourse. Meanwhile, illegal immigrants in the meatpacking industry often work in factories that are freezing, isolated, and subject to deregulated (read "unsafe") working conditions. Often they are tracked by BCIS and citizens' watch groups and are deported or allowed to stay according to arbitrary criteria. Additionally, conditions in the Border Industrial Program, a transnational factory area established through a partnership between the United States and Mexico, are both "free"—that is, deregulated—and dangerous and exploitative for workers. Just as international companies in this program *(maquilas)* have enjoyed relaxed environmental and labor standards, female *maquiladora* workers have been subject to brutal conditions. Hundreds of these women have been rape-murdered or kidnapped. The murder investigations of these "women of Juárez" have been sluggish, but their border crossing is certainly policed. The lack of heat in these factories, the speeding up of conveyor belts so that injuries are commonplace, and the vulnerability of these workers to both the market and the police form the parameters these workers' daily existence.[76] In all of these cases, workers are exploited

74. Other jobs rated among the most dangerous are mining and meatpacking work.

75. Legislation has been proposed to modify guest workers' conditions, but this is at the very beginning stages; moreover, the proposed legislation still does not go far enough to protect these workers from abuse, starvation, poor medical care, and exposure to the elements.

76. See Human Rights Watch, "Human Rights Watch Welcomes U.S. Government Meat and Poultry Study," http://hrw.org/English/docs/2005/02/03/usdom10117_txt.htm; "Abusive Child Labor Found in U.S. Agriculture," http://hrw.org/English/docs/2000/06/20/usdom 580_txt.thm; NCRLC, "U.S. Agricultural Workers," http://www.ncrlc.com/Agricultural.Workers. html.

and seemingly abandoned by the state; yet at the same time they are subject to much greater surveillance and control.

Similarly, workfare participants may have to travel far for their jobs, have no day care and no negotiating power, and make less money than on welfare; yet they are subject to racial profiling, to accusations that they are unwilling to work or that they have abandoned their children because they are working, to the scrutiny of housing authorities, and to the whims of their employers. Correspondingly, African American men are often the last hired and first fired and are subject to racial discrimination; furthermore, they face more racial prejudice than many other groups in the low-tier sector. At the same time, women workers—who predominate in the service sector—make the lowest wages and must often juggle domestic duties with long hours and precarious employment status. Their docility is not only a condition of their employment[77] but also often presented as a moral requisite in terms of traditional norms (e.g., in immigrant communities),[78] the welfare/workfare state, and constant demands for assimilation by xenophobic Americans.[79] In all cases, the jobs pay poorly, are part-time or on contract, have no health insurance, and are located in deregulated workspaces so that injury rates are high., Finally, poor health arising from workspace conditions can result in employment being terminated.[80] This is not just economic exploitation—it is also political exploitation, which comes in the form of comparing male to female workers (this split is invoked especially against African American males) and "native" to immigrant workers (poor American workers serve as the paradigm of moral degeneracy, laziness, and so on). In this way, racism, ethnocentrism, and sexism have come to be openly acceptable and to inform public policy. Groups are *used* against one another in ways that extract political value even while obscuring the sexism, racism, and xenophobia of bureaucrats, politicians, and employers. Those who are

77. See Bonacich, "A Theory of Ethnic Antagonism, 547–59; Simone de Beauvoir, *The Second Sex*, trans. and ed. H. M. Parshley (New York: Vintage Books, 1989); Colette Guillaumin, *Racism, Sexism, Power, and Ideology* (New York: Routledge, 1995); Sassen, *Globalization and Its Discontents;* Wilson, *When Work Disappears.*

78. Spivak notes that many immigrant women workers believe that they are making an "ethical choice" to be submissive toward men in intimate relationships and employment. See Spivak, "Cultural Talks in the Hot Peace."

79. On gendered aspects of American xenophobia and the particularly stringent demands for assimilation placed on foreign women, see Honig, *Democracy and the Foreigner.*

80. Saskia Sassen, J. Oloka-Onyago, and Deepika Udagama, "Globalization and Its Impact on the Full Enjoyment of Human Rights," UN Press Release, http://www.globalpolicy.org/socecon/un/wtonite.htm.

targeted by these attitudes simultaneously serve as exemplars of model workers *and* as people who are inherently criminal, lazy, and a threat to society.[81] Divisive tactics are used to in effect "ghettoize" each group; at the same time, ascetic discourses, norms, and policies result in the disciplining of the entire working class.

Public policies and attitudes toward poor workers in the United States suggest a continuum in the ascetic ideational structure. The language of flexibility implies a sort of freedom for workers and employers at the same time that it demands austerity and sacrifice. This sacrifice is presented as something we all undertake and accept. The pursuit of low-wage policies is portrayed as a choice: full employment but under flexible and deregulated conditions, *or* an expensive welfare state with greater worker protections but massive unemployment.[82] Flexible work conditions give the appearance of an agreement between two equal partners, worker and employer, wherein commitments are short and the worker is free to find another job when the first one ends. Also implied is that workers have the mobility to travel from place to place in order to seek work. However, flexibility also can include termination at will, short-term contracts, wages that are not market rate or minimum wage, and odd or irregular hours.[83]

Additionally, flexibility describes increasingly informal work conditions including sweatshops, factories that do not meet labor codes, and primitive work conditions in the case of agricultural workers.[84] Deregulation—deregulated workspaces, deregulated pollution controls, deregulated wage ceilings and employment contracts, and so on—complements a flexible labor force. It may seem paradoxical that notions of flexibility and deregulation (which suggest freedom) are connected to ascetic ideas (which imply constraint); but it must be remembered that an ascetic ethos seemingly frees the individual. The ascetic citizen is hard-working and economically independent and has achieved self-mastery.

Yet because of the precarious nature of these arrangements and conditions, low-wage workers have lost the stability that low-skilled manufacturing jobs once provided. With the labor market becoming increasingly feminized, racialized, and filled by immigrant workers, the

---

81. Some recent examples are Frances Fukuyama, Dinesh D'Souza, and Samuel Huntington's arguments about moral values, the work ethic, and assimilation. Each of these authors makes openly racial comparisons between groups of immigrants and African Americans.

82. Wilson, *When Work Disappears*, 152–53.

83. See Bauman, *Globalization*, 104–5, 112–13, 118; Wilson, *When Work Disappears*, 152–53.

84. See, for example, Sassen, *Globalization and Its Discontents*.

ascetic imperatives of low-wage strategies demand hard work, suffering, and economic instability and affect certain segments of the population more than others. In turn, the working class as a whole has now become subject to these disciplinary effects and norms. The language of the global economy is being disseminated to all workers and classes of people, but the austerity the new economy demands really only affects the American born and immigrant poor (within the United States).

It is significant that deregulation, flexibility, and the transition from AFDC (Aid to Families with Dependent Children) to TANF (*Temporary* Assistance to Needy Families) together imply minimal government intervention in the labor market and welfare-to-workfare recipients' lives. Authors across the political spectrum have argued that the state is less powerful now than ever before. Nonetheless, can be said that two processes have emerged as a result of economic globalization and the increasing disenfranchisement of this new working class (new not only demographically but also in terms of what constitutes blue-collar employment).

First, deregulation actually requires a *strengthening* of certain elements of the state even as others grow weaker.[85] Early on Karl Polanyi showed that there has never been a truly free market (his famous phrase is "laissez-faire was planned; planning was not")[86]—and more recently, Sassen has demonstrated how global capital still depends on governments to protect assets and guarantee contracts and transnational agreements, as well to provide a military to enforce these arrangements. Domestically, less attention is paid to the state's role in meeting the needs of global capital by ensuring a cheap supply of docile workers who cannot protest labor conditions, bargain for wages, or even unionize in many cases.[87] This role is tied to the second trend: the surveillance and domination of those who do not benefit from the increased mobility of economic globalization.

As capital demands control, protection, and security from the state, this creates a hierarchy in which those who are destined to stay in their locality—the working poor, the disenfranchised—are policed.[88] It may seem counterintuitive to argue that the groups discussed above have less

85. For example, the state may cede power to transnational corporations that can evade regional legislation; or it can be altered by international governmental organizations; or it can lose strength because of the presence of unauthorized immigrants.

86. Karl Polanyi, *The Great Transformation* (Boston: Beacon Press, 2001), 147.

87. For example, in workfare, low-wage policies, guest-worker policies, and deregulation (which allow for sweatshops and more informal workspaces).

88. See Bauman, *Globalization*, 18–24.

geographical mobility, but consider these facts: immigrant guest workers are tied to their employer sponsor; refugees and other resident aliens must stay put in order to establish residency and fulfill other legal requirements (this is particularly true of asylum applicants in major U.S. cities, who are now required to wear electronic ankle bracelets);[89] and, as Wilson has described poignantly, many residents of inner cities remain where they are not by choice but because of limited savings, poor transportation, and a dearth of employment options.[90] Inner-city residents (including poorer immigrants) are also less mobile when walls are built in areas suspected of high drug trafficking, when the criminalization of homelessness disallows the use of public space, and when gated communities and semiprivate commercial spaces are monitored by private security firms. In fact, one could argue that only the most "immobile" groups would endure nonunion, physically intensive, low-paid, and financially unstable work.[91] The arbitrary nature of government power in bringing these conditions about matches the contingency of global capital. In this way, state power—and I will argue, prerogative power—is strengthened while democratic practices become increasingly devalued or criminalized and spatially displaced.

The actual policing of the poor involves the following, among other things: welfare caseworkers who push recipients not only to become more self-disciplined (that is, to practice sexual abstention, save money, and abstain from alcohol) but also to accept low-paying jobs in lieu of welfare; BCIS policing of immigrants' status but not their work conditions; the rapid arrest and deportation of certain immigrants; racial profiling in the poorest areas of cities, where there is inadequate public transportation, a severe shortage of job opportunities, and a decaying infrastructure; and interference by housing authorities with regard to rules, but again little regard for the conditions in which residents live. Adding to all this, ordinary citizens are contributing to a sort of negative civil society that upholds the precarious political status of these workers: employers can threaten to fire them or turn them into the BCIS, vigilante groups can harass immigrants, and the media make them all feel as if they do not fit in economically or politically. These cases are not reflections of a bureaucracy

89. Daniel Zwerdling, "Electronic Anklets Track Asylum Seekers in U.S.," NPR, http://www.npr.org/templates/story/story.php?storyId=4519090.

90. See also Bauman, *Globalization,* regarding the limited mobility of the poor; see also Jones, *American Work.*

91. See Jones, *American Work,* 370.

run amuck. Rather, they represent state ideology and control of a population that is increasingly disenfranchised (if enfranchised at all, in the case of illegal immigrants or foreign residents); an asymmetrical power dynamic in which these groups have limited agency; and the increasing dehumanization of certain groups in the population.

Welfare reform, low-wage policies, and economic deregulation are all tied to one another in their ideational justification: the ascetic ideals that have shaped government policy, liberal thought, and the development of capitalist values. Ascetic demands are being placed on the poor that are not placed on mainstream Americans. It is supposed that these values foster a work ethic in the poor and encourage them to try for economic independence; in actual fact, these coercive mechanisms do *not* free the poor and only illuminate their status as "bare life" (even if on a spectrum)—that is, as biological beings or less-than-citizens—and thus how they become objects of prerogative power. In this way, modern policies based on asceticism do not indicate a more humane society but rather the inhumanity of sovereign power. In the next section, I will investigate ascetic ideas in Marx, Nietzsche, and Weber in order to demonstrate how asceticism has historically been linked to economic values as well as to the deployment of sovereign power.

Asceticism

In this section, I explore how the development of modern asceticism in the work of Marx, Nietzsche, and Weber, as well as the debates regarding its origins and purposes, explains our contemporary practices. My conclusion will be that ascetic values are less significant for their moral qualities than for being the organizing ethos of modern politics and economics in the United States. First, I investigate how authors have made conceptual distinctions between modern asceticism, the development of the modern state,[92] and a market economy. These distinctions are more recently apparent in the theoretical division between welfare and warfare. In contradistinction to these differentiations, I discuss the idea of a political theology—the notion that all of these realms have been historically intertwined even when there are no direct causal connections, such that ascetic values provide

---

92. Which, following Max Weber, was rationalized by asceticism but is modern precisely as a consequence of its separation from religion as a basis of legitimacy.

an ideational nexus between the modern state (including the deployment of prerogative power) and the capitalist economy. This connection is particularly evident when the roles played by work as well as natural law theory are examined and it can be seen that ascetic ideas have never been strictly confined to a religious realm but were apparent in early liberal thought and notions about a market economy. The manifestation of a double standard in morality is more complex than it would appear: ascetic principles and practices are conceived of in terms of the entire population and not just the poor. Nevertheless, this double standard justifies the political and economic disenfranchisement of the poor rather than reflecting a mere cultural division. To put it differently, the double standard of modern asceticism illuminates the distinction between citizen and bare life.

I argue first that ascetic values are linked to the development of the state and prerogative power and that the traditional linkages among asceticism, welfare, and democracy do not hold. Rather, ascetic values are what justify the use of prerogative power. In this way, those subject to ascetic prescriptions and punishments (forced sterilization in the past, and nowadays deportation, court-ordered removal of children from the family, systematic racial profiling, and so on) have the status not of citizens but rather of biological life (or bare life, in Agamben's terms). Second, although welfare is commonly viewed as a corrective to the problems of capitalism or even the antithesis of capitalism, I demonstrate that its origins, structure, and implementation are intimately bound up with the development of a market economy. That is, welfare policies serve to normalize, discipline, and hierarchize clients in conjunction with capitalist ideology and demands. In this way, they work in combination with the ideology of the U.S. low-wage policy, which demands labor flexibility and the acceptance of precarious job arrangements.

Ascetic prescriptions have existed since the ancient Greeks. Plato and Aristotle both describe the value of hard work, the need to achieve balance and moderation in one's life, and the importance of not being enslaved to one's passions. These ideas are echoed in modern theoretical tracts, for example, in those of Adam Smith, Friedrich Nietzsche, and Jean-Jacques Rousseau. However, the sort of asceticism that encourages working beyond subsistence, going beyond what one would normally do, and practicing an extreme form of self-denial at a *mass level* did not arise until modernity, as Max Weber shows. Asceticism was at first the reserve of magicians, seers, and priests, and as Weber argues, it was practiced to attain an altered state of the sort achievable through drugs or alcohol.[93] Thus, its origins were not negative. In stark contrast, the ascetic values that became part of political theory and policy beginning in the 1600s were harsher, more self-abnegating, often coercive, and applied to the masses rather than embraced by religious figures alone. As Weber tells us, the *meaning* of these ideas may have been lost but the self-denial, hard work, and other expectations remain today.[94]

Although liberal prescriptions were especially cruel toward the poor (for example, in Hobbes and Locke), these values affirmed the new paradigm of an ideal political member (eventually, a citizen): hard-working, productive, and ensuring that one person's pursuits did not harm others. The same prescriptions served as a critique—particularly in Locke, Smith, and Rousseau—of the landed nobility and laid the basis for a politics that protected the fruits of one's labor and provided for the rule of law and for political leaders chosen for their political skills rather than noble lineage. The focus on hard work and on shunning material excess provided a new moral basis for politics: survival (Hobbes), the preservation of life and pursuit of material well-being (Locke), or a new sort of self-interest based on productive activity that contributed indirectly to society (Smith, de Tocqueville). In other words, politics was no longer the pursuit of something higher or noble as in ancient Greece or even feudal times; rather, it was based on bare life, survival, and "self-interest properly understood."

As Agamben explains, this transformation of political aims heralded a politics of "bare life," which in ancient times had been consigned to *oikos* (the household). In ancient Greece, *oikos* was the locus of subsistence, biological needs, and irrational emotions. Those who embodied the biological (women), or were deemed irrational (women, children), or were slaves (prisoners of war), were relegated to *oikos*. In contrast, political life was conceived of as transcending the body and biological need and as in opposition to individuals chained to their biology and irrationality. Thus, bare life on the one hand and political life on the other. Bare life was the exception, political life the rule.[95] In contemporary times, however, bare

93. H. H. Gerth and C. Wright Mills, eds., *From Max Weber: Essays in Sociology* (New York: Oxford University Press, 1958), 270, 271.

94. Max Weber, *The Protestant Ethic and the Spirit of Capitalism*, trans. Talcott Parsons (New York: Routledge, 2001), 124–25. For a slightly different interpretation of Weber's argument, see Brown, *States of Injury*, 136.

95. Agamben further claims that the origin of the distinction between bare life and human life lies in the division between animal and human. See Agamben, *The Open: Man and Animal*, trans. Kevin Attell (Stanford: Meridian/Stanford University Press, 2004).

life has become the basis of the political. Thus, Foucault comments that "what might be called a society's 'threshold of modernity' has been reached when the life of the species is wagered on its own political strategies. For millennia, man remained what he was for Aristotle: a living animal with the additional capacity for a political existence; modern man is an animal whose politics places his existence as a living being in question."[96] Or, as Agamben states, bare life is the exception that has become the rule.[97]

Nietzsche's conception of two types of asceticism captures this historical development. In *On the Genealogy of Morals,* Nietzsche distinguishes between two types of asceticism; one that is grasped desperately by the weak and that is motivated by *ressentiment;* the other that signifies freedom from desire, jealousy, and other petty feelings. In essence, the first is saying "no" to life and the second, according to Nietzsche, is an affirmation of living. Nietzsche locates the negative sort of asceticism in the Church and the figure of the ascetic priest. He calls priestly morality slave morality: "While every noble morality develops from a triumphant affirmation of itself, slave morality from the outset says No to what is 'outside', what is 'different,' what is 'not itself'; and *this* No is its creative deed."[98] In this way, Nietzsche separates religion from political power or, at least, the politically powerful.

Weber disagrees with Nietzsche that the more negative form of asceticism proceeded from the *ressentiment* of the weak;[99] like Nietzsche, however, he claims that ascetic values had purely religious origins.[100] In part, Weber argues this to challenge Marx's apparently simplistic formulation of a base and superstructure.[101] Religious asceticism at a mass level did not simply spring up as an economic tool of the bourgeoisie, Weber argues, but the reverse: religious values had an "elective affinity" with capitalism, and thus, gradually, these values became the spirit of capitalism. Yet this union then led to religion's demise—or its marginalization to a private, devalued, irrational realm—because "the paradox of all rational asceticism, which in an identical manner has made monks in all ages stumble, is

96. Foucault, *The History of Sexuality,* 143.

97. Agamben, *Homo Sacer,* 9.

98. Friedrich Nietzsche, *On the Genealogy of Morals,* trans. Walter Kaufmann (New York: Vintage Books, 1989), 36.

99. Gerth and Mills, *From Max Weber,* 270, 271.

100. See, for example, ibid., 268.

101. I do not believe that Marx actually relied on a simplistic base/superstructure notion at all. His theory is far more complex, and he only mentions base/superstructure once in his entire oeuvre.

that rational asceticism itself has created the very wealth it rejected."[102] Wealth thus becomes its own means leading to "irrational rationality" or to the increased rationalization of everything, accompanied by abnormally hard work, when there is no longer meaning in these things. What is significant in terms of Weber's argument against Marx, however, is that religious asceticism had no economic origins and yet served as the ethical meaning for the development of capitalism.

Weber further maintains that, contra Marx, these values are inherently at odds with state power, which requires a devotion that is viewed as idolatry by church leaders. On the other hand, the religious requirement for brotherly love is considered threatening to the state, which demands that citizens be willing to give their lives in wartime, suspending the notion of brotherliness.[103] Because the modern state has a monopoly on legitimate force and violence, it is first and foremost concerned with power: "In the final analysis, in spite of all 'social welfare policies,' the whole course of the state's inner political functions, of justice and administration, is repeatedly and unavoidably regulated by the objective pragmatism of 'reasons of state.' The state's absolute end is to safeguard (or to change) the external and internal distribution of power."[104] He concludes that the values of ascetic religious sects are viewed as threatening to modern polities. Nonetheless, the story Weber tells about bureaucracy and its increasing influence in every area of life shows that the impersonal character of rational work and conduct as valued by ascetic sects is perfectly suited to modern bureaucracy in economic enterprises *and* the state. Weber can only argue that modern rational asceticism is at odds with state power if he conceptually separates political bureaucracy from the state. This separation is echoed in contemporary writings in which the welfare state is distinguished from the "warfare state" and domestic politics is viewed as absolutely distinct from international political action.[105]

Given Weber's incredibly complex and even beautiful treatment of the development of asceticism in the West, it would appear that Marx has nothing to offer. However, Marx's own view of asceticism as a tool of the bourgeoisie illuminates certain important facts that Weber ignores. In the "1844 Manuscripts on Economic and Philosophical Thought," he notes that varying forces—cultural, religious, economic—preach to the

102. Gerth and Mills, *From Max Weber*, 332.
103. Ibid., 336.
104. Ibid., 334.
105. See, for example, Kaldor, "Reconceptualizing Organized Violence," 93.

poor the virtues of thrift, sexual abstinence, and low wages.[106] Yet at the same time, the rich and even middle classes show no such restraint. While Marx does view religion as the locus of "moral values," he sees it as working *in conjunction* with economic and political forces to justify the extreme poverty that has come about through industrialization and capitalism. In contrast to Nietzsche, Marx argues that a moral code that is *dictated* by one group to another cannot be an affirmation of agency or will. When it is, such a code is less an ethos than a tool of hegemony and domination.

Although Weber did recognize the inherent violence of modern asceticism,[107] he did not view this asceticism as informing modern political beliefs and practices. This did not conform to his notion of power, nor did it to his account of history. Part of the problem with his conception of history, however, is that he applies the word "capitalism" arbitrarily to any moment in world history. What is new to him is not the economic form itself, but rather its rationalization and thus its proliferation. Marx, on the other hand, uses the word capitalism not ahistorically but rather as marking a particular moment in time that is geographically and culturally specific. Capitalism, he recognizes, is more than economic; it touches on every area of life, and vice versa. This is why his argument seems to capture the idea of multiple causality better than does Weber's. Religious asceticism certainly had its own origins, unrelated to capitalism as Weber contends; yet clearly, it has also been used as a political tool and as a justification for exploiting and disenfranchising the poor. What Marx implies is the idea of a political theology: the intermingling of religion, economics, and politics in a significantly different way than in the past. In fact, Carl Schmitt (the man who coined the term "political theology")[108] would later argue that it is precisely the ethical orientation of the state that keeps it from being the ideal state Weber describes: one solely focused on power.

Weber clearly recognized that ascetic values had become increasingly harsh in modernity. His denial that asceticism was linked not only to capitalism but also to modern politics seems to have arisen from his desire to distance himself from Marx. If the liberal state does indeed have the same values as the capitalist ethos, then it would appear that the base/superstructure formulation is correct. Nevertheless, Weber aptly demon-

---

106. Foucault similarly remarks that the origins of poverty were believed to be "neither scarcity of commodities nor unemployment but the weakening of discipline and the relaxation of morals." Foucault, *The Foucault Reader*, ed. Paul Rabinow (New York: Pantheon, 1984), 131.

107. Gerth and Mills, *From Max Weber*, 336, 342.

108. Carl Schmitt, *Political Theology*, trans. George Schwab (Cambridge, Mass.: MIT Press, 1985).

strated that state power has dynamics of its own and that bureaucratic rules and rationalizations may mirror economic forms of bureaucracy, albeit with a different logic.[109]

But it is in the work of John Locke that one can see that the three areas—worldly asceticism, a market economy, and liberal governance—were never entirely distinct from one another. Rather, each informed the others as they developed over time, notwithstanding there were tensions among these realms.[110] Significantly, Locke was motivated by religious beliefs loosely based on Calvinism.[111] He employed religious language and values in his political and economic theories but was not an orthodox religious adherent. Evidence of this is his personal and political religious toleration[112] and his belief in freedom of conscience. Nevertheless, like ascetic protestant groups, he described outer-worldly asceticism in much the same language: we are all God's creatures, and therefore there is a moral imperative to ensure the survival of all; we are tools of God and thus must be productive through labor (which is why property is a *moral* and political element in his thought); and idleness and waste is a sin.[113] His ascetic prescriptions for a virtuous life—hard work, temperance, moderation, and the prohibition against unlimited accumulation—were aimed at several groups: the landed nobility, the Catholic Church (which had become corrupt), and albeit more guardedly the Anglican Church. He also had in his sights those selfish and arbitrary kings who were motivated by personal gain rather than the common good.

In particular, Locke (like Smith) is criticizing the idle rich and decrying the waste of tillable lands. In his view, productivity and hard work are to

109. In fact, Weber's intellectual heir Jürgen Habermas argues this precisely: that the state and the economy have developed their own separate spheres and logics. Any political domination of workers for the purpose of capitalist exploitation would merely be a form of "colonization" rather than inherent in the political system.

110. This is not to argue that C. B. Macpherson is correct to portray Locke as a materialistic capitalist who formulated his ideal government in order to meet the simple requirement to protect private property. Macpherson in his depiction is merely applying the base/superstructure formulation to a more complex reality. See Macpherson, ed., Introduction to John Locke, *Second Treatise of Government* (Indianapolis and Cambridge: Hackett Publishing, Classic Series, 1980).

111. For a discussion of this, see Richard Ashcraft, *Revolutionary Politics and Locke's Two Treatises of Government* (Princeton: Princeton University Press, 1986); see also John Dunn, *The Political Thought of John Locke.* For the parameters of the debate on Locke's religiosity, see David Wootton's Introduction to John Locke, *Political Writings,* ed. David Wootton (Indianapolis and Cambridge: Hackett Publishing, 2003).

112. See, for example, Ashcraft, *Revolutionary Politics,* 105–19.

113. See ibid. See also Thomas A. Horne, *Property Rights and Poverty: Political Arguments in Britain, 1605–1834* (Chapel Hill: University of North Carolina Press, 1990).

be the foundations of a liberal polity and nascent market economy in which rationality is a corollary. That is, rationality is necessary if consent is to be won for this new political arrangement, but it also is something that becomes *evident* through one's hard work. Here, Locke is presenting a slightly more secularized version of the notion of election in ascetic Protestantism (where one's hard work and material wealth are signs of election to grace by God). Correspondingly, political leadership should be based on rationality and wisdom rather than on noble lineage (although Hobbes is more adamant about the latter point than Locke). Given Locke's radical politics, it is hard to deny that he is criticizing the wealthy and democratizing politics by making work the key category of political inclusion rather than wealth.

On the other hand, Locke was certainly critiquing the (apparently) idle poor. Like the Protestant sects, he viewed poverty more as a function of one's sinfulness or individual problems than as a result of unemployment or other structural problems. Although his treatment of the poor in the *Second Treatise* was laudable, his contributions to the Poor Law demonstrated his contradictory views of the poor: everyone should have the right to live, but the poor should be treated punitively. The idle poor should be forced to work and be subject to constant surveillance and regulation; furthermore, it ought to be permitted to whip them, lop off their ears, compel them to do hard labor on ships, or deport them to the colonies.[114] Thus, while his critique of the rich may disempower them politically, the consequences for the poor are significantly harsher. The difference between the liberal treatment of the poor and the administration of poor relief during feudal times was one of ethical orientation. In earlier times, "masterless men" were viewed as a threat to society and the poor were merely given aid.[115] In contrast, the liberal justification for controlling and coercing the poor had two sources: first, a desire to tame the irrational elements, to civilize the poor and make them productive and industrious, thus fulfilling God's wishes and the norms and standards of this new political membership; and second, the notion of the general welfare of the people, the common good.

The first requirement was not merely cultural or private; it also involved the regular exercise of state power at the same time that the law

114. See Locke, "Draft of a Representation Containing a Scheme of Methods for the Employment of the Poor" (446–61) and "The Fundamental Constitutions of Carolina" (210–32), in *Political Writings;* Terence Hutchison, *Before Adam Smith: The Emergence of Political Economy, 1662–1776* (Oxford: Basil Blackwell, 1988), 72.

115. See Bauman, *Globalization,* regarding the first, and Polanyi, *The Great Transformation,* regarding the second.

was suspended (as with the possibility of losing an ear). Nevertheless, the Poor Laws were viewed as more enlightened than those of in the past, in that they aimed to educate and guide rather than merely apply force. The hope was that individuals would internalize these norms. As de Tocqueville remarked later on: "Under the absolute government of a single man, despotism, to reach the soul, clumsily struck at the body, and the soul . . . rose gloriously above it; but in democratic republics . . . tyranny . . . leaves the body alone and goes straight for the soul."[116] While this captures the change in political aims, what is truer is that liberal asceticism aimed at the body in order to reach the soul. Foucault would later call this "disciplinary power," the power to shape, enlighten, and make docile.[117] Labor serves this function as a pedagogical tool and "would revive for the lazy individual a liking for work, force him back into a system of interest in which labour would be more advantageous than laziness"; this was a moral lesson aimed at spiritual conversion.[118] On the one hand, ascetic policies demonstrate the close link between the market economy and state. On the other, this raises two questions: How can coercive power be justified when applied to noncriminals in a liberal democracy? And how can the suspension of law be brought about through bureaucratic (that is, rational ascetic) means?

The second requirement—that sovereignty be deployed for the common good—may appear inconsequential, but I will argue that it is of the utmost significance in defining modern political power and in justifying coercive action against some members of a polity. Convention has it that liberalism heralded a new era, free from arbitrary power save for the use of prerogative power in international relations and war. This belief is reflected in Weber's conceptual division of the state on the one hand and bureaucracy on the other, warfare on one side and welfare on the other. But this is faulty reasoning. It is not that prerogative is *absent* in the modern state; rather, it is now deployed for the common good rather than on behalf of an individual monarch. As Wolin argues, welfare and warfare in the modern nation-state are not mutually exclusive but one and the same.[119] Both point toward reason of state guided by concerns of welfare

116. Alexis de Tocqueville, *Democracy in America*, ed. J. P. Mayer, trans. George Lawrence (New York: Perennial Classics, 2000), 255.

117. See Foucault, *Discipline and Punish*, trans. Alan Sheridan (New York: Vintage Books, 1979).

118. Ibid., 122.

119. Wolin, "Democracy and the Welfare State," 166–70. In a different context, Richard Tuck also argues this; see Tuck, *The Rights of War and Peace* (New York: Oxford University Press, 1999).

or the common good—what Wolin calls Wohlfahrtsstaatsräson. Indeed, this notion of the common good is what enables Locke to argue that his ideal political government is far more democratic than that of Hobbes or of those (such as Hooker) who justified the divine right of monarchs. Locke argued for the division of governmental power, for checks and balances, and for the subjection of political leaders to the law, and in this he seemingly moved away from both Hobbes and Hooker.[120]

First, sovereignty would not be deployed by any one person, and thus an impersonal character (a key feature of liberalism and bureaucracy) would be lent to sovereignty that had not existed before. Second, political leaders would be chosen for their wisdom, education, and political skills, thus ensuring the good of all. Henceforth, sovereignty and political power would be exercised not for personal reasons or the defense of the king's body but rather for all citizen-subjects. The fact that the leaders would be subject to their own laws and that the people could (in theory) rebel in cases of egregious abuse on the part of the government further reinforced the case that sovereignty was now being configured *impersonally*, on behalf of all people and to achieve a common good. This reasoning justified, for example, the coercive nature of the Poor Laws, the purpose of which was to realize the common good under the enlightened goal of improving and disciplining the poor. In this way, "replacing the adversary of the sovereign, the social enemy was transformed into a deviant, who brought with him the multiple danger of disorder, crime and madness."[121]

Indeed, this is why Locke argues that in these circumstances, prerogative power can certainly be exercised.[122] Prerogative power involves decisions by one or more leaders in times of emergency (such as war) and/or when the law does not account for a specific situation. It is *legitimate* arbitrary power.[123] In the first case, it can involve a temporary suspension of the law. Prerogative power does not follow the rule of law; rather, it depends on its suspension and is capable of unleashing the full force of the state's violence. But as Wolin's term implies and as Locke's writings clearly spell out, prerogative power, which we usually assume is intended for foreign relations and for times of war, is conceived as operating domestically just as much as internationally. Here, Weber is certainly correct that the modern state affirms its legitimacy and monopoly on violence in the face of both internal and external threats. Yet Weber does not reconcile

---

120. Locke, *Second Treatise of Government*.
121. Foucault, *Discipline and Punish*, 299–300.
122. See Locke, *Second Treatise of Government*, Chapter XIV.
123. This wording follows Brown's in *States of Injury*, which I have cited above.

the arbitrary power and violence exercised as prerogative power with the cool and impersonal detachment that constitutes a highly rationalized bureaucracy. The two appear to be opposites; and of this, one consequence is that ascetic values (for example, through rationalization, the Protestant ethic, welfare policies) remain firmly in the civil, economic, and religious spheres rather than in what is clearly the most political of all spheres: the ability to make war or use violence legitimately.

However, when we adopt Wolin's hypothesis, these relationships can be viewed differently. First, we must concede that bureaucracy is not specifically economic or capitalist even if the bureaucratic form is highly compatible with capitalist needs.[124] Second, Weber would still argue that the two spheres of power—bureaucratic and sovereign/prerogative—have separate functions. Foucault's contribution to this argument is that modern power is now dispersed, local, and like a network rather than vertical, as in the past. Put another way, sovereignty no longer has the same forms it once did.[125] In fact, if Wolin is right, in a liberal capitalist polity bureaucratic power and sovereign power have the same goal and raison d'être: the common good. It follows that warfare and welfare are merely two aspects of modern power for the same purpose. When viewed this way, the logics of prerogative power and bureaucracy are not at odds. Finally, although bureaucracy's rationality appears to be the opposite of prerogative power as typically defined—as characterized by irregularity, arbitrariness, and violence—bureaucracy can serve as a vehicle for the deployment of prerogative power at a domestic level (as with Locke's writings on the Poor Laws, which involve bodily harm, internment, and deportation). As Wolin and Weber both note, bureaucratic rules in themselves may be formally structured and rational, but their content and implementation can be highly irrational and arbitrary.[126] Accordingly, bureaucratic power is the *arm* of modern sovereignty and prerogative rather than their opposite. Foucault's description of modern power as a web whose disciplinary forms eventually move outward from bureaucratic offices to nonjuridical loci (such as the doctor's office, the police station, the welfare office) demonstrates how this power is increasingly diffuse, normalizing, and impersonal (i.e., "no one person is responsible").

124. Bureaucracy functions in modern states, but democracy or capitalism are not prerequisites.
125. Although Foucault would argue that sovereignty is vertical and his formulation of modern power is something different.
126. Wolin, *Democracy and the Welfare State*, 157–59; Gerth and Mills, *From Max Weber*, 333–34.

Given this, it may be tempting to revert to a Hobbesian thesis that sovereign power in fact supersedes all other relations in importance. Nevertheless, in a polity such as the United States (*especially* the United States) "the economy is the ontological principle of modern ideologies and not a neutral construct that merely describes different organizations."[127] Indeed, the term "economic polity" rightly describes the "ontological and ideological assumption of underlying reality to which ideally the life of society should be attuned and the conception of power that should respond to private and public in nonadversarial way; this polity unlike Plato or Aristotle's polities is dedicated to the ever expanding increase of power . . . late modern forms of power that are aided by application of scientific knowledge . . . [are] endlessly reproducible and increasingly independent of civic virtue."[128]

In the United States, the modern state and capitalism work together tightly, yet there are certain tensions: capitalism is nonterritorial whereas the modern nation-state has been rigidly territorial; capitalism undermines feelings of patriotism whereas the modern nation-state demands unwavering loyalty; and so on. But I would argue that rather than amounting to a neat separation of two spheres,[129] these constitute *inherent* contradictions in the partnership between liberalism and capitalism, not one sphere colonizing the other. Bureaucracy and state power can be found in any modern nation-state, but liberalism and capitalism have a much closer relationship; each realm has informed the other throughout the historical development of both. Thus, in the United States the "spirit of capitalism" informs the deployment of sovereignty.

The State of Nature—the site of prerogative power's deployment and the conceptual locus of bare life or subsistence—illustrates the political consequences of this alliance between capitalism and sovereignty. The liberal concept of the State of Nature represented the economic and political baseline for a new politics that envisioned nothing more than going beyond preservation and that placed utmost importance on the right to live. In other words, politics was not conceived of as a radical transcendence of the biological; no search for a higher truth, for justice or the Good, was involved. If the State of Nature was a subsistence economy (and that was Locke's view), then it was the project of civil society to rise

127. Wolin, *Democracy and the Welfare State*, 154–55.
128. Ibid., 155.
129. As Jürgen Habermas has argued in *Theory of Communicative Action*, vol. 1, trans. Thomas McCarthy (Boston: Beacon Press, 1984); and *Theory of Communicative Action*, vol. 2, trans. Thomas McCarthy (Boston: Beacon Press, 1985).

above that state. Locke's new polity included neither the rule of the people nor any daily political activity; it did, though, cast hard work as a sort of civic duty and social contribution as well as (noted earlier) a sign of "election." Certain groups remained in the State of Nature owing to their irrationality or economic dependence—women, children, the poor, "ideots"; members of civil society transcended that state through their hard work, productivity, and rational conduct. On the one hand, bare life, mere survival; on the other, the work of civilization and civil society, which rose above bare life. On the one hand, individuals who needed guidance or who had to be molded, punished, coerced, and/or assimilated to join the new norm of political and economic membership; on the other, those . who had already proven that they were tools of God. Correspondingly, liberal democratic governance (guided by the rule of law) administers civil society, and prerogative power (the suspension of law) is deployed in the State of Nature. Thus, as Agamben (among others)[130] argues, the State of Nature does not precede civil society but is internal to it.[131] It follows that those who become objects of prerogative power domestically are the disenfranchised, those viewed as inhabiting the State of Nature.

To return to the subject of asceticism, the following observations can be made. First, it is clear that modern asceticism was not a tool of the weak and oppressed to rid the nobility of their political power per Nietzsche. The bourgeoisie or burghers whom Weber names as social carriers of this new "ethos" were neither powerless nor the most powerful. Second, the highly rational, ascetic ethos that dominated new religious sects and political and economic treatises carried with it values that were targeted at the *entire* population, not the poor per se as Marx argued. In fact, as Foucault contends in *The History of Sexuality, Vol. 1,* the allegedly repressive discourse surrounding sex was aimed at and a product of the bourgeoisie first. Freud's own experience with middle-class and wealthy clients bore this out; consider here his thesis in *Civilization and Its Discontents* that repression and ascetic ideals make *all* of civilization unhappy yet productive. This is not to say that Marx was wrong about a double standard; the point is that this argument must be made in a more nuanced manner.

If ascetic recommendations are meant for the entire society, then what we have is not merely an ethos but an approach to structuring political and economic life around what Agamben calls "bare life." An ascetic political and economic structure may be aimed at everyone, but it is

130. Notably Tuck, in *The Rights of War and Peace.*
131. Agamben, *Homo Sacer,* 18.

applied *coercively* to the poor, who serve as the exemplary group outside the norm. In this way a threshold is established, with one group—subject citizens—viewed as active participants in the work of civilization and allowed autonomy and the benefits of liberal democracy, and the other group perceived as requiring guidance, discipline, and protection. The second group become objects of prerogative power and face not only the suspension of the law but also, possibly, bodily harm.

By the time Bentham and Malthus were writing, ascetic values had been conditioned by other factors: the growth of the market economy, an increase in poverty and geographical dislocation, and the perception of scarcity. Ascetic values served as dogma and were preached to the poor by ministers, politicians, and the newspapers of the time. Both Marx and Nietzsche commented on this, although they came to very different conclusions. This explains how asceticism has become the "ethos" of bare life and modern power. It applies to all, albeit unequally and in different forms. Marx was right to consider this ethos a domineering and hypocritical double standard. But he failed to recognize the implication of the ascetic ethos that is the foundation of modern politics: that anyone can become bare life.[132] The control and management of the species is directed toward all. The development of eugenics was a logical outgrowth of all this. It may comfort some of us to think that radical asceticism is a tool of class domination exerted on the poor alone. The more disturbing reality is that asceticism is our society's key organizing principle. In the United States, prerogative power based on bare life is aimed at the disenfranchised and at those perceived as biological: poor immigrants of color, racial minorities, and women, among others.

The entire complex of my argument—that prerogative power is exercised at the bureaucratic level as well as the executive level; that it works in conjunction with capitalism, with asceticism as its guiding principle—points to a historical shift in sovereign power and its aims. In the past, "the sovereign exercised his right of life only by exercising his right to kill, or by refraining from killing. . . . The right which was formulated as the 'power of life and death' was in reality the right to *take* life or *let* live. Its symbol, after all, was the sword."[133] In contrast, modern power is based on the right to live; this is particularly true of liberalism, whose most fundamental element is natural law (for example, the right to self-preservation). The sovereign right to kill "is now manifested as simply the

132. See ibid., 114.
133. Foucault, *History of Sexuality*, 136.

reverse of the right of the social body to ensure, maintain, or develop its life. Yet wars were never as bloody as they have been since the nineteenth century, and all things being equal, never before did regimes visit such holocausts on their own populations."[134] On the one hand, power administers, manages, optimizes, and measures life; on the other, "wars are no longer waged in the name of a sovereign who must be defended; they are waged on behalf of the existence of everyone; entire populations are mobilized for the purpose of wholesale slaughter in the name of life necessity: massacres have become vital."[135] In this way, modern forms of genocide or state racism are logical outcomes of contemporary political forms.

Ascetic values in the liberal capitalist state may once have had some ethical motivations, but they have not been ethical per se. Rather, they are a function of biopower and disciplinary power. Disciplinary power developed first and "centered on the body as a machine: its disciplining, the optimization of its capabilities, the extortion of its forces, the parallel increase of its usefulness and its docility, its integration into systems of efficient and economic controls, all this was ensured by the procedures of a power that characterized the *disciplines:* an *anatomo-politics of the human body.*"[136] Biopower involves the ordering, administration, and management of the human species politically. It is "the growing inclusion of man's natural life in the mechanisms and calculations of power."[137] "Only because politics in modernity had become bio-politics was it possible for politics to be constituted as totalitarian in a way never before possible."[138] Consequently, rational asceticism signified not just the introduction of a new morality but "the entry of life into history, that is, the entry of phenomena peculiar to the life of the human species into the order of knowledge and power, into the sphere of political techniques."[139] As Foucault remarks, this was not the first synthesis of the biological and political; this has always been the case to varying degrees. Nevertheless, with changing agricultural techniques and the introduction of modern science and medicine, famines and epidemics in the West were largely eliminated as regular features of daily life, and for the first time the optimization of life was possible.[140] Hand in hand with this, biopower reflected the basis of power on "bare life."

134. Ibid., 136.
135. Ibid., 137.
136. Ibid., 139.
137. Agamben, *Homo Sacer,* 119, quoting Foucault.
138. Ibid., 120.
139. Foucault, *History of Sexuality,* 142.
140. Ibid., 142.

In our current political system, women and racial minorities—including poor immigrants of color—are conceived of first and foremost in terms of their biology or skin color. They are the object of biopower because of their "biology" as it has been historically and socially constructed, because their "biological existence" is "reflected in political existence."[141] For example, in the United States today, women are viewed as responsible for the family and for sexual reproduction (as evidenced in our current welfare laws). This has involved the "hysterization of women's bodies," which translates into the "medicalization of bodies and sex, carried out in name of responsibility they owed to the health of their children, the solidity of the family institution and the safeguarding of society."[142] Accordingly, biology and sex constitute "woman's body, ordering it wholly in terms of the functions of reproduction and keeping it in constant agitation through the effects of that very function."[143] That is not to say that men are any less "biological" than women; the point here is that the liberal capitalist state regulates women's biological functions and freedoms in the areas of sexuality (for example, birth control, abortion); imposes hetero-sexuality and marriage as the norm; promotes "family" values; and administers physical protection and physical violence (among other things) for political and economic reasons.

In this way, women's political identity is formulated *as* women and a norm of femininity is constructed. The relation of women to the state is as reproducers, dependents, child care workers, and wives. Much the same can be said of poor immigrants and racial minorities, whose identity is formulated in terms of their skin color and economic condition. This is particularly evident in the growing popularity of biological racism over the past twenty years.[144] Less recognized is the biologization of poverty—the assumption that poor people in general have lower IQs, are inherently lacking in morals and a work ethic, and are deficient in myriad other ways. These assumptions are most evident in the treatment of the U.S. homeless as not simply poor but pathological, deviant, and a form of

141. Ibid., 141.
142. Ibid., 146, 147.
143. Ibid., 153.
144. See Wilson, *When Work Disappears*, Introduction; Jones, *American Work*, Epilogue; Jim Naureckas, "Racism Resurgent: How Media Let *The Bell Curve's* Pseudo-Science Define the Agenda on Race," http://www.fair.org/extra/9501/bell.html; Joseph Barnes, "Book Review: *The End of Racism* by Dinesh D'Souza," *Zmagazine*, http://www.zmag.org/zmag/articles/dec95reviews.htm; Adam Miller, "Professors of Hate," *Rolling Stone* 693 (1994); Charles Lane, "The Tainted Sources of 'The Bell Curve,'" *New York Review of Books* 41, no. 20 (1994).

social pollution.[145] In contrast, the political relationship of mainstream individuals to the state fits the norm of universal citizenship held by the autonomous individual.

Asceticism functions under nonmarket conditions; in Nazi Germany, for example, biopower and totalitarianism were one and the same. Yet ascetic demands also suit capitalism, and this in the United States has led to an *entirely different* synthesis of the political and the economic. In particular, prerogative power has been strengthened in response to the needs and demands of global capital. In this country, power and domination are both obscured and diffuse. Certain political institutions and democratic practices are disappearing or becoming marginalized; and meanwhile, the state is being fortified by its connection to capitalism, notwithstanding that this coupling has its tensions. As a consequence, the domination of the poor is becoming more and more possible rather than less and less, and exploitation is not merely economic but also political.[146] If the State of Nature is the conceptual location of prerogative power, and if those who are viewed as occupying that conceptual sphere can become objects of prerogative power, it cannot be said that the poor or women or racial minorities are being targeted because of what they just *are;* rather, they are being targeted because of their political condition—specifically, their de facto disenfranchisement and precarious political status. They easily become "bare life" and the objects of prerogative power in ways that an ordinary, autonomous citizens cannot.

Although bare life is not the only organizing principle of modern politics, it is becoming increasingly predominant. This is not to deny acts of resistance on the part of the oppressed or a long history of democratic organizing and grassroots activity. These acts of resistance—from micro-resistance to mass protest—tell us that even in a state that is increasingly deploying absolute power, the fragmentary nature of late modern power is continuous and porous. Nevertheless, as neoliberalism and neoconservatism have become predominant institutionally, in policymaking, and even as a general mindset, it can be argued that the state's organizing principle has increasingly become bare life and its ethos asceticism, around which species thinking and biopower have developed.[147] It also means that welfare prescriptions and low-wage policies have less to do with

145. See Leonard Feldman, *Citizens Without Shelter* (Ithaca: Cornell University Press, 2004); Arnold, *Homelessness, Citizenship, and Identity.*

146. See Wolin, *Democracy and the Welfare State,* 158.

147. This argument does not negate materialist analyses or critiques of the nation-state, for example; but it does hold that their foundations are first and foremost bare life.

morality, humanity, and enlightenment than with control, surveillance and a re-engineering of humans into docile bodies. It demonstrates that prerogative power is exercised domestically, and on a regular basis rather than only during states of emergency. It is a form of assimilation that offers no hope for citizenship, autonomy, or democracy. Those who do not fit the norms of biopower are not viewed as moral or rational beings nor even as human. To be worthy of humanity and the species, one must first be accepted by civil society as a rational and autonomous being. Women, the poor, and exploited and oppressed racial minorities have not fallen under that rubric. Instead they have come to represent the biological, the irrational, and thus the inhuman. The combination of capitalist demands (disciplinary power), biopower (ascetic demands), and political theology (the intermingling of prerogative, the baseline of bare life, and ascetic orientation toward the human species) has allowed for a disturbing level of inhumanity in the treatment of individuals who have passed beyond the pale of law.

With the proliferation of mechanisms of power on behalf of sovereignty, the possibility of *sustained* democratic power as an active force in the United States has become increasingly diminished. Illustrations of this: the decline of unions and their increasing impossibility for guest workers and low-wage workers; the view that immigrant self-help or political groups are "separatist" and a threaten to national unity; the denigration of poor African Americans who protest job conditions as "uppity" or ungrateful;[148] and the perspective on protesters against globalization, on behalf of the poor, or against the war on terrorism as marginal, crazy, or traitorous.[149] The decline of democratic conditions is a sign of prerogative power's regular deployment, and of a polity in which the state of exception and the state of emergency have become permanent features.

---

148. See both Wilson, *When Work Disappears*, and Jones, *American Work*, on this subject.

149. Indeed, John Stuart Mill predicts the docility and individualization that occurs: "In [Christianity's] horror of sensuality, it made an idol of asceticism, which has been gradually compromised away into one of legality. It holds out the hope of heaven and the threat of hell as the appointed and appropriate motives to a virtuous life: in this falling far below the best of the ancients, and doing what lies in it to give to human morality an essentially selfish character, by disconnecting each man's feelings of duty from interests of his fellow creatures, except so far as a self-interested inducement is offered to him for consulting them. It is essentially a doctrine of passive obedience; it inculcates submission to all authorities found established; who indeed are to be actively obeyed when they command what religion forbids, but who are not to be resisted, far less rebelled against, for any moment to ourselves." John Stuart Mill, *On Liberty*, ed. Elizabeth Rapaport (Indianapolis and Cambridge: Hackett Publishing, 1978), 47.

Asceticism, Low-Wage Policies, Deregulation, and Welfare

The ascetic values, discourse, and policies that serve as the guidelines for welfare on the one hand, and for guest-worker policies, low-wage policies, workfare, and the deregulation of work conditions, on the other, are fundamental to the historical development of sovereignty and modern power. Not only do these policies lack compassion, but they also justify the deployment of prerogative power at the domestic level *and*, significantly, at the bureaucratic level. This challenges two widely held assumptions: that prerogative power is only exercised in the international realm; and that because it is characterized by arbitrary decision making and the suspension of the law, bureaucracy and its modalities must *preclude* the existence of prerogative power. Furthermore, it challenges Foucault's idea that sovereignty as an exercise of power is distinct from disciplinary and biopower (although Foucault hints that it is possible for them to be connected and Agamben argues that Foucault's later work indeed implies this possibility).[150] Ascetic prescriptions are a form of biopower, and minorities, poor women, and immigrants of color match the profile as subjects for the types of control these deployments exert. This is why changes in immigration, welfare, and labor policies do not signify the abandonment of the poor per se, but rather a transmogrified political space in which the suspension of law is more prevalent.

In the current political environment, ascetic demands and values are not only preached to the poor but also imposed on them through welfare/ workfare laws and low-wage and deregulation policies. Nietzsche's distinction between the asceticism that is a will to power and priestly or slave morality is helpful because the asceticism urged on the poor is presented to them as life-affirming—that is, they are told that if they comply with these standards (save money, abstain from sex, work hard even if wages are low), they will succeed and be "free." Marx recognized the hypocrisy of these demands that the poor save, abstain from alcohol and sex, and eat less while the wealthy often were not held to these standards. To apply Nietzsche to Marx, it can be said that the asceticism preached to the poor is not a will to power but instead is characterized by *ressentiment*. In Nietzsche's words, those who promote asceticism (policymakers, welfare caseworkers, editorial writers) say "no" to the poor. In the same way that Nietzsche conceives of the weak in society formulating an ethos that is simply a reaction to the more powerful Other, the response to the poor

---

150. Agamben, *Homo Sacer*, 5, 6.

comes paradoxically[151] from a position of weakness or uncertainty. In part, this is because economic power is not always stable; the poor represent a loss in what is conceived of as a zero sum game. A welfare recipient can represent "a purely receptive, expending, and consuming agency, an *apparently* useless mouth."[152] The resentment of the rich is based on feelings of Schuld, debt, and guilt that have been projected back onto the poor. Related to this is that the well off view not just their work as a sign of grace but their spending as well. In contemporary times, gambling, stock-market speculation, and investment in various properties can be viewed not as pure excesses but as sacrifices, contributions, and manifestations of "self-interest properly understood." George W. Bush confirmed this after the attacks of September 11, 2001, when he urged all citizens to continue spending money and shopping.

More specifically, ascetic categories are racialized and gendered, not to mention determined by economic class. The vices of poverty, sexual wantonness, economic dependence, and family disintegration (among other things) are marked as especially feminine and racial. The vice of greed, on the other hand, is transformed into economic independence and responsibility, and these values are associated with men. Economic independence and notions of responsibility and rationality distinguish these categories from "vices." The middle classes and the wealthy feel that they have *earned* the right to their excess. In this way, the fetishization of the stock market is interpreted as a logical consequence of work in the new economy, even while poor working families are criticized for spending beyond their means, for not buckling down.[153]

Thus, the state's treatment of women, racial minorities, and immigrants brings to the surface its attitude toward poverty and also the position of these groups politically. This is not to say that state power and ideology is unified and consistent—it is not—nor is it to say that all of these individuals are uniformly subject to state power. Rather, in a general sense, it demonstrates to varying degrees the political identity of these groups and explains the difficulty of *sustained* democratic action.

151. Paradoxically because this interpretation of women on welfare as Other comes from numerous privileged sources.

152. Jacques Derrida's comment on how some view beggars. Derrida, *Given Time: I. Counterfeit Money*, trans. Peggy Kamuf (Chicago: University of Chicago Press, 1992), 134.

153. In one *New Yorker* article from ten years ago, a poor family is criticized for going to McDonald's once a week. The same article recommends that they eat beans rather than meat in order to save money.

Conclusion

What must be emphasized is that ascetic values are the guiding ethos for the entire population and not just the poor, racial minorities, and women. For this reason, there is outrage at white-collar crime and the middle and upper middle classes feel smug that they are thin, have invested wisely, and have only one child, for example. Ascetic values inform actions at all levels. In fact, this explains how ascetic values involve reversals: immigrants are exploiting "us" by taking jobs and sending all their earnings out of the country; poor women have out-of-wedlock children and use welfare as their income (as Simone de Beauvoir remarks, "Woman has been assigned the role of parasite—and every parasite is an exploiter");[154] and poorer African Americans represent pathology, disorder, and crime.[155] In this way, work—the key category of asceticism—becomes obscured by the alleged exploitative behavior of these "marginal" groups. That is, dependence is construed as exploitation. Ironically, Beauvoir notes, these groups have historically been paid less for the same work by (mainstream) men and thus their dependence is a fait accompli.[156]

"We" are able to judge "their" actions and endorse moral prescriptions only if we can tell ourselves that we have adhered to these norms ourselves. The double standard I have investigated in this chapter is thus not blatant hypocrisy; nonetheless it is still a double standard at its base, and one that hinges on work. Labor has become a key category of modern asceticism and the values associated with it—it is the "spirit of capitalism," as Weber has shown. Jobs associated with the private sphere and/or groups that have traditionally been viewed as the "serving classes" are devalued precisely because of ascetic standards. In a labor market guided by neoliberal policies and in which the service industry is now dominant, the economic contributions of the working classes have been obscured as well as feminized and racialized. First, these groups are defined by their biological identity over and above their labor, or to put it differently, the labor they perform is viewed in biological terms: gardening is natural to Mexicans, Dominican women make great nannies, women were made for service work and helping others, and so on.[157] This work is seen as

154. Beauvoir, *The Second Sex*, 614.
155. See Toni Morrison, "On the Backs of Blacks," 98; Jack Miles, "Blacks vs. Browns," 119–24; Frances Fukuyama, "Immigrants and Family Values," 156, 161, 163; all of these in *Arguing Immigration*, ed. Nicolaus Mills (New York: Touchstone, 1994).
156. Beauvoir, *The Second Sex*, 114, 680–81.
157. See Jones, *American Work*, 375.

"immanent" (Beauvoir's term) or "preservation" (Heidegger's) precisely because it is subsistence level, tied to domesticity or service in some way, often absolutely necessary, frequently performed in isolation or in the home, and viewed as a natural extension of the self. Low wages are justified for exactly these reasons.[158] Second, the associations between biology (that is, the natural) and excess, sin, and vice fate these groups to immorality[159] and, it follows, as transgressors of ascetic norms. This explains why they are assumed to resist adapting to ascetic norms[160] and must be forced to do so for their own good and the good of society. Clearly, the "protection" of the welfare state and the "positive" gains for workers through low-wage policies are aimed at producing a docile workforce. And the mechanisms for achieving this are coercive and hierarchical rather than therapeutic or humane.

The prescription of asceticism, while intended for the entire populace, has been aimed at the working poor and welfare recipients as the exemplar of a group that is being molded into good, docile citizens and simultaneously being punished for "excesses." Despite sexism, racism, the yawning gap between rich and poor, bleak employment opportunities for women, and the crisis in affordable housing, these groups are being blamed for their poverty. The ascetic values underlying policy and cultural solutions imply that the poor will achieve some sort of self-mastery and thus, fitness for citizenship, only if they buckle down. This espousal of asceticism is an attempt to master groups falling under the rubric of the biological by eradicating or neutralizing difference, and the power dynamic is one of coercion more than independence or self-will. The dynamics of power in the liberal capitalist state have allowed for the coexistence of seemingly contradictory power mechanisms, both democratic and nondemocratic. However, this seemingly paradoxical coexistence is an integral part of liberal capitalism: "bare life" is crucial to political identity, power, and the economy.

This brief intellectual history of ascetic ideas has demonstrated how and why the moral imperatives of welfare and the ascetic practices linked to workfare and work in the global economy do not signal the decreasing importance of the state, much less sovereignty, in late modern politics. The purported disappearance of the nation-state has been claimed on two fronts: in the context of the global economy, and in the dismantling

158. Not to mention the history of the family wage.

159. This idea is indebted to Beauvoir, *The Second Sex*, 474.

160. Despite evidence and arguments to the contrary—see, for example, Beauvoir's arguments throughout *The Second Sex* as well as Wilson's research on how African Americans have internalized the Protestant work ethic in *When Work Disappears*, 69, 178–82.

of welfare and affirmative-action programs. These developments do not demonstrate the absence of state, but rather the increasing influence of economic logic in matters of sovereignty, be they internal or external.[161] Ascetic ideas provide the crucial nexus between matters of sovereignty and the deployment of prerogative, on the one hand, and the dictates of capitalism, on the other. The growing predominance of a neoliberal ethos in this way brings politics to the level of bare life and facilitates the greater influence of biopower and disciplinary power, thus enabling the suspension of law. In the next chapter, I examine more closely the development of the idea of prerogative power and the justification for its use.

---

161. Since the end of the Cold War. See Cheryl Shanks, *Immigration and Politics of American Sovereignty, 1890–1990, Kritikos* 2 (2005).

DOMESTIC WAR: LOCKE'S CONCEPT OF PREROGATIVE

The tradition of the oppressed teaches us that the "state of exception" in which we live is the rule.

—WALTER BENJAMIN[1]

In this chapter, I revisit the concepts introduced in the previous chapter in order to examine the dynamics of late modern sovereignty in the United States. A dominant strand of contemporary theory distinguishes between the largely extrajuridical exercise of sovereignty abroad and the domestic exercise of power, which significantly follows the rule of law, treats citizens equally, and holds democratic values as the highest. In this line of argumentation, it is contended that the development of a spirit of capitalism and the increasing rationalization of law have led to the deployment of domestic power diffusely and impersonally and that both depend on the rule of law. Political power is legitimated through appeals to abstract notions of justice and the common good, and this underscores rationality as well as a moral framework that rewards an individual's hard work, honesty, and integrity. It would seem that this emphasis on rationality and on the ascetic values that form the basis of liberal capitalism's ethical structure disavow irrationality, violence, and arbitrary power. The concept of a social contract symbolizes this rationality and also implies mutuality between the government and the

---

1. Walter Benjamin, "Critique of Violence," in *Reflections*, quoted in Giorgio Agamben, *Homo Sacer: Sovereign Power and Bare Life*, trans. Daniel Heller-Roazen (Stanford: Stanford University Press, 1998), 55.

governed.[2] However, as discussed in the previous chapter, Western political theorists of the modern state never really conceived of the absence of prerogative power within state boundaries. Rather, liberal theorists and theorists of the modern state such as Max Weber reconceived how this power could be deployed under modern conditions.

This becomes evident when we explore who is subject to prerogative power, and why. The question of prerogative is relevant to the War on Drugs, the War on Terror, the criminalization of homelessness, the monitoring of workfare recipients, low-wage policies directed at the poor, and our guest-worker programs; all of these combine to control marginalized populations while coordinating with the demands of global capital. In this chapter, I examine the conceptual roots and justifications for prerogative power in the liberal writings that I discussed in the previous chapter, with the goal of solving a number of puzzles. First, I explore theories about prerogative power and its implementation, beginning with the early liberals. I have chosen this as a starting point in order to answer two questions: How has prerogative power been deployed in liberal democracies? And why have liberal theorists justified its exercise domestically? I focus in particular on John Locke's arguments about prerogative because he advocates both the rule of law *and* the use of prerogative power.[3] His recommendations relating to the poor and to colonial administration demonstrate how he (partially) resolves this seeming paradox. Building on my arguments from the previous chapter, I elucidate how these policy prescriptions demonstrate that the conventional distinction made by political theorists between welfare and warfare is misguided: a liberal polity does not separate these spheres neatly; rather, it unites them in the notion of the common good.

Indeed, to Locke, prerogative power was the most expedient way to accomplish an end in certain circumstances; as he noted, written law cannot account for every event or problem. Hegel and, later, Weber also recognized that beyond liberal democratic power, the state must still act

2. Regarding this distinction, see Carole Pateman, *The Disorder of Women* (Stanford: Stanford University Press, 1992); Sheldon Wolin, "Democracy and the Welfare State: The Political and Theoretical Connections Between Staatsräson and Wohlfahrsstaatsräson," in *The Presence of the Past: Essays on the State and the Constitution* (Baltimore: Johns Hopkins University Press, 1989).

3. "Locke is without doubt the only political theorist, among the major advocates of limited monarchy, to make prerogative a central element of his political theory (whatever most of his interpreters might think), and to construct from it a systematic constitutional theory of extralegal power." Pasquale Pasquino, "Locke on King's Prerogative," *Political Theory* 26 (April 1998): 199.

as a state. In contemporary times, Wendy Brown has formulated the exercise of prerogative power in Weberian terms. For her it is the "legitimate arbitrary power in policy making and legitimate monopolies of internal and external violence in the police and military. As the overt power-political dimension of the state, prerogative includes expressions of national purpose and national security as well as the whole range of legitimate arbitrary state action from fiscal regulation to incarceration procedures."[4] In fact, with the consolidation of nation-states into larger territories, with their monopoly on violence, and with the development of scientific applications for exerting power, the exercise of prerogative power has become viable on a scale never before possible. In this way, the deployment of prerogative power or raison d'état does not represent a historical rupture; rather, it has been accommodated to liberal democratic notions. Even so, clear tensions have developed among certain democratic values that are the basis of liberal theory, on the one hand, and institutions and the exercise of prerogative power, on the other, even as they are tied together in two ways: first, prerogative power has been conceived of as the precondition for liberal democratic power; and second, liberal power and prerogative power, although they differ in ethical orientation, have biological life as their basis.

A second puzzle is how prerogative can be deployed with the rationalization of political power (as theorized by Weber and Habermas) and, more broadly, with the development and exercise of disciplinary power and biopower (Foucault's notions). This line of argument holds that bureaucratic power has dispersed political power and thus acts of pure sovereignty appear few and far between, especially on the domestic front.[5] If prerogative power was at one time in the hands of feudal lords and, more significantly, was the defining power of absolute monarchs, the question is this: How is it exercised now that we have "cut off the king's head"?[6] As Brown notes, in late modernity "modes of power are far easier to determine than particular agents."[7] Yet when we consider Locke's theory of prerogative power in combination with his recommendations for the poor and for colonial subjects, we quickly see that the use

4. Wendy Brown, *States of Injury: Power and Freedom in Late Modernity* (Princeton: Princeton University Press, 1995), 176.
5. Richard Tuck argues that raison d'état is at the heart of the liberal tradition. See Tuck, *The Rights of War and Peace* (New York: Oxford University Press, 1999).
6. Michel Foucault, "Truth and Power," in *The Foucault Reader*, ed. Paul Rabinow (New York: Pantheon Books, 1984), 63.
7. Brown, *States of Injury*, 167.

of prerogative even in his time was deployed through administrative (now bureaucratic) means. In this way, institutions that represented the rule of law could also suspend the law, and sovereign agents were diffuse rather than concentrated in the figure of a single leader.

There is also the charge that capitalist functions and values have largely *replaced* the state, citizenship, and political participation. This claim is prevalent in a world of economic globalization. It appears that the nation-state's boundaries are becoming blurry, that cities like New York, Los Angeles, Tokyo, and London are more dominant than any country's capital and transnational arrangements; thus, the European Union and the North American Free Trade Agreement (NAFTA) have come to hold more power than any one state. Accordingly, it is claimed, national sovereignty has been undercut by transnational contracts and deals and by corporate political and economic actions abroad that have made state power obsolete. Thus it would appear that sovereign power—and, more importantly, prerogative power—is on the decline in a highly rationalized world that is increasingly operating under capitalist norms and guidelines.

But it is the individual as subject (in the philosophical sense) of prerogative power—the refugee in the holding cell, the homeless man who cannot occupy public space, the Roma woman sterilized by an East European government, the displaced masses in refugee camps—who draws attention to the role of the state and prerogative power. These individuals, whose numbers have increased significantly in the second half of the twentieth century (Hannah Arendt is famous for declaring that the stateless are "the most symptomatic group in contemporary politics"),[8] defy the logic of the nation-state and liberal capitalism. They are all examples of individuals being subject simultaneously to both the law and its suspension. Their displacement is an inevitable consequence of the uprootedness of these two realms, yet their conditions are still political. I argue below that this signals not the absence of prerogative but its bureaucratic facilitation. These individuals have entered a space that Giorgio Agamben calls "bare life," in which they are conceived of biologically rather than as citizens and thus human beings.[9] Citizens are subject to the rule of law; those considered biological or "bare life" are subject to the sovereign power usually reserved for states of emergency. The power dynamics of liberal capitalist states have enabled the coexistence of two

---

8. Hannah Arendt, *The Origins of Totalitarianism* (New York: Harcourt Brace Jovanovich, 1979), 277.
9. See Agamben, *Homo Sacer.*

seemingly contradictory power mechanisms: the liberal (the rule of law) and the prerogative or nondemocratic (the suspension of law). This seeming paradox is integral to liberal capitalism today: the poor, rootless subject of power (bare life) is crucial to political identity and to power as it has become constituted.

The first crucial element of modern power is that arbitrary power must now be authorized through legal—and often rational—means. Second, the subject must be considered bare life—that is, less than a citizen—if the suspension of law is to be justified. In this way, those whose status has been criminalized or who have been politically excluded or devalued can face arbitrary power and the suspension of law. Those who are conceived of as bare life are not dehumanized through criminal acts per se but rather by their political status. For this reason, I believe this term is more appropriate than the word *enemy*, given that subjects of domestic prerogative have not formally been declared enemies. Bare life is "biological life"—Agamben's term—but this is not a politically neutral rubric. This term is also useful in that it links the State of Nature to the private sphere and household labor[10] and undermines the notion that the State of Nature is temporal, preceding civil society. Given this conceptual framework, I propose that citizenship in today's liberal nation-state is not founded on contracts or consent per se, but instead on the criteria of *ius soli* and ius *sanguinis* (that is, criteria which rest on status more than on choice; roughly, ius soli is citizenship by birth and *ius sanguinis* is citizenship by descent).[11]

Prerogative Power in Liberal Thought

In this section, I explore the links between bare life and prerogative power in early liberal thought. As I discussed in Chapter 1, by taking human nature and human needs as its bases, liberal thought brought politics down to the level of life. This trend began as early as the preliberal Hobbes. In classical, Roman, and feudal times, politics was a transcendence of the biological involving a nobility of the spirit and communion with others; later, liberalism addressed self-preservation, the right to live, and the preservation of others. Property rights—the basis of liberal thought

10. This formulation may be problematic in other contexts, but I believe it is adequate for the purposes of this text.

11. Even *ius soli*, the allegedly more democratic of the two, has been criticized as feudal, privileging the fact of birth over free choice.

in Locke—thus are not driven purely by a concern for wealth, as C. B. Macpherson mistakenly contends; instead they are directed toward sustaining life first and foremost, as Richard Ashcraft has demonstrated. Few have noticed that Locke did not believe in unlimited accumulation of land *unless* it was compensated for by money (for example, hiring labor), thus allowing for the survival of all (§31, 36, 37, 46, 50).[12]

Indeed, the early liberals posited that all moral obligations—from helping the poor or one's neighbor to opposing the abuses of an absolute monarch—were rooted in natural law. Thus, political power ought no longer serve the interests of elites, but rather those of the general public. That is, political power ought to be founded on rights, including that of property (albeit property should not be the axis). Thus, political power should be constituted by rights such as free speech, a free press, and freedom of religion. Clearly, political power was being conceived of as a moral claim.[13] Ashcraft contends that "the truly radical claim advanced by Locke . . . is that poor relief is a socially constitutive and necessary feature of any legitimate society, since societies are only legitimate to the extent that they realize the purposes and objectives of natural law."[14] In this way, subsistence was conceptualized as a right and not a privilege and communal responsibility superseded that of the individual. But it must be emphasized here that morality was derived in the first place from natural law, which was reducible to human need and preservation. Thus, morality reflected an increasing concern with species thinking and with biological aspects of the populace (concerns that would develop into biopower). As I will discuss later, the rights that originated in natural law led to the development of citizenship rights in the form of *protection* and, thus, a passive form of political membership.[15]

Why the emphasis on bare life when politics formerly aimed at the soul? As Foucault expressed it (and I quoted in Chapter 1): "For millennia, man remained what he was for Aristotle: a living animal with the additional capacity for a political existence; modern man is an animal whose

12. John Locke, *Second Treatise of Government*, ed. C. B. Macpherson, (Cambridge: Hackett Publishing, Classic Series, 1980), 20–21, 22–24, 28, 29–30. See also Richard Ashcraft, *Revolutionary Politics and Locke's Two Treatises of Government* (Princeton: Princeton University Press, 1986), 262–83 n151 (266–67 in particular); Tuck, *Natural Rights Theories* (Cambridge: Cambridge University Press, 1981), 170–72.

13. Richard Ashcraft, "Liberalism and the Problem of Poverty," *Critical Review* (1993): 11, 12.

14. Ibid., 7.

15. As Verity Smith (Ph.D. candidate, University of California, San Diego) notes, early theories of natural law worked backwards from the international order toward more local assumptions regarding the State of Nature. Verity Smith, private correspondence, May 2004.

politics places his existence as a living being in question."[16] The rise of princely (that is absolute) power on the one hand and religious wars on the other precipitated preliberal and liberal treatises. The call for the separation of church and state by Hobbes and Locke,[17] among others, removed any pretensions to a politics of the spirit or a radical transcendence of biological man. This is not to say that biological man was unaccounted for in the past; as both Agamben and Foucault have remarked, biological life has been a significant feature of politics for the past two thousand years. Nevertheless, in ancient philosophy and governments, *oikos* (the household) was conceived of as the *precondition* for politics, not as constituting the substance of the political. This was still considering politics in terms of bare life—here, as the opposite of bare life—yet there remained a conceptual separation between bare life and politics.

In ancient Greek political philosophy the political was conceived of as a transcendence of the biological and natural. *Oikos* represented subsistence living and animal need. As Aristotle stated: "It is evident . . . that mastery and political [rule] are not the same thing . . . household management is monarchy . . . while political rule is over free and equal persons."[18] Aristotle's conception of the household was similar to Locke's (but not Hobbes's) notion of the State of Nature: familial relations with the father as head of the household, a subsistence economy, and mere living. However, one realm implied the other; that is, Western politics constituted itself through the exclusion of bare life.[19] If premodern politics founded the separation between man and animal (as in animal need), modern politics was established through the growing union of the two. In this way, bare life perhaps remained in the State of Nature (as liberal writers implied certain individuals lacking rationality did), but it was not "natural" per se. Thus, modern politics does not signal a rupture from the past but rather the "the growing inclusion of man's natural life in the mechanisms and calculations of power."[20] Liberal theory made biological life a key feature of its politics in a way that had not been true in the past. Furthermore, in the notion that the populace itself must be allowed to survive, all were considered equal in this right even as it was conceived

16. Foucault, *The History of Sexuality, Volume I: An Introduction,* trans. Robert Hurley (New York: Vintage Books, 1980), 143.

17. Although the subject of Locke's tolerance is obviously not that simple.

18. Aristotle, *The Politics,* trans. Carnes Lord (Chicago: University of Chicago Press, 1984), 43.

19. See both Pasquino and Tuck on the relation between the State of Nature and the constitution of political power in Locke. Tuck, *Rights of War and Peace.*

20. Agamben, *Homo Sacer,* 119.

of as a passive right. In this way the conditions were created for both totalitarianism and mass democracy.

For Hobbes and Locke, the State of Nature was a conceptual apparatus that allowed them to express these human needs as well as their views of arbitrary or prerogative power. They envisioned prerogative power as absolute, as following no particular law or rule, and as justified by the political position of the one making prerogative decisions. For Hobbes the fact that men have "a perpetuall and restlesse desire of Power after power, that ceaseth onely in Death,"[21] did not make them evil per se; however, it did make the State of Nature essentially equivalent to a State of War. While sovereign power also had its origins in the State of Nature—and while it remained there by not being subjected to the laws[22]—its authority led to the creation of civil society and to hopes for the preservation of all. Here, Hobbes was building a politics on the *absolute* right of the Leviathan to exercise prerogative power. His sovereign could do no wrong because it embodied human nature (the State of Nature) and the body politic. Hobbes's portrayal of the Leviathan as the head of this body was firmly rooted in political conceptions of the time that the "king has two bodies," one natural and mortal and one that represented sovereignty: political, absolute, and unerring.[23] This conception could be found in legal decisions dating back as early as the 1300s but most notably during the Tudor period, as Agamben has explicated in his work.

Ernst Kantorowicz has argued that jurists of the time created this legal fiction by taking the idea of Christ and transposing it onto the king.[24] Yet funeral rites for kings and emperors dating back to pagan times demonstrate that this notion of two bodies is not exclusively Christian. Rather, Agamben explains, the funeral of a king and the subsequent burning of his effigy were rituals that appeared to show that the body and dignity of the king were immortal and that sovereignty was perpetual. But the fact that this ritual dates back to the Romans has an unexpected implication for the intellectual history of sovereignty: the "metaphor of the political body no longer can be viewed as a symbol of perpetuity of *dignitas* but rather the cipher of the absolute and inhuman character of sovereignty."[25] This

21. Thomas Hobbes, *Leviathan*, ed. Richard Tuck (Cambridge: Cambridge University Press, 1999), 70.
22. Ibid., 122.
23. See Ernst H. Kantorowicz, *The King's Two Bodies: A Study in Mediaeval Political Theology* (Princeton: Princeton University Press, 1997). See, for example, chaps. 7 and 8 and pages 505–6.
24. See ibid., chap. 3.
25. Agamben, *Homo Sacer*, 101.

is why the Leviathan remains in the State of Nature as something beyond the human and beyond conventional law. Accordingly, the State of Nature is theorized not as existing prior to the establishment of a commonwealth but rather as internal to it.[26] This is also why it is acceptable to kill the Leviathan when he has not fulfilled his duties. First, the absence of a truly strong Leviathan leads to a suspension of civil life and a reversion to the State of Nature in which each person has the inalienable right to defend himself. Second, *power* may be everlasting but the body of the king is not meant to be. Sovereign power in modernity is thus impersonal and absolute in a way that it could not be in the past.[27] What is presupposed in defining the State of Nature on the one hand and civil life on the other—which will be discussed below—is that there are two types of life. First, there is "sacred" or bare biological life, which is not quite human and remains outside the commonwealth. The sacred realm is analogous to the liberal conception of the State of Nature in that the rule of law no longer applies and that when a subject enters this realm, he or she is considered bare life.[28] Consequently, killing this individual cannot be an act of homicide or a transgression of the law. A citizen, in contrast, is subject to and protected by the rule of law. Because the Leviathan's full powers are exercised in the former area, the true manifestation of political power occurs in the State of Nature.

It may appear that Hobbes's sovereign can thereby exert absolute power on a citizenry without consequence, but Hobbes, like Locke, contends that the laws of nature are immutable and eternal[29] even if some—such as the right to revenge—are handed over to the sovereign authority in civil society. For this reason, contrary to conventional readings, in which Hobbesian politics is antithetical to the rule of law, I find that Hobbes does conceive of a sort of rule of law; he essentially argues that the sovereign

---

26. Ibid., 105.

27. Interestingly, comparable sentiments regarding the perpetuity of sovereignty can be found in an important Supreme Court decision upholding the presidential prerogative in foreign relations. In the World War II–era *Curtiss-Wright* decision, Justice George Sutherland stated: "'Rulers come and go; governments and forms of government change; but sovereignty survives. A political society cannot endure without a supreme will somewhere. . . . It results that the investment of the federal government with the powers of external sovereignty did not depend upon the affirmative grants of the Constitution.'" The president's power does not have to be approved by Congress, but it must be exercised "in subordination to the applicable provisions of the Constitution." Sutherland, quoted in Major Fergus Paul Briggs, United States Marine Corps Reserve, "Formal Power and Prerogative: The Presidency and National Security" (May 9, 1988), http://www.globalsecurity.org/military/library/report/1988/ BF.htm, chap. 3.

28. See Agamben, *Homo Sacer*, 109.

29. Hobbes, *Leviathan*, 110.

should make decisions and laws based on his or her knowledge of mankind[30] and in accordance with the guidelines of natural law *except* when there are threats to the unity of the polity.[31] These threats can be internal or external—a point made clear by Hobbes's constant emphasis on the need for domestic unity. He acknowledges that this power may be abused; but he also contends that if the sovereign is protecting the population from internal and external threats, then this is a necessary evil. While Hobbes does not guarantee any fair application of the laws, he is perhaps more consistent than Locke in allowing for unlimited prerogative power that cannot be challenged, scrutinized, or overthrown. The limit of a sovereign's worth always comes down to preservation and security— that is, the threat of death. In the end, Hobbes provides for the conditions of liberal democracy—for example, equality before the law, the right to self-preservation, the separation of church and state, and the notion of a social contract—but not for democratic practices. Hobbes's theories not only were preliberal but also conceptualized modern power and its basis—bare life—as no other theorist previously had done.

Locke, in contrast, provides a much more complex view of these issues. First, he believes that men can live in peace outside of civil society; thus, a sovereign power is instituted not to inspire awe in its subjects but rather to protect the material means by which preservation can be maintained as well as the body (which is property as Locke defines it). Arbitrary power—the abuse of prerogative power—thus constitutes a state of war, unfreedom, and irrationality. The foundation of civil society is not survival in Hobbes's terms, and it is not protection from other human beings; rather it is the protection of material goods in order to allow for self-preservation and the preservation of all.[32]

While both authors are still concerned with bare life, what is being protected ostensibly changes the purpose and nature of government (for Locke, "government has no other end but the preservation of property";

30. Ibid., 10, 11.
31. Ibid., 127.
32. Note that the protection of property was indeed a concern of Hobbes's as well, but with certain key differences from Locke's theories of property: (1) property does not exist in the State of Nature for Hobbes; and (2) like the Levellers, Hobbes was also concerned with how property rights, created by civil law (ibid., 203), fit into a world once owned in common. The purpose of civil laws was to protect private property and thereby prevent what would happen in the State of Nature—a war of all against all (ibid., 188). This meant, then, that property was necessarily exclusive (see Ashcraft, "Liberalism and the Problem of Poverty," 28). However, there were no absolute rights to property as the sovereign defined property rights. Only in this way could all be equal.

§94).[33] Thus, the terrifying power that Hobbes sees in other men is not the same terror to Locke; for the latter, the danger is a potentially abusive prince who can arbitrarily take away one's means to live. Locke distances himself from Hobbes by arguing that to protect against the abuses of political leaders in civil society, those leaders must be subject to the laws of citizens (§93).[34] He further ensures this by advocating the separation of powers and a system of checks and balances; these serve to institutionalize the rule of law rather than the capricious rule of a prince. In this way, he prepares the ground for Max Weber's more complex analysis of bureaucracy in which custom, family ties, and arbitrariness are rejected in favor of the rule of law, leadership by convention rather than nature, and impersonal fulfillment of the law. A prince who is constantly exercising his prerogative in flagrant disregard of any law, be it conventional or natural, brings himself into a State of War with the populace. Finally, Locke provides for rebellion against any political leader who has overstepped his legal boundaries. None of these provisions can be found in Hobbes, nor would they have been consistent with his political prescriptions. Nevertheless, in Locke's polity, to put it cynically, the people are allowed "to rebel but not rule."[35]

Locke's system of government is far closer to that of the United States than Hobbes's, yet there remains the problem of prerogative power. Locke indeed provides for prerogative power, albeit with limits. In the past, prerogative represented the decisions of one man whose power was based on a supposed relation to Adam and Eve and thus to God; a more reasoned exercise of prerogative would come from a leader or leaders who were chosen for their political acumen rather than for their lineage. In contrast to the exclusive rule of the prince, the rule of law and equality before the law would determine daily political life, with prerogative to be exercised only during emergencies or when the law was too vague or outdated or had not foreseen a special circumstance. Significantly, where prerogative power once meant the usurpation of goods and men for a prince's own needs, the liberal deployment of prerogative power would have the common good and national security and well-being as its guidelines. Hence, prerogative power would still deal with bare life—but for the good of all, not the few.

33. Locke, *Second Treatise*, 51.
34. Ibid., 50 (§93). This distancing is not absolute, however; see Tuck, *Natural Rights Theories*, 172–76.
35. Wolin, "Democracy and the Welfare State," 168.

As discussed in the previous chapter, Sheldon Wolin calls this Wohl-fahrtsstaatsräson—reason of state guided by welfare—marking the transition from princely power to the protection of all.[36] In this way, warfare and welfare are not conceptually or practically separated; rather, they are one and the same. Foucault's notion of governmentality is analogous to Wolin's Wohlfahrtsstaatsräson:

> In contrast to sovereignty, government has as its purpose not the act of government itself, but the welfare of the population, the improvement of its condition, the increase of its wealth, longevity, health, and so on; and the means the government uses to attain these ends are themselves all, in some sense, immanent to the population; it is the population itself on which govern-ment will act either directly, through large-scale campaigns, or indirectly, through techniques that will make possible, without the full awareness of the people, the stimulation of birth rates, the directing of the flow of population into certain regions or activities, and so on.[37]

The common good according to this view would not be monolithic but would imply a multitude of concerns, such as the health of the popu-lation, birth rates, and economic well-being.

While Locke's limitations on prerogative power sound reasoned and measured, one significant provision challenges this sober quality. He argues that in the hands of a wise prince, citizens should allow unlimited prerogative power:[38]

> But since a rational creature cannot be supposed, when free, to put himself into subjection to another, for his own harm . . . *prerogative* can be nothing but the people's permitting their rulers to do several things, of their own free choice, where the law was silent, and sometimes too against the direct letter of the law, for the public good; and their acquiescing in it when so done: for as a good prince, who is mindful of the trust put into his hands,

36. Ibid., 166, for example.
37. Foucault, "Governmentality," in *Power*, ed. James D. Faubion, trans. Robert Hurley et al. (New York: New Press, Essential Works of Foucault, 1954–84, vol. 3, 1994), 216, 217. See also Pasquino on the point of the common good.
38. A point that Straussians praise.

and careful of the good of his people, cannot have too much *prerogative,* that is, power to do good.[39]

Locke goes on to argue that in fact, *"prerogative is nothing but the power of doing public good without a rule."*[40] Wolin notes that Locke achieves this trick by assigning prerogative to the domain normally dealing with external affairs: the federative power, which represents the power that assumes man's alienation of his right to self-defense from the State of Nature.[41] Wolin further argues that in Locke's provisions for prerogative power and its unlimited use, this reasoning "amounts to a criticism of the political system of his own creation, to a deconstruction of his own theory."[42] In contrast to Hobbes's consistency in theory, this is perhaps true. Locke's goal in this was to eliminate the predominance of arbitrary power in political rule, yet he was advocating this very thing *provided* the ruler was a wise one.

Locke would defend himself in the following ways. First, the leadership of his ideal state is divided, in contrast to Hobbes's Leviathan. In this way, checks and balances are built into his system of governance. This is further reinforced by the fact that Locke's leaders are subject to the law just like any other members, except in times of emergency. While it could then be argued that Locke's idea of prerogative power is essentially the same as Hobbes's in that it exists outside the law and all conventions, Locke would respond that in contrast to the capricious rule of a selfish prince, the determinant of any action in *his* state would be the *common* good and *national* security (in present-day parlance). Although Hobbes has the welfare of the populace as a guideline as well, Locke seemingly ensures this outcome through his provision for the right to rebellion. Third, a leader is not chosen because of his noble lineage but rather for his wisdom and rationality; it follows that this leader is bound to act differently than a prince. Last, Locke provides for the use of prerogative power only as a *state of exception* (and arguably, this is Hobbes's ideal also). This last provision would be of key importance for future theorists and modern governments (and all of these points would later be used in the Founders' justification for prerogative).[43]

39. Locke, *Second Treatise,* 86, §164.
40. Ibid., 87, §166.
41. Wolin, "Democracy and the Welfare State," 168.
42. Ibid., 169.
43. See Federalist Papers nos. 21, 24, 69, and 74; see also Briggs, "Formal Power and Prerogative."

For both Hobbes and Locke, the limitation on prerogative or absolute power is danger to one's self-preservation—that is, death—but this of course presents a paradox.[44] By the time one has become the object of prerogative power, one has been stripped of political status and can face death. This is the point where Locke and Hobbes clearly provide for rebellion. Yet it is also at this point that it is clearly too late. Anyone who faces death as the object of prerogative power has already been stripped of political status and thus is no longer protected by the law; furthermore, that person has entered the political space of arbitrary power and potential violence, where freedom to act or rebel is precarious at best. To take up Wolin's point, liberal theory from Locke onward has provided a potentially dangerous loophole that can subsume the democratic or pluralistic in its pursuit of order, stability, or purity of the national body in the future.[45] This is further reinforced by the design of liberal government: the government is *representative* of the people rather than constituting rule of the people, and the greatest contribution a member can make is through economic participation. Locke was an activist for an expanded franchise, yet his ideal civil society was not an inherently political one; or, to put it differently, the means and ends of preservation were the raison d'être of quotidian political activity. Added to his rather apolitical vision of popular sovereignty was his emphasis on rationality rather than consent per se; for him, legitimacy was derived from the degree of rule-boundedness or rationality (in the Weberian sense) rather than from direct consent. That is, prerogative power was justified in liberal democratic terms not because explicit consent had been given but rather because decision making must be wise and for the common good.[46] In this regard, both Wolin and Friedrich argue that the linkage of rationality with the exercise of sovereign power is distinctly modern and a historical innovation.[47] Rationality was not necessarily absent in the past; however, especially in the Weberian sense, rationality for Locke assumed a primacy that had

44. On this paradox, see Michael Walzer, "The Obligation to Die for the State," in *Obligations: Essays on Disobedience, War, and Citizenship* (Cambridge: Harvard University Press, 1970); Leonard Feldman, "Violent Substitutions: Hobbes, Girard, and Agamben on the Sacrifices of Politics," paper presented at the Western Political Science Association, Portland, Oregon, March 2004.

45. "Here perhaps we see Arendt's influence on Wolin's thought in an interesting extension/permutation!" Smith, private correspondence, May 2004.

46. For a more contemporary defense of the absolute necessity for constitutional dictatorship in a modern democracy, see Clinton Rossiter, *Constitutional Dictatorship*, (Princeton: Princeton University Press 1948).

47. Carl Friedrich, *Tradition and Authority* (New York: Praeger Publishers, 1972).

not been there before.[48] This emphasis on rationality over explicit consent can also be found in Locke's analysis of labor and property.

Bare Life in Liberal Thought

Locke's emphasis on rationality was not only a precondition for political leadership but also tied to expectations that members of civil society labor: "God, who hath given the world to men in common, hath also given them reason to make use of it to the best advantage of life, and convenience. The earth, all that is therein, is given to men for the support and comfort of their being. . . . That *labour* put a distinction between them and common: that added something to them more than nature, the common mother of all, had done; and so they became his private right" (§26, §28).[49] If one follows the line of argumentation in Locke's chapter, he contends that through reason—and *not* consent—we should recognize that labor makes property.[50] He goes on in §30 to call this the "law of reason." Those who sinfully waste land (such as capricious princes) violate this law, and so do those who are idle. Thus, he makes work and rationality central components of his political theory: work transforms raw material into property; labor and the fruits of labor are to be protected by liberal government; labor rather than noble title are to determine who contributes to civil society; and rationality is exemplified through productive labor and also provides the crucial link for the establishment of property and governance.

Nevertheless, the categories of productivity (and thus socially meaningful labor) on the one hand and rationality on the other, would lead to the political subordination of the poor and of anyone else not making an economic contribution (for example, women and slaves).[51] The poor were caught in a trap: they were "equal," but they were equal in a society with preexisting inequalities (holdings), and thus they could not labor in a society in which labor presupposed property rights.[52] Early liberal writers arrived at a dual conception of citizenship: the guarantee of one's

48. Although I do not wish to conflate seventeenth-century interpretations of reason and twentieth-century definitions.

49. Locke, *Second Treatise*, 18, 19.

50. This leads to Locke's defense of colonization. See Tuck, *Rights of War and Peace*, 171–73.

51. For example, see Carole Pateman, *The Disorder of Women* (Stanford: Stanford University Press, 1989).

52. See Locke, *Second Treatise*, 287.

preservation laid the basis for passive (or protective) citizenship; however, the provision for equal political power among economic independents constituted *full* citizenship. Full citizenship did not necessarily mean daily political activity; it did, though, ensure treatment before the law as an autonomous citizen who needed neither guidance nor protection; who had access to the franchise; to whom public office was open; and so on.[53] Rationality was a precondition for productive labor *and* was evidenced through this activity. Given these tensions at the time, aid, charity, poor relief, or dependence on one's husband (all forms of economic dependence) by no means entitled the recipient to participate in the market, since he or she was not the economic or political equal of others. In this way, the categories of work (specifically defined work) and rationality had become central criteria of political power, and both criteria led to internal exclusion.

Locke's thought process is perhaps more complicated than this, however. It is not necessarily that he excluded women, the idle poor, and "ideots"[54] *because* of how he defined work but that notions of rationality at this time mutually reinforced the division between productive and nonproductive (that is, subsistence) labor.[55] Modernity signaled a primacy of the rational that had never before taken such precedence; dichotomies were established such that one concept defined the other: civilization versus barbarity (most notably in Mill),[56] agriculture and cottage industry versus hunter–gatherer societies, or individuals whose existence was guided by rationality versus individuals whose biology chained them to their bodies and who were thus capable only of exercising rationality sporadically (this notion can be found in authors ranging from Hobbes to Rousseau to Freud). All of these categories could be reduced to species thinking: lower forms of the human species represented wildness and irrationality and were satisfied with subsistence-level existence; in contrast, higher forms of the species transcended subsistence-level economies and carried

53. This conception of citizenship is comparable to Rogers Brubaker's: "Citizenship, for my purposes, is a legal institution regulating membership in the state, not a set of participatory practices or a set of specifically civic attitudes." Brubaker, "State, State-System, and Citizenship in Germany," in *Citizenship and Nationhood in France and Germany* (Cambridge, Mass.: Harvard University Press, 1996), 51.

54. Locke, *Second Treatise*, 34.

55. With regard to the distinction between productive and nonproductive labor, see Adam Smith, *The Wealth of Nations*. In Locke's defense, he was more progressive about the role of women than his contemporaries and even future political theorists such as Jean-Jacques Rousseau; he was also one of the first political theorists to conceive of child development and education.

56. On this, see Karuna Mantena's work (e.g., *Alibis of Empire: Social Theory and the Ideologies of Imperialism* [Princeton: Princeton University Press, forthcoming]).

out the important work of civilization building. Groups deemed irrational and biological thus needed guidance even as they served an integral function in society. In other words, there was bare life and "life beyond bare life." Inasmuch as political status was determined by these categories, "citizenship was not founded on egalitarianism" or a social contract, but rather on birth (ius soli) or blood (ius sanguinis); hence modern sovereignty and citizenship were founded on bare life and the promotion of life.[57] The criterion was not only biological life but also what biological life had provided: the foundation for political and economic life and identity. Thus, in these writings, women were protected by the law but not as autonomous members; they were defined politically but had no independent political status. The status of the poor was perhaps harsher.

Since Locke was the first prominent liberal thinker to both write and actively participate in reformulating the Poor Law, his writing is especially interesting. The Old Poor Law at this time was actually the terminus of a series of laws enacted between 1597 and 1601; it was the last one, the "43rd of Elizabeth," that was considered the foundation of the Poor Law. This law required each parish to tax the landowners who resided therein in order to alleviate poverty. Additionally, the 1662 Act of Settlement allowed parish overseers to return strangers to their original parish, thus reinforcing local administration of the Poor Law.[58] Although Locke's reforms were radical for his time,[59] and although his advocacy of education for poor children went above and beyond what many of his contemporaries felt the poor deserved, his policy recommendations and promulgations demonstrated that the poor had no political status and were to be treated as bare life. His proposed reforms demonstrated how prerogative power is exercised domestically, through bureaucratic means (if a term not used at the time is permitted here) and as a permanent state of emergency rather than a temporary one.[60] First, he believed that the poor were to blame for their poverty as exemplified by their "relaxation of discipline and corruption of manners," "their debauchery," and their "idleness." He believed that if alehouses were closed, if vagrancy and begging were outlawed, and if aid were difficult to obtain, poverty among the able-bodied

57. Agamben, *Homo Sacer,* 129.

58. Thomas A. Horne, *Property Rights and Poverty: Political Arguments in Britain, 1605–1834* (Chapel Hill: University of North Carolina Press, 1990), 64.

59. Ibid., 157. See also, for example, Ashcraft, *Revolutionary Politics,* chap. 7.

60. See Locke, "Draft of a Representation Containing a Scheme of Methods for the Employment of the Poor" and "The Fundamental Constitutions of Carolina," in *Political Writings,* ed. David Wootton (Indianapolis: Hackett Publishing, 2003).

would end.[61] What's more, he advocated that paupers wear badges and that their children between three and fourteen be sent to "working schools"; older paupers would be assigned to "houses of correction" and work hard labor. Anyone violating these rules could be whipped or have their ears lopped; or they could be forced to work hard labor on ships or be deported to the colonies.[62]

Locke believed that local artisans and farmers should be forced to employ the able-bodied unemployed, but he also held that the latter should be paid a reduced rate.[63] As Terence Hutchison remarks: "These proposals, which might be considered profoundly illiberal, included rounding up adult males found begging 'in maritime counties,' and sending them for compulsory service and hard labour at sea for three years, together with shipping and compulsory labour for children under fourteen found begging outside their parish, as well as a series of similar measures involving conscription and regimentation of the poor and unemployed."[64] Compare these measures to Locke's definition of political freedom: "A Liberty to dispose, and order, as he lists, his Person, Actions, possessions, and his whole Property, within the Allowance of those laws under which he is; and therein not to be subject to the arbitrary Will of another, but freely follow his own."[65] Autonomy is central to the notion of liberty; conversely, "protection" amounts to the suspension of the law. Hobbes similarly believed that self-preservation was a right and not a privilege, but he also argued that the poor were to be subject to coercion:

> But for such as have strong bodies, the case is otherwise: they are to be forced to work, and to avoyd the excuse of not finding employment, there ought to be such lawes, as may encourage all manner of Arts; as Navigation, Agriculture, Fishing, and all manner of Manifacture that requires labour. The multitude of poor, and yet strong people still encreasing, they are to be transplanted into Countries not sufficiently inhabited: where nevertheless, they are not to exterminate those they find there; but constrain them to inhabit closer together, and not range a great deal of ground, to snatch what they find; but to court each little

61. Horne, *Property Rights and Poverty*, 64.

62. See Terence Hutchison, *Before Adam Smith: The Emergence of Political Economy, 1662–1776* (Oxford: Basil Blackwell, 1988). See also Locke, "Draft of a Representation," and "The Fundamental Constitutions of Carolina."

63. Ashcraft, "Liberalism and the Problem of Poverty," 7.

64. Hutchison, *Before Adam Smith*, 72.

65. Locke, *Political Writings*, 306.

Plot with art and labour, to give them their sustenance in due season. And when all the world is overcharged with Inhabitants, then the last remedy of all is Warre; which provideth for every men, by Victory, or Death.[66]

Hobbes's and Locke's arguments that sustenance and the means of preservation were absolute and inalienable rights were radical for their time and more radical than our own conceptions of welfare. The United States does not have a right to live, or a right to food, housing, or water. However, what is significant for the purposes of this argument is that prerogative power in this context was not the spontaneous act of a capricious sovereign but a regular and crucial function of liberal civil society, as exemplified by poor law and colonial administration. This was possible in that the foundation of liberal political and moral edicts became bare life, with the allowance for prerogative power exercised on a scale never before imagined.

Thus, despite the egalitarian motivations in allowing all to live, there were two subjects of political power: first, relatively autonomous members, which established the basis for modern citizenship as we know it; and second, those who needed guidance, a strong hand, and "protection" and who thus could be subjected to arbitrary power. At the time Hobbes and Locke were writing, the poor could be forced to work, held without having committed a crime, or deported. In this way, indigents, women, and the insane were not merely left by the wayside but served as the biological norm on which politics was founded. They needed guidance and "protection" while autonomous members did not; thus, they were not rational individuals who had broken the law but subjects whose way of life and very being needed care, handling, and remolding. Perhaps poor men could escape this category by becoming rich, but the political status of African slaves, Native Americans, and women was far more static. The hard work and execration of luxury of ascetic beliefs was perhaps applied to the whole population by thinkers such as Locke. However it also reflected a desire to tame the "natural" and "irrational" elements embodied in all of these groups. In the poorhouses, it was only a more naked form of coercion.

Certain thinkers argue that Locke's proposals for the indigent were an anomaly and thus cannot be considered part of his political thought;[67] others contend that notwithstanding these undemocratic features, Locke's

---

66. Hobbes, *Leviathan*, 387, chap. 30.

67. Jeremy Waldron, presentation to the Harvard Department of Government's Political Theory Colloquium, Spring 2002.

work must be considered in its historical context and for its radical implications.[68] The second argument is indeed true; *however,* these policy reforms cannot be ignored in light of Locke's discussion of prerogative power.[69] Locke's reasoning regarding both the care and the internment of the poor shows a new form of reason of state: Wohlfahrtsstaatsräson, that is, reason of state guided toward the good of the people. In other words, this new reason of state is the exercise of prerogative power deployed for seemingly democratic justification—the security and well-being of the public—even as its implementation is profoundly nondemocratic. The exercise of prerogative power domestically thus becomes justified given its "democratic" aims.[70] Although it could be objected that Poor Law policy was codified and institutionalized, thereby undermining the definitional requisite that prerogative power is arbitrary (or flexible), Wolin also convincingly demonstrates that the dictates of the welfare state are founded on highly arbitrary decisions and reasoning. On the other hand, this assertion of authority does not preclude rationality.[71] Both these observations challenge the welfare-versus-warfare dichotomy, as discussed in Chapter 1. Those who become objects of prerogative power are stripped of political status (if they had it in the first place) and are subject to the whims of their husbands, judges, poor law officials, ship captains, and colonial governors, among others. The laws merely *enable* the deployment of prerogative power rather than constituting its enactment; and they evidence the deployment of prerogative beyond a unitary sovereign figure. In this context, bare life serves as the precondition for the political just as prerogative power is the precondition for liberal democracy.

Accordingly, there is less tension between democratic power and prerogative power in the liberal democracy Locke envisioned than in, for example, Alexis de Tocqueville's observations about democracy. De Tocqueville clearly recognized that with an *active* democratic citizenry—made possible by strong local governments and citizens' groups and a weak federal government—the state might not be effective during times of war or domestic threat. Locke provides the conditions for a procedural democracy in which the equality of all before the law, the rule of law, and

68. As Ashcraft would argue.

69. As Tuck recognizes; see his *Rights of War and Peace,* 168, 171, 172, 177.

70. Max Weber would call this a politics of ultimate ends, where the means are ignored. See H. H. Gerth and C. Wright Mills, eds., "Politics as a Vocation," in *From Max Weber: Essays in Sociology* (New York: Oxford University Press, 1958).

71. See Friedrich, *Tradition and Authority,* regarding conventional views that Enlightenment thinking and rationality are inherently antiauthoritarian and antitradition. Rather, modern sovereignty is founded on both rationality and state or prerogative power.

the end of preservation are the key elements of government and civil society; de Tocqueville, however, recognizes at least two dangers in this arrangement. First, he warns that a population of isolated individuals focused only on material well-being and not the good of the larger community will pave the way for a highly centralized and thus despotic government. As individuals become increasingly isolated and feel less connection toward one another, each will become independent and weak, "proud and servile."[72] As the love of equality and the hatred for privilege grow endlessly, they will come to favor "the gradual concentration of all political rights in those hands which alone represent the state." He rightly sees the danger of this centralization: "Every central power which follows its natural instincts loves equality and favors it. For equality singularly facilitates, extends, and secures its influence."[73] It is not equality per se that is the problem but an equality of material conditions that holds bare life as its standard. To put it simply, equality in and of itself does not ensure democratic activity and participation.

With the increased power of the central government, the focus turns to security and well-being rather than debate, dissent, accountability, or responsibility; indeed, the love of order could "induce private persons to sacrifice more and more of their rights for the sake of tranquility."[74] This centralization and substantively empty legislation, favoring procedure and equality over democratic activity, would also be aided by the tyranny of the majority of which Montesquieu and de Tocqueville warned as well as by the development of a new aristocracy in the form of industrial wealth. Sounding very much like his contemporary Karl Marx, de Tocqueville cautioned that as industrial enterprise increased and required legislative protection and a new and better infrastructure, the state itself would become the "leading industrialist."[75] In this way, two contradictory revolutions would occur: one weakening supreme power, the other strengthening it.[76]

Marx aptly formulates how this is possible: a state's emancipation from private property, or religion, does not eradicate either; in fact, it presupposes their existence: "Far from abolishing these *effective* differences, it [the state] only exists so far as they are presupposed . . . it manifests its

---

72. Alexis de Tocqueville, *Democracy in America*, ed. J. P. Mayer, trans. George Lawrence (New York: Perennial Classics, 2000), 672.
73. Ibid., 673.
74. Ibid., 677.
75. Ibid., 686.
76. Ibid., 688.

universality only in opposition to these elements."[77] It follows that political emancipation is not human emancipation and that man leads a double life as an abstract citizen, on the one hand, and a member of civil society, on the other. The material expression of this atomized political identity is private property, and this "leads every man to see in other men, not the *realization,* but rather the *limitation* of his own liberty."[78] Marx recognizes that state domination exists in this arrangement, but he contends that it proceeds directly from capitalism. By his account, the end of the state is to make the rich richer and the poor poorer in the name of technological progress, abstract philosophy, and national greatness.

Marx does not analyze the exercise of political power beyond capitalist ends, but he does describe in detail the conditions of bare life—mere, biological life stripped of political rights. First, workers are divested of all political status: they have no vote, laws prohibit "combinations" and meetings of three or more people; and work conditions are not protected. When workers do attempt to unionize, the state does not hold back its violence or consider the letter of the law; it has no need to. Second, workers are consigned to a life of bare survival: "Light, air, etc.—the simplest *animal* cleanliness—ceases to be a need for man. *Dirt*—this stagnation and putrefaction of man—the *sewage* of civilization . . . —comes to be the *element of life* for him. Utter, *unnatural* neglect, putrefied nature, comes to be his *life-element.* None of his senses exist any longer, and not only in his human fashion, but in an *inhuman* fashion, and therefore not even in an animal fashion."[79] Here we see what biological life (disenfranchisement) *is* in contradistinction to humanity or notions of what it is to be a human being (citizenship). The connection between bare life and disenfranchisement suggests how status rather than criminal activity opens these subjects to the violence of the state.

The less humane aspects of liberalism were developed as industrial capitalism became more firmly established in the West and as the treatment of workers became more scientific and inhuman, as evidenced by the population theories of Malthus and Ricardo and their intellectual heirs. Ascetic prescriptions for the entire population—hard work, productivity, thrift, frugality, and prudence (Locke, Smith) were, in practice, exercised only on the poor. The idle rich were not targeted. The democratic activity

77. Karl Marx, "Economic and Philosophic Manuscripts of 1844," in Friedrich Engels and Karl Marx, *The Marx-Engels Reader,* 2nd ed., ed. Robert C. Tucker (New York: W. W. Norton, 1978), 33.
78. Ibid., 42.
79. Ibid., 94.

that could have restrained arbitrary state power—activity that de Tocqueville witnessed in the United States—gradually became subsumed by urbanization, the growth of the nation-state, and the emphasis on material gain. Political life as democratic *activity* and as a significant check on governmental and prerogative power—to the degree that it existed—began to decline with the development of bureaucracy, the growth of scientific policies and administration, and the increased role of state-sanctioned capitalism. In this way, the less democratic aspects of liberal theory were developed and consolidated alongside liberal governments and constitutions.

Most academics tend to treat Hobbes as the theorist of sovereignty and international relations and Locke as the theorist of civil society and domestic politics. What is forgotten is that Hobbes's treatment of power is distinctly modern and anticipates liberal writings; thus, his theories illuminate how the State of Nature is a crucial part of civil society rather than something prior to or outside of it. At the same time, Locke's provision for prerogative power has largely been neglected[80] (including by Agamben), along with its implications for a new reason of state embodying the welfare of the people and operating both domestically and externally. This is why Hobbes is usually not mentioned in discussions of contemporary citizenship and why Locke is excluded from contemporary debates about the modern nation-state. Neither theorist is merely "liberal," however; each has contributed to the intellectual history of the growth of the modern nation-state. Each calls for the alienation of a man's natural right to defend himself and for the state to have a monopoly on force and violence. Thus, each author anticipates the growth and consolidation of territorial sovereignty and the categories of *ius soli* and *ius sanguinis* that mark modern citizenship and political belonging, notwithstanding the fiction of the social contract.[81] Locke's subordination of consent to rationality in property is one indication of this. Indeed, Locke's ideal polity is much more suited for modern warfare and other exercises of prerogative power than the truly democratic conditions that de Tocqueville observed in the United States' early history.

Yet the contradictions between liberal democracy and the exercise of prerogative power cannot really be seen in Hobbes's writings. It is Locke

80. Obvious exceptions: Sheldon Wolin, Wendy Brown, Richard Tuck, and Straussians such as Harvey Mansfield. As Pasquino states, Locke's arguments about prerogative are "a concept and a chapter that most interpreters pass over in silence." See Pasquino, "Locke on King's Prerogative," 199.

81. See Brubaker, *Citizenship and Nationhood*, 32; ius soli is ascriptive and challenges the liberal notion of consent.

we must turn to in order to view the inherent contradictions with which we live right now: a government that is subjected to law and yet, at the most crucial political moments, is not; the rule of law and checks and balances, but at the same time, arbitrary power that knows absolutely no rules and takes no guidance with regard to means; and a purpose for all political rule—the good of the people—that is so loosely defined that it could mean anything, in contradistinction to the rationalization of modern life. In the end, prerogative power as the power exercised when there is a state of emergency has become the exception that proves the rule. As it has been theoretically formulated and historically developed, prerogative power is the precondition for liberal government and democratic activity. This is evident not only in Locke, but also in certain of the Founders' arguments for presidential prerogative such as those of Alexander Hamilton.[82]

In discerning what this means for political subjects, the social contract, as a political theoretical concept, only makes sense if there is passage from the State of Nature to civil society in a temporal sense. The difficulty of this construct has been discussed in much of the recent literature on citizenship. For example, Bonnie Honig notes that immigrants are the only people who can truly consent to being American citizens.[83] That a group who can be subject to prerogative power "enters" civil society through naturalization evidences the fact that one sphere does not precede the other. Much of the academy positions the State of Nature as outside of civil society, and meanwhile, the exercise of prerogative power in a liberal polity is widely viewed as being the exclusive reserve of international relations and politics; yet it should be evident to readers by now that neither of these assumptions is true. The State of Nature has long been incorporated into civil society, and prerogative power has always been formulated in terms of both international *and* domestic relations. Hobbes and Locke ideally conceived of the use of this power in times of a state of emergency, thus constituting its exercise as an exception even if their own theories undermined this exceptional status. Let it be noted, though, that their substantive theoretical shift to the biological and rational prefigured the development of biopower and disciplinary power. The crucial element

82. See, for example, Federalist Papers nos. 34 or 69, by Alexander Hamilton; see also Briggs, "Formal Power and Prerogative"; Nasser Hussain and Austin Sarat, "The Literary Life of Clemency: Pardon Tales in the Contemporary United States," paper presented at the Association for the Study of Law, Culture, and Humanities, March 2005, Austin, Texas; Jeffery Alan Smith, *War and Press Freedom: The Problem of Prerogative* (New York: Oxford University Press, 1999).

83. See Bonnie Honig, *Democracy and the Foreigner* (Princeton: Princeton University Press, 2001), 92–98.

that links these deployments of power is bare life. Thus, we end up with subjects who enter the State of Nature within civil society—bare life—juxtaposed against autonomous subject-citizens who make their "life beyond bare life."

Prerogative Power in the Modern Nation-State

In early liberal writings, then, the notion of prerogative power and violence were designed to deal not simply with external enemies but also with internal enemies.[84] In the face of internal instability, the possible abuse of power was worth the risk. Thus, dual strands of power have developed in liberalism and the modern nation-state—the legitimacy and will of the people, and the power of the state. Where the two clash, the power of the state trumps the power of the people except in times of revolution. Nonetheless, as de Tocqueville noted, people *willingly* give more power to a centralized state as long as they are treated equally.

Governmental power in the United States was at first closer to the Tocquevillean conception of democratic governance and legitimacy. As described in Book I of *Democracy in America,* the town meetings, the significant degree of local political participation, the strength of secondary associations, and the freedom of the press were all possible in a country in which states' rights took precedence. The country at this time was decentralized and had no national military or coin. The economy was largely agrarian or composed of small entrepreneurs and so did not require a strong state. This was probably one of the most democratic periods in modern Western history with regard to political participation and activity.[85]

Around this time, the issue of prerogative was disputed by the American Founders; it was mostly settled by the time the presidency was established in the late 1700s. Concerns about the abuse of prerogative were directed not only at the executive but also at the legislative branch and, later, the Supreme Court. The abuse of prerogative was not conceived of as being the unbroken power of a single leader or king; rather, it was broadly theorized as a *concentration* of power in any single branch or political body.[86] For this reason, the presidency was made stronger in the late

84. See Federalist Paper no. 24 on the United States' "natural enemies."

85. Of course, as with Ancient Greece, the most democratic circumstances coexisted with the most nondemocratic: racism, slavery, genocidal practices toward Native Americans, the exclusion of women, incredibly harsh treatment of criminals, and so on.

86. Briggs, "Formal Power and Prerogative," chap. 2.

1700s in order to check legislative tyranny and, indirectly, the tyranny of the people. Two key elements of this prerogative were contained in Article 1 of the Constitution: the authority to declare war, and the authority to grant clemency. Because the powers of the executive were never defined as clearly as those of the legislative branch, the president could potentially have "unlimited power."[87] Yet the authors of the Federalist Papers were careful to distinguish the U.S. presidency from the British monarchy.[88] As with the difference between Hobbes's and Locke's sovereigns, the key differences were that the president was subject to the rule of law, could be held accountable for his actions, and was to act according to the common good.

The presidency and the federal government were nevertheless weak up until the Civil War. Then, with the increasing control of the federal government during and after the Civil War, and with the development of the United States into a modern nation-state, the tension between local, dispersed power and state power became more pronounced.[89] At the same time, the presidency from Lincoln onward became stronger, setting a historical precedent that was (arguably) not challenged until after the Nixon administration: a strong, activist presidency checked but not hindered by the legislature in both national and international affairs.[90]

The development of industrial capital led to further demands for centralization. The increase in federal power had a homogenizing effect, and the idea of *national* identity became much more important. This trend accelerated with a second expansion of bureaucracy (with the beginnings of the welfare state) and federal power during the Great Depression.[91] The dispersion and augmentation of bureaucratic power reflected the transformation of the United States from a country in which states' rights were of supreme importance to a modern nation-state; it also gave rise to a branch of the government that was shaped by nondemocratic power. As Wolin has pointed out, the exercise of sovereignty is just as important domestically as it is internationally: "In the final analysis, in spite of all

87. Ibid.
88. For example, see Alexander Hamilton, Federalist Paper no. 69, March 14, 1788.
89. See Agamben's discussion of Lincoln in *State of Exception*, trans. Kevin Attell (Chicago: University of Chicago Press, 2005), 20. This transformation had been predicted earlier by Tocqueville.
90. For Agamben on Lincoln, see *State of Exception*, chap. 1. For Briggs on an activist presidency and the legislative acts following the Nixon presidency that attempted to curb future presidents' actions (and largely failed), see "Formal Power and Prerogative." chap. 1.
91. See James T. Patterson, *America's Struggle Against Poverty, 1900–1985* (Cambridge, Mass.: Harvard University Press, 1986), chaps. 2 and 4.

'social welfare policies,' the whole course of the state's inner political functions, of justice and administration, is repeatedly and unavoidably regulated by the objective pragmatism of 'reasons of state.' The state's absolute end is to safeguard (or to change) the external and internal distribution of power."[92] With the development of bureaucracy, sovereignty is much more dispersed even as governmental actors—be they presidents, Supreme Court justices, governors, or the police—can be held accountable for their actions.[93] In this regard, Giorgio Agamben points out that the zone of indistinction between the juridical order and the state of exception in a liberal democracy must be highlighted, even if it is not absolute or unbroken as in a monarchy, a fascist regime, or a dictatorship.[94]

In contrast to monarchical prerogative, in a modern polity the rule of law facilitates the suspension of law; in this way prerogative (and the State of Nature) is inextricably linked to the rule of law instead of signifying its absolute negation.[95] In this sense, prerogative is not akin to Carl Schmitt's notion of dictatorship; rather, its analysis must be grounded in a more ambivalent "democratic" context.[96] In a Weberian sense, prerogative can be rational in that the rule of law and some sort of juridical process is required in order to suspend the law. However, it can be irrational in a few senses: it indicates the suspension of law and thus can be marked by unpredictability (although not necessarily); it can be fiscally costly despite rhetoric of rolling back the state;[97] and it can be initiated by an individual or individuals unhindered by the checks and balances of government. Finally, prerogative can lead to benevolent acts, although the precariousness of this benevolence must be highlighted. The

92. H. H. Gerth and C. Wright Mills, *From Max Weber,* 334.

93. That the exercise of prerogative is not conceived of as the president's power alone is evident in contemporary treatments of the subject. For example, on states' governors exercising the right to commute death sentences, see Nassar Hussain and Austin Sarat, "The Literary Life of Clemency: Pardon Tales in the Contemporary United States," paper presented at the Association for the Study of Law Culture, and Humanities, Austin, March 2005; on the Supreme Court's exercise of prerogative, see Rogers Smith, "Bush v. Gore," in "Roundtable Discussion: The Uses and Abuses of the Constitution, Special Issue on the Constitution," *Common Place* 2 (July 2002), http://www.common-place.org.

94. Agamben, *State of Exception,* chap. 1.

95. Nevertheless, this does not produce a black-and-white situation of within the law/ outside the law but rather a juridically undecidable situation. See ibid., 21.

96. The mistake that is made is to call this absolute power in Carl Schmitt's sense of a dictator. Both Agamben and Pasquino discuss how this power can still be called prerogative or the state of exception even though it differs from monarchical prerogative and dictatorship in Schmitt's conception. See Pasquino, "Locke on King's Prerogative"; Agamben, *State of Exception.*

97. For example, the fiscal irrationality of criminalizing the homeless even though it often costs three times as much as simply providing housing subsidies and welfare.

subject of prerogative power—whether treated compassionately, indifferently, or violently—has been stripped of all legal rights, be they de facto or de jure.

Consequently, prerogative power and nationalism have not been conceived of as merely categories of political power reserved for international relations; in fact, they inform domestic politics. This has been especially evident in the United States since the attacks of September 11, 2001, although this event merely illuminated (and heightened) what had already been present. This strand of liberal thought justifies nondemocratic (arbitrary, violent) power in the liberal context and presupposes internal enemies. The dual nature of this power has been deepened with the historical development of capitalism and the growth of bureaucracy in almost all areas of life. Capitalist enterprise not only takes bureaucratic form but also demands that the state work with it in an efficient and precise way.[98] Internal stability and the justification of coercion become more important in this context.

Furthermore, the growth of the modern nation-state reinforces the priority of stability over both justice and democratic practices. Accordingly, questions of national security can be solved by means that are less than democratic—in the form of prerogative power—because it is reasoned that only with national security can democracy flourish. The extreme examples of this are the internment of the Japanese during World War II and the surveillance and detainment of Middle Easterners residing in the United States today. Less obvious is the surveillance and policing of poor inner-city workers, welfare-to-workfare recipients, guest workers, and poor working-class immigrants, not to mention the indefinite detainment of some refugees and immigrants. As I discuss in Chapters 4 and 5, the War on Drugs, the War on Terror, and the criminalization of the homeless (and poverty in general) are mutually reinforcing power dynamics that work in conjunction with neoliberal policies affecting poor workers.

Conclusion

In an era of increasing economic globalization, it is conventional wisdom that the nation-state is disappearing and that governments are being left merely to administer what the market cannot. The neoliberal dream is small government and the increased flow of goods and capital; the assumption is that these will aid the cause of progress and freedom. Yet

98. See H. H. Gerth and C. Wright Mills, *From Max Weber*, 215.

the United States is by no means disappearing as a nation-state. Rather, democratic activities and practices are diminishing as the state is increasingly strengthened by its links to capitalism—even as this union also has inherent contradictions. As I will argue in the following chapters, unionization and worker protections are being discouraged at the same time that cheap labor and deregulated conditions are being encouraged; immigrant organizing is viewed as separatist and as a threat to national security, while immigrant labor is actively recruited; and general political and economic protests are now very often seen as disloyal or traitorous even as low-wage policies create the conditions for these protests. Meanwhile, the events of 9/11 have provided the necessary link between the protection of global capital and policing, domestic surveillance, and the suspension of law. Thus, while the nation-state has indeed been weakened by deregulation, it has also strengthened its prerogative power. This is sufficiently clear when we view prerogative not as anomalous to the modern state, and not as violating some "social contract," but rather as significantly foundational to modern power, the liberal state, and modern citizenship.

Indeed, the demand for increased deregulation requires greater administrative and bureaucratic power at the expense of democratic or liberal power; and as I argued earlier, modern sovereignty is being deployed through bureaucratic means domestically. The nation-state *has* been weakened through the creation of new legal forms and institutions that "negotiate between national sovereignty and the transnational practices of corporate economic actors,"[99] as well as through the predominance of institutions such as the International Monetary Fund, the World Bank, and the North American Free Trade Agreement. However, the centralization of power and legal processes is absolutely vital if these global processes and institutions are to function, even as this centralization grows more "dispersed" (located in major cities rather than national capitals, for example). In essence, the nation-state has far from disappeared and in fact has strengthened its role with regard to questions of citizenship, immigration, protection of economic interests, and military power.

Thus, it is not that political power is disappearing with a more economic focus but that it is increasingly directed at the life of the species, biology, and bare life. As I argued earlier, this is not an anomalous development. Historically, the arbitrariness that liberals wanted to get rid of was

99. Saskia Sassen, *Globalization and Its Discontents: Essays on the New Mobility of People and Money* (New York: New Press, 1998), xxvii, xxviii.

the exercise of prerogative power for selfish or personal reasons. A politics that conceived of sovereignty as concerning the body of the populace solved this problem. But it also demonstrated the inhuman character of sovereignty in that power itself was being perpetuated beyond any one person; this was provided for by concept of State of Nature and by locating what is most political in that State, where life is at subsistence level and the possibility of war is high. For this reason, I contend that a key component of the state's organizational principle is bare life and that its ethos is asceticism, around which species thinking and biopower have developed, culminating in a spectrum of violence leading to oppression of the poor, racial profiling, and the close control and surveillance of poor female welfare recipients.

Welfare prescriptions and policies toward the poor have less to do with morality, humanity, or enlightenment than with control, surveillance, and an engineering of docile bodies. This demonstrates that prerogative power is exercised domestically and on a regular basis, rather than in a state of emergency. The War on Drugs and the War on Terror (which, it must be remembered, was given significant legislative power in 1996 with the Antiterrorism and Effective Death Penalty Act and the Illegal Immigration Reform and Immigration Responsibility Act—IIRIRA), in combination with antihomeless legislation, are evidence of wars without end, waged domestically. These power dynamics demand assimilation while precluding citizenship, autonomy, and democracy. Indeed, those who do not fit the norms of biopower are not viewed as moral or rational beings or even as human. To be worthy of humanity and the species, one has to have been accepted in civil society as a rational and autonomous being. Women, the poor, and exploited and oppressed racial minorities have not fallen under that rubric. Rather, they represent the biological and irrational and thus the inhuman. In sum, the combination of capitalist demands (disciplinary power), biopower (ascetic demands), and political theology (the intermingling of prerogative, the baseline of bare life, and ascetic orientation toward the human species) is allowing for a more systematic and yet covert level of inhumanity in the treatment of individuals who have passed beyond the pale of law.

In theory and policy, John Locke conceived of the use of prerogative domestically. Furthermore, he conceptualized prerogative power as the wise decision making of one leader for the common good; yet his recommendations for the Poor Law and colonial administration advocated the use of sovereign authority through administrative organs. Today, it is evident that prerogative is being deployed in a liberal democracy. The Founders and Locke believed that they were providing democratic safeguards through their notions of the common good, constitutional checks, and the possibility of prosecuting political actors who abused prerogative power. Yet "war" is still being waged today against individuals who are de facto or de jure disenfranchised. And it is really the treatment of the subjects of prerogative that is the litmus test of democracy.

EXPLOITATION AND THE NEW WORKING CLASS

In the previous two chapters, I argued that ascetic values have served to justify the suspension of the law with subjects who are considered bare life. In terms of the globalization of the economy, the growing predominance of the service sector, and changes in the working class, it is significant that bare life is linked to the conceptual split between productive and reproductive (or unproductive) labor. Low-tier jobs in a global economy increasingly resemble reproductive, household, or subsistence labor by virtue of their location (for example, in the home, casual factories, or sweatshops); their labor relations (which are characterized by isolation, hierarchy, and a profound asymmetry of power, including the reinforcement of traditional gender roles); their flexibility (which makes them "informal" rather than "formal" work); the subsistence wages they pay (which foster dependence); and the demographics of the working class (groups that have historically performed unpaid or low-paid labor in coercive circumstances). This chapter explores the dynamics of power in the low-tier labor market in terms of the political status of workers. I contend that exploitation is not merely economic but political, even as ascetic values and ideological manifestations of biopower (such as racism) obscure this exploitation. More broadly, I hope to connect my analyses of our current ideational system and late modern sovereignty (and its increasingly economic orientation) to a theory of exploitation.[1]

Marx's notion of exploitation, as I interpret it, involves not only the extraction of surplus value[2] but also the conditions described in his earlier work:[3] political disenfranchisement or statelessness; a double standard of asceticism (as with the Protestant ethic) whereby workers are held to standards that the wealthy are not;[4] and an inverse relationship between productivity and income so that the poor never rise above subsistence living. Even so, Marx's analysis of exploitation may not seem to be a useful critical tool for assessing today's work conditions in the United States. In this chapter,[5] I interrogate the notion of economic and political exploitation, given that this concept may seem outdated in or irrelevant to today's economy.[6] This perception that exploitation is "old paradigm" or passé is grounded in two ideas: that communism and thus Marxism are dead;[7] and that in a liberal democracy, any contract an individual enters is through individual choice. Against this, I will be arguing that the neoliberal discourse and policies that became predominant in the 1980s—which I will link to ascetic ideas of the past and their contemporary manifestations—have changed the lenses through which we view work and freedom in the global economy. The neoliberals would tell us that conditions of employment are increasingly deregulated and nonunion and thus "free." However, an examination of how work in the United States has changed will make it clear that a new, increasingly disenfranchised working class

1. I believe that instead of challenging Agamben's notion of bare life, I am expanding it. I would note, though, that Andrew Norris has pointed out to me that work is precisely *not* a key part of Agamben's analysis of the Muselmänner; work in concentration camps was often useless. Nevertheless, it is not work per se that creates the situation of bare life but its denigration in combination with the (relative) suspension of law. To put it differently, the suspension of law *fosters* economically exploitative conditions while also masking them. One example of the confluence of these two terms is an agricultural guest worker who is *legally* exposed to pesticides that are not permitted for U.S. citizens because of their toxicity.

2. As delineated in Karl Marx, *Capital*, vol. 1, trans. Ben Fowkes (New York: Vintage Books, 1977).

3. In particular, "On the Jewish Question," "Economic and Philosophic Manuscripts of 1844," and "The German Ideology," in Karl Marx, *The Marx-Engels Reader*, ed. and trans. Robert Tucker (New York: W. W. Norton, 1978).

4. Marx, "Economic and Philosophic Manuscripts of 1844," *Marx-Engels Reader*.

5. I would like to thank Daniel Engster, my colleague in Political Science at the University of Texas, San Antonio, for his comments on this chapter, as well as those who participated in the American Political Theory Conference in St. Louis in 2005, notably Paul Gomberg.

6. See Slavoj Žižek, "Why We All Love to Hate Haider," *New Left Review* 2 (March–April 2000), for an insightful discussion about why critiques of capital are considered outdated.

7. Ibid.

has been forming. This disenfranchisement and exploitation is not merely bad luck (a Hayekian or Schumpeterian argument);[8] in fact, it is part and parcel of the synthesis of liberal asceticism, neoliberal economics and policies, and the deployment of state power. Given these transformations, this is why I will be investigating the links between the state and the economy, between public policy and business enterprises, as well as examining how race, class, and gender figure into these new power dynamics.

As I have discussed in previous chapters, many have argued that the nation-state is becoming obsolete and that sovereign power is waning.[9] Indeed, the question of sovereignty is an important one, given all the competing claims about the disappearance of the nation-state. This purported disappearance does not explain the U.S. bombings of Afghanistan and Iraq or the War on Terror; yet it does allow certain gray areas of sovereignty at the domestic level to remain unexamined. These gray areas are most obvious in the example of Guantánamo Bay; they are much less so in the criminalization of homelessness (that is, the criminalization of poverty), the detention of certain immigrants (especially Haitians) indefinitely and without legal representation, the War on Drugs (which has led to the incarceration of significant numbers of African American men in their prime), and the plight of guest workers in general. These gray areas are ignored for various reasons. First, ascetic values obscure the relations between welfare or workfare and the urban poor on the one hand and immigrants and the Bureau of Citizenship and Immigration Services (BCIS) on the other. That is, the power exerted by welfare/workfare agencies and the BCIS is viewed as moral aid, as a means to morally strengthen individuals, and thus as not a form of sovereignty. Second, and related to this point, gray areas are ignored because bureaucracy and bureaucratic prerogative are not perceived as the same as sovereignty and prerogative power. Indeed, welfare and immigration services are viewed as crucial to democracy (the former help the poor, the latter allow for naturalization) and thus the opposite of prerogative (that is, arbitrary) power. Third, any arbitrary actions or policies that *are* exposed are taken to be anomalies or exceptions, departures from liberal democratic practice that can be resolved through reform. Yet when one focuses on liberalism rather than democracy,

8. See Friedrich Hayek, *The Essence of Hayek*, ed. Chiaki Nishiyama and Kurt R. Leube (Stanford: Hoover Institution Press, 1984); Joseph A. Schumpeter, *Capitalism, Socialism, and Democracy* (New York: Harper Perennial, 1976).

9. On the left, scholars such as Fredric Jameson, Saskia Sassen, Wendy Brown, Roland Axtmann, and Zygmunt Bauman critically examine this idea. Clearly, then, this question is not the exclusive territory of neoliberal thinkers.

the antinomy between one sort of governance (liberal) and another (pre-rogative) is no longer so clear-cut.

In addition to the conventional view that the nation-state and thus sovereignty are disappearing is the idea that blue-collar work is vanishing, along with the working class itself. It can be argued that with the loss of most traditional manufacturing jobs, low-tier positions are disappearing; however, this is because work, as a significant concept to liberal inclusion (see Chapters 1 and 2), has been defined in ascetic terms, thereby obscuring *how* work has changed. In liberal terms, work has been defined mono-lithically as full-time, well paid, masculine (and therefore not service work), in one place, regulated by law, and rationalized by fixed hours (rationali-zation developed from protestant asceticism, after all). This type of employment is no longer the norm. Lower-tier work that is available is devalued as subsistence labor and thus viewed as merely a precondition for the first type.[10] It is often part-time or irrregular contract work and performed in casual conditions (such as industrial homework); thus, it is not recognized as *real* work. This is true in terms of political rhetoric and academic studies, and also in terms of bureaucratic classifications such that unemployment benefits, for example, cannot be claimed in cases of job loss for these types of employment. Similarly, those who are filling low-skilled or unskilled manufacturing jobs or performing nonmechanized agricultural work—women, minorities, and immigrants—are viewed in terms of their identity and so are not considered working class. Their identity and the corresponding stereotypes not only preclude recognition of them as workers (or the working class) but also hide how work and the workforce have changed over the past two decades. For all of these reasons, the term exploitation—which I will explore both theoretically and practically—has fallen into general disuse. Nevertheless, I believe that it captures the synthesis of these new work conditions as well as their political and economic consequences. In this chapter, I critically analyze issues of exploitation, linking Tommie Shelby's notion of exploita-tion to Edna Bonacich's concept of a split labor market; I will then relate their work to ascetic ideas in order to present a different perspective on the U.S. labor force and work conditions. In the conclusion, I will connect the theories of exploitation that I develop in this chapter and the next to the exercise of prerogative power domestically in the United States today.

10. This idea is of course indebted to Carole Pateman's work.

The 1980s rang in a series of changes that contributed to the new types of blue-collar work and the demographic transformation of the working class in the United States. In the final few years of the Cold War, the globalization of the economy took on new dimensions and neoliberal policy seemingly transformed the national questions from ideological or political ones into economic ones, including how the United States was to remain competitive in the world economy. Soon after, immigration laws were changed in order to reflect economic concerns rather than international politics.[11] The steady dismantling of the welfare state began at this time with a renewed focus on individual responsibility, as discussed in the previous chapters. In this political and economic context, the very nature of work began to change and the view began to take hold that the nation-state was declining and that government would soon become merely an adjunct of the economy. All of this has altered the nature of work and the situation of poor workers; for these reasons, Marx's ideas are perhaps more relevant now than at any time in the twentieth century.

Yet in recent times, Marx's analysis of capitalist society and exploitation has been largely discredited, as have his predictions about the working class.[12] The most obvious reason for this has been the end of the Cold War, which supposedly drove the final nail in the coffin of communism. But even before this, it was being argued that the conditions of the working class (in the United States, for example) demonstrated how Marx had been wrong on several of his most crucial points. First, Marxism was viewed as having failed because the revolutionary potential of the working class had been neutralized over time ("assimilated" in Habermas's terms) as a result of the institutionalization of unions and the rise of worker protections in factories (beginning in the late 1800s) and workers' political rights (beginning in the early 1900s).[13] The potential of the working class to make revolution had also been politically and economically neutralized (albeit indirectly) as a result of the emergence of individual civil rights beginning in the 1940s and the development of a mass welfare state just before that. The contention was that in the postwar era, workers not only enjoyed full legal rights but also could be economically independent (not

11. As Cheryl Shanks notes, the last link between immigration and the Cold War was made in 1985; since then, policy has increasingly had an economic logic. See Shanks, *Immigration and Politics of American Sovereignty, 1890–1990* (Ann Arbor: University of Michigan Press, 2001).

12. This notwithstanding a revival of interest in Marx's work in the late 1990s. See John Rees, "The Return of Marx?" *International Socialism* 79 (Summer 1998): 3–11.

13. See ibid., 3.

in the Marxist sense of owning their means of production but in the more minimal sense of not needing welfare or other aid).[14]

Second, it can be inferred that Marx was wrong about the link between the state and the economy; that is, the base/superstructure formulation was refuted through these reforms. Liberalism is not capitalism, and the state has its own logic and life, as Max Weber maintained. In fact, these reforms arguably demonstrated that the state was on the workers' side and that it rewarded hard work and an honest living. The state could be seen as correcting the harsher effects of capitalism and as protecting individuals who participated in the labor market. Thus, it could be argued, the state operates independently of capitalist enterprise. Furthermore (or hence), the contradictions of capitalism did not deepen and culminate in revolution; in fact, it seems that the working class became the *paradigm* of good citizens: hard working, honest, and independent. This dealt a blow to one of the most significant Marxist arguments: that exploitation is facilitated by the state precisely because workers are disenfranchised. Moreover, conditions in the United States showed not only the autonomy of state power in confrontation with capitalist power and the neutralizing effects of the welfare state but also that Marx had been fundamentally wrong about exploitation being inherent to capitalism. If workers were indeed unhappy and truly exploited, they would certainly rise up; in a democratic society, they had every opportunity to do so. Yet arguably, from the 1940s through the 1960s, many workers enjoyed secure employment (including salary and benefits), were not vulnerable to economic crises, and could lead a middle-class life. For this reason, the security and well-being of the American working class was an important ideological tool in the Cold War. It could be argued that, precisely for these reasons, the Soviet Union focused on racism and sexism rather than worker exploitation in its propaganda against the United States.[15]

Jürgen Habermas echoed these criticisms in his earlier work, albeit from a position that clearly takes Marx's ideas seriously. His argument in *Theory of Communicative Action*[16] is that class conflict is mediated and

14. See, for example, Thomas McCarthy, "Translator's Introduction," in Jürgen Habermas, *Theory of Communicative Action*, vol. 1 (Boston: Beacon Press, 1984), xxi.

15. Conversely, it is interesting that the United States would only recognize *political* repression as a human rights violation when processing refugee and asylum applications during the Cold War. While this category has been retained, it has been problematized by the profusion of ethnic wars breaking out after the Cold War and by the demise of clear ideological and political lines.

16. Habermas, *Theory of Communicative Action*, vols. 1 and 2, trans. Thomas McCarthy (Boston: Beacon Press, 1985).

pacified by the state and that as a consequence, other, more marginal problems arise (such as the state's overinvolvement in welfare clients' lives). However, while he is correct that many problems arose that Marx never predicted, he is wrong in contending that class problems and exploitation have thereby been neutralized, particularly by the state. In fact, the decline of the welfare state—especially for women and immigrants—has meant fewer protections and more vulnerability for those who would make up the working class. That is, the state's role has not been as a mediator of class conflict per se. Habermas also criticizes Marx for taking one historical stage and extrapolating a theory of class exploitation from that, and he may be right. However, the historical conditions that Marx described—the absence of workers' rights and protections, the real or effective disenfranchisement of workers, and the lack of job security—have certainly resurfaced, albeit in new ways, thus distinguishing this new group (group meaning a complex array of people) of workers from the working class of the 1940s, 1950s, and 1960s.

The problem is also definitional: the notion that there is economic exploitation of workers loses force because the target population has been white, male, fully enfranchised, and working in manufacturing jobs with adequate salaries and benefits.[17] When work is conceived of in this way, it is difficult to argue that exploitation is occurring; rather, these jobs are disappearing and those particular people are unemployed.[18] When there are exposés of superexploitation (for example, of garment workers in Los Angeles or foreign workers enslaved on a Texas ranch), these cases are treated as anomalous and unconnected to one another. As further obfuscation, instead of comparing the "old" working class of the 1940s or 1950s (for example) to the "new" working class and its conditions, there are frequent comparisons between African American low- or unskilled laborers and service workers and immigrants who do similar work (in the literature, it is evident that both are considered "guests" in this country). This has led to what Bonacich has described as ethnic antagonism brought about by the split labor market (discussed below).[19] The feminization of

17. See Carole Pateman, *The Disorder of Women* (Stanford: Stanford University Press, 1992), chap. 8.

18. See William Julius Wilson, *When Work Disappears* (New York: Vintage Books, 1997), xiii, xix, 16, 17, 19, 22, 25–29, 52–54, 220, 224–25.

19. See Edna Bonacich, "A Theory of Ethnic Antagonism: The Split Labor Market," *American Sociological Review* 37 (October): 547–59. Unlike Bonacich, however, I do not think that racism, ethnic antagonism, or sexism simply originate in the labor aristocracy's attempts to prevent low-paid labor from undercutting them. Rather, I believe that these antagonisms are often expressed and fomented at elite levels, and not merely for economic gain but also in an effort to alleviate anxieties about sovereignty.

labor correspondingly results in a gender split that corrodes or fundamentally alters relations between minority men and women as well as
immigrant couples,[20] thus concealing exploitative work conditions.

Indeed, Marx's critique has become relevant again with this new
working class. With the globalization of the economy, the nature of blue-
collar work has changed as well as the labor force doing this work.
Although the majority of the working class is still white, a new ideal type
of worker has emerged for a more flexible job market. First, those who
compose the new working class are historically disenfranchised (for example,
women, African Americans, and other racial minorities), have never been
enfranchised (immigrants without documentation, for example, or guest
workers), or are recently enfranchised but politically vulnerable. Second,
the new ideal worker is from a group typically associated with domestic
or reproductive work. Third, these workers are viewed as gendered others
or racial minorities so that whites who fill these positions are racially
degraded ("white trash") and/or viewed as gender transgressors who have
not lived up to their potential (men who should be breadwinners but are
not). The precarious political status of all these workers, which allows for
the greater political and economic exploitation that Marx foresaw, was not
possible during the 1950s and 1960s to the same degree (for mainstream
workers anyway).

Related to this, owing to changes in the demand for labor in the United
States, blue-collar work is now dominated by the service industry and
includes agricultural work and unskilled manufacturing, among other
things. This employment is more dangerous and physically intensive
than in the recent past (because of deregulation in certain sectors—such
as agricultural work and meatpacking positions—and the proliferation
of sweatshops and illegal factories).[21] Exploitation in these areas is ignored
owing to the reliance on old definitions of work, not to mention the
invisibility of these individuals for various reasons that will be discussed
below. Anti-immigration sentiment further allows exploitation of immigrants,

20. See Saskia Sassen, *Globalization and Its Discontents: Essays on the New Mobility of People and Money* (New York: New Press, 1998), chaps. 5 and 6; see also Wilson, *When Work Disappears*, 88–95, 97–107, 100–105.

21. See Alvaro Bedoya, "Captive Labor," *Dollars and Sense* 249 (September–October 2003): 30–34; Kirstin Downey, "New Risks Widen Definition of Dirty, Hazardous Work," *Boston Globe*, June 1, 2003, E3; Human Rights Watch, "Human Rights Watch Welcomes U.S. Government Meat and Poultry Study," http://hrw.org/English/docs/2005/02/03/ usdom10117_txt.htm; "Abusive Child Labor Found in U.S. Agriculture," http://hrw.org/English/docs/ 2000/ 06/20/usdom580_txt.thm; National Catholic Rural Life Conference, "U.S. Agricultural Workers," http://www.ncrlc.com/AgriculturalWorkers.html.

given the lack of support for their residence in this country. Finally, racial factors and language barriers not only heighten this obscurity but also allow for greater vulnerability and, thus, exploitation. Ultimately this demonstrates that there *is* a connection between political power and economic exploitation even if a base/superstructure relation is overly simplistic.

Furthermore, given the precarious nature of these new jobs, declining unionization, and the U.S. low-wage policy, the conditions that Marx described in the 1840s, such as workers' disenfranchisement, inability to unionize, subsistence-level wages, long hours, and dangerous conditions, have become the norm again. These conditions do not merely reflect the caprice of big business but are part of neoliberal policies and thus demonstrate the state's role in economic exploitation, not to mention the connection between exploitation and disenfranchisement. While economic globalization is perhaps not so new, it clearly began to effect these changes in the 1980s; paired with neoliberal policies from that decade onward, it then took on a political and economic meaning and force that it hadn't before. The push for economic deregulation, smaller government, and greater mobility of capital (among other things) has forged an unbreakable link between working conditions and political policy, between wealth and politics. Although I will not refer to Jacques Derrida's *Specters of Marx*[22] at length in this chapter, his reasons for writing that book are pertinent if there is to be any hope for alternative discourse or movements; Marx may be viewed as outdated, irrelevant, and an academic curiosity, but his intellectual and critical potency cannot be denied.[23] This is true at practical levels, whether we are diagnosing problems of the working class or the directions its organizing efforts should take. But it is also true in the sense that any attempts to master and fix public discourse on one economic and political paradigm will inevitably meet its ghosts, the return of the repressed. A closer look at how globalization has changed the U.S. economy will illustrate these points.

What Is Globalization?

Globalization can be viewed in at least two different ways. First, it is the very real *historical* processes that have marked a closer integration of

22. Jaques Derrida, *Spectres de Marx* (Paris: Galilée, 1993).
23. See Rees on Marx's importance; Nancy Fraser, "A Future for Marxism," *New Politics* 6 (Winter 1998): 98–101.

communication, trade, and cultural exchange, among other things. These processes, which are by no means new, have been aided in recent years by technological innovations that have reduced costs of travel and communication and that have resulted in an unprecedented flow of peoples and goods. This suggests why "globalization" as a historical period can be viewed as distinct from the imperial past, even if it is not a historical rupture. In particular, *economic* globalization involves the development of global finance and the global circulation of capital. Changes in the world economy involve "the rise of finance and advanced services as leading industries . . . contributing to a new international economic order, one dominated by financial centers, global markets, and transnational firms."[24] It is often ignored that these changes also produce the globalization of labor flows, the development of informal economies, and the strengthening of certain forms of state power. Perhaps for all of these reasons, as Joseph Stiglitz notes, the most controversial element of globalization is economic globalization.[25]

A second way to look at globalization is in terms of the *ideational* structure that has shaped various economic, cultural, and political processes since the 1980s, often under the rubric of neoliberalism. This ideational structure can also be viewed as promoting "cultural imperialism" or the advocacy of certain ideas and products (including franchises), which are held to be cultural markers of material prosperity and—so the reasoning goes—civilization, democracy, and a free market. While democracy is viewed as a highly desirable and inevitable outcome of a free market, economic ideas predominate under this rubric.[26] Thus it can be argued that economic ideas subsume political ones and that a free market exists at the expense of an unfree labor force. The first view of globalization points to economic processes that have developed over many decades, the second to the ideational structures that explain, validate, and even distort these very real processes. In this chapter, I will be referring to both, focusing on the economic in order to illuminate the political consequences of these very real developments as well as the ideas attached to them at this moment in history.

24. Sassen, *Globalization and Its Discontents*, xxix, xxx.

25. Joseph Stiglitz, *Globalization and Its Discontents* (New York: W. W. Norton, 2002), 10. This book shares the same title as Sassen's but is more accessible and easier to read.

26. In his recent work *Globalism: The New Market Ideology*, Manfred Steger differentiates between globalization ("the expansion of the cultural flows of ideas and trade") and the ideology of globalism ("the idea that unregulated capitalism is the inevitable, inescapable fate of successful economies"). See Teresa Walker, "Review, *Globalism: The New Market Ideology* by Manfred Steger," *Logos* 2 (Spring 2003): 148–55, http://www.logosjournal.com.

There are a number of reasons why economic globalization is viewed as having emerged in the late 1980s. First, with the end of the Cold War in sight, ideological concerns began to shift from the political toward the economic. There was a widely held view that democratic political beliefs and institutions were crucial to fostering human freedom and that markets would liberalize with regime change after the Cold War. As communism fell, the order of importance was inverted; the notion that *free markets* would ensure *democracy* became predominant. As has been repeated ad nauseum, it was declared that the "end of ideology" was at hand, perhaps even the end of history as we knew it. However, the case can be made that whatever the era, the supposed predominance of one category over another merely obscures the close and constant linkages between politics and economics—especially in liberal democracies. At any rate, neoliberalism emerged most strongly at this moment, with its advocacy of privatization, economic deregulation, and greater mobility for capital. Around this time, as Joseph Stiglitz notes, the International Monetary Fund (IMF), the World Bank, and later the World Trade Organization (WTO) became "new missionary institutions"[27] linking economic policy and politics in the international arena. Although the first two institutions were established after World War II, their functions began to change in the 1980s: they became increasingly prescriptive in administering loans, and they broadened the scope of their aid to foreign countries. In these ways, they not only influenced the economies of debtor nations but also affected their sovereignty, thereby indirectly influencing U.S. sovereignty and power. Stiglitz has summarized the effects of IMF policies: "The IMF often talked as if what the economy needed was a good purgative. Take the pain; the deeper the pain, the stronger the subsequent growth."[28] Ascetic values were thus promoted not only domestically but also globally, suggesting a similar power dynamic as the one examined in Chapter 1: one of coercion and hierarchy.

In the context of economic recession, Margaret Thatcher and Ronald Reagan did not apply these international policies to their own countries precisely; even so, their own domestic policies introduced higher levels of austerity and deepened the double standard of asceticism analyzed in Chapter 1.[29] Thatcher privatized her country's industries to an unprecedented

---

27. Stiglitz, *Globalization and Its Discontents*, 13.
28. Ibid., 122.
29. On Reagan's massive cuts, which disproportionately affected African Americans, see Linda Faye Williams, *The Constraint of Race* (University Park: Penn State University Press, 2004).

degree; Reagan made the availability of affordable housing and welfare both precarious and contingent. These two political leaders inaugurated the era in which we are now, which is marked by changes in work and welfare as well as by claims that government is shrinking. The ideas influencing these changes can be traced back to the work of Friedrich Hayek, the Austrian political economist whose writings were perhaps ahead of his time.

Von Hayek's ideas[30] about an open market are crucial for understanding the neoliberal push for deregulation since the 1980s. Hayek believed, among other things, that a system governed by the price mechanism would be inherently neutral. While there would admittedly be losers and winners in this "game," no one person would be culpable for these outcomes. Rather, all would have an equal chance to win or lose. Hayek argued that choosing this system over others was in fact value free and thus the closest approximation of justice that we could have on earth. Neoliberals, including Reagan and Thatcher, adopted many of Hayek's ideas: Reagan began to make the social safety net more difficult to access; and Thatcher launched an unprecedented campaign of privatization. Ironically, though, it was President Bill Clinton who pushed for more widespread deregulation in the United States. However, unlike Hayek, who was antinationalist and who argued for a guaranteed minimum income, neoliberals and "New Democrats" in the United States argued contradictorily for deregulation *and* nationalism, along with Clinton's welfare reforms, which affected the poor whether they were immigrants or native born.[31] Neoliberals contend that capitalism is a natural system, value free and universal. They equate deregulation with individual freedom and autonomy and call for it to be exercised at the corporate level. However, the message of mobility and freedom is not just an economic one; it is also social and geographic: everyone will benefit from this system if workers remain flexible, capital can be transferred rapidly, and employers are not confined to one country.

Deregulation, of course, implies less government intervention in economic affairs and a general decrease in political apparatuses. While Michel Foucault

---

30. See Hayek. For more contemporary views of deregulation, see Stiglitz, *Globalization and Its Discontents;* Paul Krugman, *The Great Unraveling: losing Our Way in the New Century* (New York: W. W. Norton, 2003); Zygmunt Bauman *Globalization* (New York: Columbia University Press, 1998); among others.

31. Dani Rodrik puts it differently, arguing that of the three things—economic globalization, national sovereignty, and democracy—only two can coexist. In Rodrik's terms, I am arguing that neoliberals have chosen the first two above the third. See Rodrik, "Feasible Globalizations," http://ksghome.harvard.edu/~.drodrik.academic.ksg/Feasglob.pdf.

did not focus on economic globalization per se, he argued in his writings that the proliferation of bureaucracy and extrabureaucratic authority displaces sovereignty as traditionally conceived. Proponents of deregulation also portray the state as shrinking in terms of centralization and sovereignty. Indeed, Wendy Brown notes that because power has become more decentralized, and because it appears as "just one player on the global chessboard," the state now seems impotent in ways that it formerly had not. Hence, "the central paradox of the late modern state thus resembles a central paradox of late modern masculinity: its power and privilege operate increasingly through disavowal of potency, repudiation of responsibility, and diffusion of sites and operations of control."[32] On the one hand, this dispersal of state power reflects the more diffuse networks of global capital. On the other hand, absolute power is strengthened as the two realms increasingly become intertwined; the contingencies of daily life arising from economic globalization are precisely what strengthen the prerogative elements of the state: "Power is generated by uncertainty."[33] Sheldon Wolin points out that the increased privatization not only of public enterprise but also of social services (such as hospitals and schools) would seem to decentralize state power; but then he adds that "this obscures power exercised by agents who appear to be responding to profit motives and market forces but who in reality are fulfilling disciplinary needs of the Economic Polity," which are secured by insecurity.[34] As I suggested in the previous chapters, the notion of political theology does not allow the neat conceptual (or practical) separation of these spheres; in fact, it shows the power of ascetic ideas across boundaries. A closer look at how globalization has changed the U.S. economy will illustrate these points.

Dynamics of Globalization

As discussed in Chapter 1, the greater mobility and "freedom" of capital has been accompanied by the greater placeboundedness and unfreedom of labor. The greater fluidity of capital, which allows it to circulate more rapidly, creates a demand for the growth of the service industry at both

---

32. Wendy Brown, *States of Injury: Power and Freedom in Late Modernity* (Princeton: Princeton University Press, 1995), 194.

33. Sheldon Wolin, "Democracy and the Welfare State: The Political and Theoretical Connections Between *Staatsräson* and *Wohlfahrsstaatsräson*," in *The Presence of the Past: Essays on the State and the Constitution* (Baltimore: Johns Hopkins University Press, 1989), 162.

34. Wolin, "Democracy and the Welfare State," 174.

high and low levels of employment. This spawns what could be called a "new economic regime," because the service industry "imposes itself on the entire economy."[35] This is especially true of the financial service industry. The service economy has become ascendant while traditional manufacturing has been downgraded. And as labor relations become more informal and lower paid, a corresponding polarity develops in urban space so that there is a split between businesses that cater to wealthier customers and those aimed at low-income individuals. The former group is most often served by established businesses; the latter often has its needs met in the informal economy. Inequalities in wealth produce a class with a great deal of disposable income; they also lead to gentrification and a demand for services that can only be performed physically (from dog walking to child care to the hand sewing of garments and bags to the crafting of custom Nikes). Thus, the demand for physically intensive labor arises in low-tier manufacturing and service work besides proceeding from the needs of the elite.

As superprofits accrue, commercial spaces and business services become increasingly expensive, pushing out middle-of-the-road firms (that is, those making moderate profits). The result is a conglomeration of high-end services and businesses and a downgrading of low-end manufacturers, services, and businesses. As Sassen notes, inequalities in businesses' profits have always existed, but "what we see happening today takes place on another order of magnitude and is engendering massive distortions in the operations of various markets, from housing to labor."[36] As a result, moderately profitable companies may choose to operate informally— in spaces that are not zoned for commercial use, for example. Some obvious examples of the displacement of moderate-profit businesses: the disappearance of independent booksellers, as large chains such as Barnes and Noble and Borders come to dominate the market; the ever increasing presence of Wal-Mart as it branches out from retail to banking and other services; and the conglomeration of banking services, which pushes out local banks. To put it differently, there is a tendency to monopoly in the formal sector in these circumstances.[37]

Related to these dynamics, the relocation of manufacturing and other businesses to foreign countries not only affects less developed regions of the world but also transforms terms and conditions of employment in

---

35. Sassen, *Globalization and Its Discontents*, 88.
36. Ibid., 89.
37. This has been defended by revitalizing Joseph Schumpeter's ideas in recent years.

the more developed countries.[38] There is an overall increase in low-wage jobs, with work performed in less formal conditions than in the past. This is true in industries ranging from the garment industry to construction. This production can be subcontracted to "low rent" operations either in sweatshops or in the home. At the same time, low-cost operations pop up in cities to service the groups that cannot frequent the boutiques and specialty shops in gentrified areas. These low-cost operations also need low-wage labor; thus, in both gentrified and poorer areas there is a demand for these workers, making "immigrants a desirable labor supply."[39] Certain labor-intensive industries, which are "downgraded," are also strongly present in major cities (for example, the garment industry).[40] These trends point to the growth of informal employment conditions and an informal economy in highly developed countries.[41]

A more informal economy "refers to those income-generating activities occurring outside the state's regulatory framework that have analogs within that framework."[42] As Sassen remarks, Third World immigration is often seen as the *cause* of informal economic activities and business.[43] However, these economies may be formed by the needs or opportunities created by major actors in the globalized economy, including employers who recruit potential immigrants from their home countries.[44] Indeed, informal economies fill the vacuum created by the decline in manufacturing jobs; they also reflect the transformation from an industrial economy to one dominated by the service industry.[45] Pushing these changes have been the polarization of earnings and wealth, shifts in consumer demand, and the split in industry described above. In sum, the greater disparity in incomes—and in the economy in general—has generated the need for an informal economy; that need has not been generated by the presence of poorer immigrants as a cheap labor supply.

So it is not the presence of undocumented workers that makes a workplace informal.[46] Moreover, informal employment cannot be defined as side work; in fact, this sort of work has an analog in the mainstream

38. Sassen, *Globalization and Its Discontents*, 120.
39. Ibid., 124.
40. Ibid., 125.
41. See ibid., 131.
42. Ibid., 153.
43. Ibid., 154.
44. Ibid. See also Alejandro Portes and Rubén Rumbaut, *Immigrant America* (Berkeley and Los Angeles: University of California Press, 1996).
45. Sassen, *Globalization and Its Discontents*, 154.
46. Ibid., 157.

economy: "It is not the intrinsic characteristic of those [work] activities, but rather the boundaries of state regulation that determine their informalization."[47] What has actually happened is that changes in the economy—with the decline of mass production and the shift to a service economy—have altered the nature of work and the employment "contract."[48] Lower-tier jobs are now characterized by less unionization, less job protection (with regard to length of employment), and lower wages.[49] Low wages expand the numbers of the working poor and thereby increase the demand for cheaper goods, which in turn drives the informal economy.[50] In this way, both gentrification and greater poverty are generating a demand for labor-intensive low-wage work.[51] When the middle class predominated economically and culturally, suburbanization and its needs were "capital intensive" rather than labor intensive.[52] Today, in contrast, in a more global economy, growth is contributing to inequality rather than to the maintenance of the middle class.[53]

Sassen summarizes the causes of an increasingly informal economy as follows: "1) the increased demand for highly priced customized services and products by the expanding high-income population; 2) the increased demand for extremely low-cost services and products by the expanding low-income population; 3) the demand for customized services and goods or limited runs from firms that are either final or intermediate buyers, with a corresponding growth of subcontracting; and 4) the increasing inequality in the bidding power of firms in a context of acute pressures on land due to the rapid growth and strong agglomerative pattern of the leading industries."[54] Increased informalization is also a response to the pressure to remain price- and labor-competitive relative to developing countries—as in the garment industry, for example. The proliferation of informal economies can thus be viewed as a response to the formal economy's failure to meet the demands of all consumers.[55] As I will argue

47. Ibid., 156.
48. Ibid., 158. See also Michelle Conlin and Aaron Bernstein, "Working . . . and Poor," *Business Week*, May 31, 2004, 58–65, for a discussion of how this affects various groups, what can be done, and why these conditions will not change any time soon.
49. With regard to wages, see Wilson, *When Work Disappears*, 30, 34, 140, 152, 154. This is particularly true of less educated men. See Paul J. Devereux, "Changes in Male Labor Supply and Wages," *Industrial and Labor Relations Review* 56 (April 2003): 409–27.
50. Sassen, *Globalization and Its Discontents*, 160.
51. Ibid., 160, 161.
52. Ibid., 160.
53. Ibid., 149.
54. Ibid., 163.
55. Ibid., 164.

below, these conditions lead to exploitation; but they also serve a need, in that they meet the needs of low-income communities by providing jobs and cheap goods in the possible absence of both.

Demographic changes in who is hired for these low-end jobs reflect the greater use of immigrant laborers,[56] the feminization of labor,[57] and the racialization of blue-collar workers.[58] As argued above, even if the majority of low-tier workers are white, the ideal type for flexible jobs has changed. This is evident in *maquiladora* manuals, for example, which laud the nimbleness and docility of "third world women" even if the latter qualities have been challenged by unionization movements. Regardless, this ideal type has still held. Ethnic, race, and gender differentiation have led not only to radical changes in the blue-collar workforce but also to social tensions and radically altered relations. This challenges the notion that racial tensions, gender divisions, and xenophobia are biological or primordial.[59] Rather, friction arises from economic insecurity and from the perception that one group is benefiting more than others; in this way, the higher-paid or more successful group is viewed as exploitative rather than the system itself or the employers. For example, both Wilson and Sassen describe how gender relations have changed as a consequence of the feminization of labor.[60] Wilson contends that the result has been a decrease in the number of marriages, because minority men feel less financially able to get married.[61] Sassen reports different effects in immigrant communities and tells us that in urban areas, immigrant women can often break free of traditional roles.[62] Nevertheless, Sassen, Gayatri Chakravorty Spivak, and Gloria Anzaldúa, among others, problematize

56. According to one estimate, immigrants now fill half of all manufacturing jobs in the United States. Jerry Ackerman, "Easing Immigrants' Culture Shock," *Boston Sunday Globe*, May 30, 2004, G7. See Kimberly Blanton, "Study Details Immigrants' Importance," *Boston Globe*, November 11, 1999, D1; "Changes on Horizon for Nation's Workforce," *Boston Globe*, February 22, 2004; Sassen, *Globalization and Its Discontents*, 91.

57. Sassen, *Globalization and Its Discontents*, 84, 91, 111, 119, 131; Devereux, "Changes in Male Labor Supply and Wages."

58. See Jacqueline Jones for a history of workplace integration and for an account of the impact that globalization (among other things) had on African American employment soon after. Jones, *American Work: Four Centuries of Black and White Labor* (New York: W. W. Norton, 1998).

59. See, for example, Barbara Fields, "Slavery, Race, and Ideology in the United States of America," *New Left Review* I (May–June 1990): 95–118.

60. On the feminization of labor, see Wilson, *When Work Disappears*, 27, 28, 117, 118, 122–23, 126, 143–44, 154.

61. See ibid., 97–107, 88–95, 100–105.

62. See, for example, Sassen, *Globalization and Its Discontents*, 120–31.

the ease with which this newfound freedom happens; significantly, they all recognize that new work conditions are indeed exploitative.[63]

Similarly, racial and ethnic tensions reflect a more insecure job market, as in the Los Angeles riots (or uprising) in the early 1990s. However, the economic context was obscured as reported in the mainstream press, without reference to economic or political factors. In fact, the only conclusion the media succeeded in drawing regarding those riots was that racial tensions are natural; this perspective then justified the view that minorities are violent, irrational, and angry. Actually, when the stakes seem high enough, what leads to conflict and competition are income inequalities, "white flight" from the cities, and the degradation of urban neighborhoods (discussed below). Another potential driver of conflict is the perception that one group is deliberately undercutting another. Tensions in 1990s Los Angeles reflected this perception: there were tensions between recent immigrants from Central and South America and African Americans;[64] as well, there was general resentment toward Korean entrepreneurs in the inner city.[65] There were also tensions between poor whites and minorities (whether immigrant or American born).[66] The racialization[67] of the workforce points to many things, among them the apparent replacement of the white working class with an increasingly diverse and lower-paid, *allegedly* lower-skilled group of workers; the intersection of race and gender and/or immigrant status; and the exploitation of African American prisoners.[68] For these groups, the key determinant in their employment is their immobility in a world of capital mobility: "Thus a particular region of the United States might offer a surplus of illegal aliens, or the destitute sons and daughters of isolated rural folk, or inner-city blacks and Hispanics, all potential employees willing to work long hours for low

63. See Gayatri Chakravorty Spivak, "Cultural Talks in the Hot Peace: Revisiting the 'Global Village,'" in *Cosmopolitics: Thinking and Feeling Beyond the Nation*, ed. Pheng Cheah and Bruce Robbins (Minneapolis: University of Minnesota Press, 1998); Soniah Shah, ed., *Dragon Ladies: Asian American Feminists Breathe Fire* (Boston: South End Press, 1997); Gloria Anzaldúa, *Borderlands* (San Francisco: Aunt Lute Books, 1999).

64. Wilson, *When Work Disappears*, 188–89.

65. Ibid., 190–91.

66. Ibid., x, 186–87, 202. See also Jack Miles, "Blacks vs. Browns," in *Arguing Immigration*, ed. Nicolaus Mills (New York: Touchstone, 1994), for a journalistic (and highly problematic) account of these tensions.

67. See Wilson, *When Work Disappears*, chap. 5.

68. On this point, see Christopher Sturr, "Philosophical Theories of Punishment and the History of Prison Reform," in Austin Sarat and Patricia Ewick, eds., *Punishment, Politics, and Culture* (Amsterdam: Elsevier, 2004); and "The Political Economy of the Prison Crisis," *Dollars and Sense* 10 (April 2006), chap. 3; see also Jones, *American Work*, 377–78.

wages."[69] The evidence shows that friction does not develop in a vacuum; rather, it is linked to class and economic instability.[70] Furthermore, as I will argue below, racism allows academics, the media, and the social mainstream to treat African Americans as foreigners in their own country, and this leads to cultural disenfranchisement, which is reinforced by political and economic disenfranchisement. Yet the changing demographics of the working class are not being viewed in their entirety, partly because these workers are regarded as marginal, illegal, or pathological, and partly because the work they perform is devalued.

Related to this, the model of work in the informal economy has become the paradigm of low-end employment in general in the globalized economy of the United States.[71] This is due in part to the "downgrading of the manufacturing sector"—in which work is generally becoming nonunionized—accompanied by an increase in sweatshops and industrial homework. For example, the garment and construction industries are both increasingly labor intensive, and work conditions in both are becoming substandard.[72] At the same time, newer industries are spinning out production and assembly jobs that are low paid,[73] unskilled, and highly repetitive.[74] In the service sector, many jobs are part-time (service workers are twice as likely to be in part-time jobs as average workers),[75] dead-end (meaning that there is no room for advancement),[76] and labor intensive: "Over sixty percent of all part-time workers in the U.S. labor force are in labor-intensive services which is also the sector that is expected to add the largest share of new jobs over the next decade."[77] This increases not only poverty but also involuntary unemployment,[78] which is lasting longer

69. Jones, *American Work*, 370.

70. See Wilson, *When Work Disappears*, 194–201, for a compelling argument regarding the importance of class.

71. For example, see ibid., xx, 25, 26, 28, 29, 53, 54, 151–54, 177, 207, 232, 235.

72. Sassen, *Globalization and Its Discontents*, 164.

73. Ibid., 121.

74. Ibid., 165. See also David Bacon, "Labor Fights for Immigrants," *The Nation*, May 21, 2001.

75. Sassen, *Globalization and Its Discontents*, 146.

76. See Wilson, *When Work Disappears*, 25, 26.

77. Sassen, *Globalization and Its Discontents*, 146, and see also 87 and 164. As well, see Bedoya's work on agricultural guest workers (for example, "Captive Labor," *Dollars and Sense* 249 [2005]: 30–34), in which he argues that we have the most labor-intensive agricultural industry of all industrialized countries.

78. Sassen, *Globalization and Its Discontents*, 146. See "Layoffs up 8 Percent as Firms Remain Wary," *Boston Globe*, August 8, 2004, G2; Diane E. Lewis, "Pact Helped Hasten Job Losses, Report Says," *Boston Globe*, December 14, 2003, H2.

than in the past[79] and which is significantly affecting American-born men in their prime of life.[80]

Pertinent here is that poor educational systems and the decline in traditional manufacturing jobs are mutually reinforcing. As Wilson notes, rapid changes in technology are rewarding high levels of education[81] and at the same time are leading to the demise of traditional blue-collar employment.[82] Furthermore, the repetitive, physically intense, and unskilled nature of newly created informal or part-time jobs does little to enhance any worker's skills or marketability. Those who take these jobs not only become "deskilled" but also are stereotyped as occupying these jobs, which launches a self-fulfilling prophecy.[83] This is true of both American-born workers and immigrants, who are placed in jobs owing to their gender (for example, caretaking jobs), nationality (for example, the correlation of Mexicans with gardening and Peruvians with sheepherding), and race (for example, the preference for African American women employees rather than African American men because the former are more "docile,"[84] or the correlation of African American men with physical or security work).

For all of these reasons, Wilson argues that many traditional jobs are now obsolete; consider that the title of his work that I am citing is *When Work Disappears*. However, I believe this is not quite the case; Sassen's work is valuable because it shows that the irregular, informal, low-paid work that replaces these traditional jobs is not simply marginal but is now the norm for blue-collar work. Like Sassen, Wilson recognizes that the jobs remaining in cities are far more precarious than in the past. Because low-wage jobs no longer have the benefits that low-skilled or unskilled jobs used to carry (such as insurance, day care, and travel costs), nor the security (protected and enforced by unions), "many inner-city ghetto residents who maintain a connection with the formal labor market—that is,

---

79. Wilson, *When Work Disappears*, 19, 20, 25.
80. Ibid., 26.
81. Ibid., 28.
82. Ibid., xiii, xix, 16, 17, 19, 22, 25–29, 52–54, 220, 224, 225.
83. See Kathleen Paul, *Whitewashing Britain: Race and Citizenship in the Postwar Era* (Ithaca: Cornell University Press, 1997), for a similar argument about workers from the West Indies who arrived in Britain and were placed in jobs that were below their skill levels. See also Ackerman, "Easing Immigrants' Culture Shock," regarding the credentials gap between developing countries and the United States and Canada, as a result of which doctors from developing countries end up working at Starbucks, scientists find work here as janitors, and so on.
84. On this last point, see Wilson, *When Work Disappears*, 118, 123–26. Also, "increasingly displaced from manufacturing industries, inner-city black males are more confined to low-paying service work"; ibid., 142.

who continue to be employed mostly in low-wage jobs—are, in effect, working against all odds."[85] And as Spivak states, with the proliferation of deregulated or flexible work conditions such as industrial homework and home-based factories, "women all over the world are absorbing many of the costs of management, of health care, of workplace safety and the like by working at home."[86] It is crucial to see part-time work, homework, and informal or more casual conditions not as anomalies but as regular features of capitalism that are increasingly predominant in a state that promotes low-wage strategies and deregulation. All of the benefits that workers have lost now come out of these lower wages and are leading to the formation of what Wilson calls "new poverty neighborhoods."

These trends have led to spatial polarization: in select areas of cities, services are highly exclusive; other areas are heavy with informal services (such as check-cashing services and gypsy cabs). In poorer areas, major banks have closed, large supermarket chains do not have branches, and other retail services have pulled out. What's more, the availability of cheap labor (immigrants or inner-city residents) helps concentrate informal business activities in an urban area.[87] Wilson describes these concentrations as "new poverty neighborhoods" because infrastructure is decaying, violence has grown, and there is increased segregation. These neighborhoods are also marked by social isolation, greater concentrations of poverty than in the past, and less social organization.[88] With fewer working- and middle-class residents, there is not enough income to maintain neighborhood services and infrastructure.[89] Wilson concludes that "the economic marginality of the ghetto poor is cruelly reinforced . . . by conditions in the neighborhoods in which they live."[90] As Sassen argues, these inequalities are not merely reflections of the polarization of incomes; they are also new social forms that signal economic and political transformation.[91] To add to the increasing poverty of these neighborhoods, the "New Federalism" has led to severe reductions in spending on urban programs, as well as shrinking tax bases.[92]

85. Ibid., 53.
86. Spivak, "Cultural Talks in the Hot Peace," 342.
87. Sassen, *Globalization and Its Discontents*, 165.
88. See Wilson, *When Work Disappears*, chaps. 1 and 2.
89. Ibid., 54.
90. Ibid., 54.
91. Sassen, *Globalization and Its Discontents*, 148. With regard to towns and cities that are abandoned once an industry leaves—"throwaway cities"—see Gar Alperovitz, David Imbroscio, and Thad Williamson, *Making a Place for Community: Local Democracy in a Global Era*, foreword by Benjamin Barber (New York: Routledge, 2002), 10–13.
92. See Wilson, *When Work Disappears*, 185.

These changes together reflect a "bifurcation of human experience,"[93] ranging from the polarization of incomes to the polarization of space, so that mobility is greater for some individuals than for others. The term "flexibility,"[94] which has been assigned to labor conditions and thus the new working class, is a cruelly ironic signifier of the greater immobility of workers, including immigrants and guest workers. Flexibility, meaning flexible hours, nonunion workspaces, low wages, and temporary contracts, is "an intention to expropriate the power of resistance of those whose 'rigidity' it about to be overcome. Indeed, labour would cease to be 'rigid' only if it stopped being an unknown quantity in the investors' calculation."[95] Similarly, the criminalization of poverty in general,[96] and the criminalization of informal workplaces, can be juxtaposed to government *encouragement* of flexible conditions. In the same vein, the presence and work of illegal aliens is something the government tacitly supports.

The state encourages all of these things through deregulation and low-wage policies and by inviting guest workers, neglecting its own zoning laws, and encouraging unauthorized immigrants (UAIS)—especially Mexicans—to cross the border. The state tolerates employer recruitment of UAIS by selectively fining these employers, by advocating open borders for these workers, and/or by expanding guest-worker programs. The government is actually permitting employers to recruit "workers" (illegal entrants) directly from detention cells.[97] These contradictions have resulted in a highly contingent political space for low-wage workers, who serve as cheap labor even while they are being policed. To put it differently, employers do not often pay the price for illegal recruitment (an exception is a recent Wal-Mart raid)[98] or for informal work, but the workers do, and in significant ways. Workers absorb the costs of the workplace, health care, and day care; not only that, but they can be deported if they want to

93. Zygmunt Bauman's term in *Globalization;* on this subject, see also Alperovitz and colleagues.

94. On flexibility, see Wilson, *When Work Disappears,* 152, 154; Bauman, *Globalization.*

95. Bauman, *Globalization,* 104.

96. See ibid., 5, 97, 108–27; Kathleen Arnold, *Homelessness, Citizenship, and Identity* (Albany: SUNY Press, 2004), chap. 4.

97. See Maribel Hernandez, "A Citizenship of Aliens: The Case of Undocumented Mexican Immigrants in Los Angeles" (Senior thesis, Committee on Degrees in Social Studies, Harvard University, March 2004), on the INS allowing worker recruitment in holding cells.

98. See "INS Agents Raid Wal-Mart Stores," http://www.cbsnews.com/stories/2003/ /24/ national/main579798.shtml; "The Wal-Mart Raid," *Christian Science Monitor,* http://www. csmonitor.com/2003/27/p08s03-com.html; Steven G reenhouse, "Nine Immigrants Arrested in Raid File Lawsuit Against Wal-Mart," Common Dreams News Center, http://www. commondreams.org/headlines03/1109-04.htm.

switch employers (in the case of guest workers) and can be arrested if they do not have papers or are waiting for papers. Similarly, the limited mobility of inner-city workers means that when businesses shut down or move to other locations, they are simply out of a job. At the same time, the increased policing of inner cities demanded by business interests ensures that inner-city residents do not travel far from their locality. For those who are homeless, their very existence is criminalized. The immobility of workers combined with the conglomeration of businesses and agricultural enterprises ensures that there is little choice in who will employ them or in the determination of wages.

For this reason, Zygmunt Bauman notes: "'Being on the move' has a radically different, opposite sense for, respectively, those at the top and those at the bottom of the new hierarchy; with the bulk of the population . . . oscillating between the two extremes—bearing the brunt of that opposition and suffering acute existential uncertainty, anxiety and fear as a result."[99] The mistake that is made is assuming that greater mobility of capital and goods is equivalent to the greater mobility of people, including migration flows. Even as the number of refugees and migrants increases with each decade, the conditions in which these transfers occur are entirely different from those of capital, communications, and business travel. One process is elite and valued, the other is devalued and often criminalized as well, and viewed in hostile terms so as to bring about an entirely different type of statelessness than the elite processes. Hence, *"rather than homogenizing the human condition, the technological annulment of temporal/spatial distance tends to polarize it."*[100] As Roland Axtmann puts it, "global capitalism is a system of structured inequality."[101] And this inequality manifests itself not only internationally but also domestically.

While the IMF and the World Bank advocate low-wage policies globally, they also affect the labor market in the United States. In fact, these employment conditions could lead one to argue, as Bauman does, that the Protestant work ethic no longer applies: "The pressure today is to *dismantle* the habits of permanent, round-the clock, steady and regular work; what else may the slogan of 'flexible labour' mean?"[102] He goes on to point out that workers can no longer expect a permanent site of employment, are increasingly isolated as coworkers are no longer a fixed group,

99. Bauman, *Globalization*, 4.
100. Ibid., 18. Emphasis in original.
101. Roland Axtmann, *Liberal Democracy into the Twenty-First Century* (Manchester: Manchester University Press, 1996), 132.
102. Bauman, *Globalization*, 112.

and cannot hope to have a single vocation. Hence, "labour must unlearn its hard trained dedication to work and its hard-won emotional attachment to the workplace as well as the personal involvement in its well-being."[103] Nevertheless, I contend that the ascetic values that form the Protestant ethic and the rationalization of work have not disappeared at all; rather, they have adapted to the new conditions so that they now link state and economic interests together more closely. Current labor conditions and the new working class are devalued precisely because of ascetic notions, which determine what counts as work (in terms of both substance and economic independence) but which nevertheless reflect the stringent demands of Protestant asceticism.

As a result of the feminization and racialization of labor, the predominance of service jobs, and informal conditions, blue-collar work is viewed as having disappeared altogether when in fact it has been reconfigured in these devalued areas. In the same way, those performing these jobs—women, racial minorities, and immigrants—are perceived in terms of their identity rather than as a working class. Ultimately, this demonstrates the importance of biopolitical classifications and concerns regarding not only work but also sovereignty. Ascetic values give meaning to these work categories; furthermore, those values declare who counts as a worker and are tied to justifications for worker immobility—that is, for the greater political control of these groups.

The immobility of workers is a result of economic conditions—very simply, many poor workers do not have the means to move from city to city in search of work—and also of government policies and interventions.[104] Gated communities and police profiling enforce the geographic separation between economic classes as well as races,[105] and this is most evident in the criminalization of homelessness.[106] The growing polarization of incomes and the split between informal businesses and wealth-generating enterprises also leads to demands for greater policing of neighborhoods, heightened protection of assets, and strengthened geographical divisions. With public space shrinking as a consequence of commercial development and

103. Ibid., 112.
104. And it is often forgotten that the mobility of capital and enterprises is not purely market driven; it is also fostered by public policy, federal bailouts, and tax breaks. See Alperovitz and colleagues, "Introduction" in *Making Place for a Community*; Nathan Newman, *Net Loss: Internet Prophets, Private Profits, and the Costs to Community* (University Park: Penn State University Press, 2002).
105. See Mike Davis, *City of Quartz* (New York: Vintage, 1992), among others.
106. See the work of Mike Davis, Leonard Feldman, Jeremy Waldron, and Kathleen Arnold on homelessness.

semiprivate spaces (for example, many shopping malls and offices and stores now have "parks" abutting the buildings), property rights have become increasingly important and are reinforcing the importance of the state as guarantor of those rights. Similarly, the War on Drugs has led to the greater disenfranchisement of inner-city males even after they have served their prison sentences; the War on Terror has heightened surveillance and the threat of rapid deportation for many immigrants, even those who are outside the category "terrorist"; and the war on narcoterrorism has effectively militarized the southern border and all who cross it. Also, immigration laws and especially guest-worker policies now monitor and control the whereabouts of immigrants while at the same time allowing for their exploitation on the job. As Bauman remarks: "For the inhabitant of the second world, the walls built of immigration controls, of residence laws, and of 'clean streets' and 'zero tolerance' policies, grow taller."[107]

Furthermore, the precarious nature of work in general has made the average citizen anxious; calls for law and order are logical extensions of the undercurrent of fear in the average person's life in the United States. When this is combined with the panic that followed the 9/11 attacks of 2001, the demand for law and order above other concerns seems logical enough. These concerns about terrorism articulate with the interest in creating a safe environment for investors. Thus, Bauman argues that state sovereignty has been narrowed to police functions: "In the world of global finances, state governments are allotted the role of little else than oversized police precincts, the quantity and quality of the policemen on the beat, sweeping the streets clean of beggars, pesterers and pilferers, and the tightness of the jail walls loom large among the factors of 'investors' confidence and so among the items calculated when the decisions to invest or de-invest are made."[108] The area around Disney World demonstrates this synthesis of geographic partitioning and the partnership of business and the state: Disney is funding a police unit aimed at "displacing the homeless."[109]

These increased police functions suggest that the state is losing sovereignty and being "reduced" to a mere policing agent. That is, the nation-state is "withering away."[110] "Contrary to oft-repeated . . . opinions,

---

107. Bauman, *Globalization*, 89.

108. Ibid., 120.

109. See Eric Brosch, "No Place Like Home," *Harper's Magazine* 296 (April 1998): 58–59; Arnold, *Globalization and Its Discontents*, chap. 4.

110. Bauman, *Globalization*, 57.

there is neither logical nor pragmatic contradiction between the new exterritoriality of capital . . . and the new proliferation of feeble and impotent sovereign states."[111] In other words, global economic interests thrive on the weakness of states. Many others also see the demise of the state as it once was. Yasemin Soysal, for example, believes that the increasing use of guest workers and the fact that guest workers never leave their host country is forcing states to create "post-national" models of citizenship.[112] Indeed, it can be posited that the mere presence of illegal immigrants undermines state sovereignty, which is also perceived as compromised by international firms and their dealings. Thus, the state is impotent in key areas of the economy, the labor market, international relations, and the distribution of power. Many Hayekians, including Ronald Reagan, Margaret Thatcher, and other neoliberals, have in fact declared that they want to reduce the state to its most necessary functions.

However, even though the state has been fundamentally altered by global capitalism, its power has not actually been reduced; rather, it has been reconfigured and obscured. It is convenient for a state to claim impotency in the present climate; it can then claim to be defenseless against the market forces that are pushing welfare states into nonexistence.[113] Yet at the same time, that same state can be strong in military matters, and it can protect corporations from bankruptcy or legal prosecutions. Clearly, the desire for a minimal state is selective and is not as contradictory as it first seems. I will argue below that this reconfiguration has strengthened the prerogative elements of state power while weakening democratic associations (such as unions) and programs for the poor (not to idealize these programs).[114]

What *is* true, however, is that state power is changing even in the case of the United States, which I believe will retain its nation-state form far longer than European countries, for example. Globalization has given rise to new legal regimes, as Sassen argues in one way and Hardt and Negri[115] in another. For Sassen, the new legal regimes are guarantors of global capital and thus can take various forms, ranging from transnational legal entities to protectors of international firms (i.e., by bailing them

111. Ibid., 67.

112. See Yasemin Soysal, *Limits of Citizenship: Migrants and Postnational Membership in Europe* (Chicago: University of Chicago Press, 1994).

113. See Brown, *States of Injury*, chap. 7.

114. Again, see Rodrik for a similar conceptual breakdown even though our conclusions are different.

115. Michael Hardt and Antonio Negri, *Empire* (Cambridge, Mass.: Harvard University Press, 2000).

out). Joseph Stiglitz explores how the most important of these institutions operate and how they could function better and more democratically. Hardt and Negri contend that globalization is creating new legal regimes and, therefore, that globalization is not merely economic but also political. At stake in these accounts is not the disappearance of the nation-state per se but rather a reconfiguration of power; in other words, the nation-state's power is now competing with other powers. For Sassen (and probably Stiglitz), this does not mean the disappearance of the nation-state just yet; rather, the aims of nation-states are undergoing change, and so are the ways in which they are deploying their sovereignty. Significantly, the old centers of power that were concentrated geographically in national capitals are now being dispersed to major world cities, which are beginning to act sometimes like miniature nation-states. According to Hardt and Negri, geographic concentrations of power are being dispersed elsewhere so as to constitute a "diffuse, anonymous network of all-englobing power."[116]

The difference between Sassen and Hardt and Negri is that Sassen contends that the nation-state is still presupposed in most international legislation as well as human rights norms and activism. Moreover, it retains its sovereignty over three important areas that make it indispensable to multinational corporations: military power, immigration law, and border enforcement. (This is especially true of the United States but much less true of the European Union.)[117] Military power is crucial as a means to back up legal contracts and enforce international agreements affecting trade; immigration law affects the supply of low-paid laborers and their employment conditions (namely, unionization and the setting of wages); and border enforcement ensures that military power and immigration law function according to plan. In contrast, Hardt and Negri contend that any conventional reading of sovereignty has no meaning in our postmodern era[118] and that power, in reality, has been constituted by the "multitude."[119] Ironically, as Gopal Balakrishnan remarks, Thomas Friedman's best-selling *The Lexus and the Olive Tree* also rests on a notion of the masses powering globalization (ironic, in that this book paints a rather rosy picture of economic globalization and its effects).[120] However, what concerns me in

116. Gopal Balakrishnan, "Virgilian Visions," *New Left Review* 5 (September–October 2000): 143.

117. Although commentators on this manuscript have noted that European integration has happened much less smoothly than some would have it.

118. Hardt and Negri, *Empire*, 30–34, 50–52, 8–92, chaps. 2.2 and 2.3, 201–3; see also Balakrishnan, "Virgilian Visions," 145.

119. Hardt and Negri, *Empire*, 52–59, 65–66; Balakrishnan, "Virgilian Visions," 145.

120. Balakrishnan, "Virgilian Visions," 148.

writing this book—and this concern dates back to Adam Smith's worries in *The Wealth of Nations*—are the power differentials between this new working class and employers on the one hand and the state on the other. This does not mean that there are not protests or efforts at unionization; I am saying, rather, that these democratic actions are being increasingly undermined or negated by the state and its partnership with big business, commercial finance, and agribusiness. Hardt and Negri are right to argue that examples ranging from the Los Angeles riots to the Zapatista movement demonstrate that revolution is not dead.[121] But when one inverts the logic behind their thesis, the questions are these: Why is unionization declining? Why have protests been viewed as treason since 9/11? And why is the welfare state being dismantled with so little objection? Isolated protests have the potential to alter the social order, but so can an unrestrained focus on capitalism combined with a renewed emphasis on ascetic values since the "demise of communism."

For all of these reasons, I argue that exploitation—both political and economic—is occurring in the United States in this age of global capitalism.

Exploitation

In much of the literature on exploitation, the author begins by discussing the two common meanings of exploitation. The first use of this word simply means to exploit an opportunity or resource, for example, and has an amoral significance. It is simply use to one's advantage and thus has no pejorative connotation. The second meaning often does have moral implications when it is applied to human beings. The debate is then over which sense is more useful—moral or nonmoral? As Tommie Shelby[122] rightly points out, a nonmoral conception of exploitation may be more useful as a functional, scientific term rather than one that is morally predetermined. This is why he offers a naturalistic theory of exploitation that may ultimately have moral implications, depending on one's perspective, that but is not moral in its conception.

The simplest amoral definition of exploitation might be a liberal one: that all should be treated equally under the law, and that when they are, workers in low-tier positions are being treated equally under laws that

121. See Hardt and Negri, *Empire*, 52–59.
122. Tommie Shelby, "Parasites, Pimps, and Capitalists: A Naturalistic Conception of Exploitation," *Social Theory and Practice* 28 (July 2002): 382.

apply solely to them. Thus, their unequal pay and more dangerous conditions are legal although not legally equal to those of the more mainstream blue-collar workers from the postwar era. Cases of illegal work (either the factory is not up to code or the workers themselves are illegal) are then excluded from the charge of exploitation owing to the "criminality" of the worker. Alternatively, arguing that a factory is exploitative simply because it is not up to code does not actually prove exploitation,[123] although I consider this to be one condition of exploitation. Additionally, it could be argued, per Marx, that exploitation is the extraction of surplus-labor, which then means that not only is the working class being exploited, but so also are a whole host of other workers. This may be true, but it does not fit either the scope or the purpose of this book. I do, though, suggest a more expanded view of Marx's own conception of exploitation, one that takes into account not merely the extraction of surplus-value but also the way the state facilitates this exploitation, as well as the ideational system—the Protestant ethic—that obscures exploitation while providing its ideational foundations.

Shelby's theory of exploitation is different than the concept of surplus-value; even so, it is true to Marx's analysis of the political and economic effects of exploitation, for he suggests that exploitation occurs not only economically but also politically. First, he compares two biological models in order to determine the most appropriate analogy for the types of exploitation that occur in contemporary society. The first is the outcome model, in which a parasite gains something at the expense of a host.[124] In this model, all one knows is who gains and who loses; one does not know how to change the relationship of exploitation. His second, preferred example is the process model, in which a host forages for food, which requires time, energy, and so forth, and scrounging occurs. Scrounging is when one organism benefits from the host's work, and this usually occurs through "usurpation, deception and stealth."[125] There are, then, two key components to this theory. The first is the "basic structure of exploitation" (BSE), which holds that "X exploits Y only if: a) Y is forced to make a sacrifice which results in a benefit for X; and b) X obtains this benefit by means of an advantage in power that X has over Y." Benefit here is defined as anything gained that improves the welfare

123. See Sassen, *Globalization and Its Discontents*, who argues that many of these factories should be legal.

124. See Shelby, "Parasites, Pimps, and Capitalists," 389, 390.

125. Ibid., 389.

of the one acquiring it.[126] Shelby then argues that when this relationship is maintained over time, it can be called a "self-reproducing exploitative relationship" (sers), which is when:

a) Y is regularly forced to make sacrifices that result in benefits for X
b) X obtains these benefits by means of an advantage in power that X has over Y; and
c) as a result of a) and b), perhaps in combination with other factors, X's power advantage over Y is maintained (or is increased) and Y remains in the conditions of being forced to make sacrifices for X's benefit.[127]

Significantly, the "key feature of exploitation is control, not consumption."[128] Given this dynamic, it can be argued that differentials in power are crucial for understanding exploitation. These differentials not only explain how political and economic exploitation can occur and benefit different parties (for example, the state and employers), but also how multiple gains can happen that involve not just economic profit but further increases in power, status, or competitive "edge."

Given power inequality, a crucial question to explore is whether coercion must occur to effect exploitation. I would argue that coercion, while a significant mechanism of exploitation, does not necessarily involve violence or danger. As both Shelby and Allan Wood contend, physical coercion is not necessary in order to bring about an exploitative relationship.[129] Marx himself recognized that exploitation in a capitalist economy is not normally characterized by violence or force.[130] In fact, the activities involved in exploitation may not necessarily be bad in themselves,[131] and consent to perform them is often given freely.[132] So it is possible to effect coercion without force or violence. For example, as authors ranging from J.S. Mill to de Tocqueville to Foucault have argued, social norms can be highly

126. Ibid., 393.
127. Ibid., 404–5.
128. Shelby, "Parasites, Pimps, and Capitalists," conference paper, Department of African and African American Studies, Harvard University, June 2001, 25.
129. See Allan Wood, "Exploitation," in Exploitation, ed. Kai Nielsen and Robert Ware (Amherst: Humanities Press, Key Concepts in Critical Theory Series, 1997), chap. 1.
130. See Susan Himmelweit, "Exploitation," in A Dictionary of Marxist Thought, ed. Tom Bottomore (Malden: Blackwell Publishers, 1997), 183; John Elster, "Exploitation, Freedom, and Justice," in Exploitation, ed. Kai Nielsen and Robert Ware, 28.
131. See Shelby, "Parasites, Pimps, and Capitalists," 26n18.
132. See Wood, "Exploitation," 12; Shelby, "Parasites, Pimps, and Capitalists," 14, 15.

coercive. On the other hand, the threat of physical force has certainly entered into many employment situations (for example, immigrant laborers are practically enslaved in some situations). Foucault's notion of power can help us understand how nonphysical coercion operates over a period of time in a liberal capitalist or modern state.

Foucault argues that power is not the equivalent of violence or even physical struggle; indeed, power can only be exercised over free subjects.[133] At the same time, an asymmetry of power can exist at many different levels. As various authors have pointed out, an individual may benefit from and be complicit in a relationship of subordination.[134] In the context of exploitation, a subject has limited agency because of circumstances (limited resources and mobility) and the narrow range of choices offered by an employer. Thus, coercion involves both voluntary and involuntary action, and an asymmetry of power is a precondition for exploitation (since there is an obvious asymmetry when exploitation has commenced).[135] The exploitee must relinquish something; in the cases mentioned above, this could be health (in deregulated workspaces, including exposure to dangerous pesticides or use of dangerous machinery), time, a sense of future security, and even freedom of mobility (in the case of illegal immigrants and guest workers).[136] In these relationships, workers are subordinate to employers in terms of legal power and recourse, as well as the setting of wages and conditions of employment. In this regard, John Elster suggests that workers often accept a job owing to circumstances and are then coerced into accepting low wages.[137] The second factor is more indicative of coercion in exploitation, although it is the first factor that sets the conditions in which a worker can be exploited. Shelby contends that in ascertaining whether an individual is being exploited, the most useful question is this: If the worker doesn't perform the action demanded, will this "prevent her from satisfaction of some *vital* need"?[138]

133. Michel Foucault, "Afterword," in *Michel Foucault: Beyond Structuralism and Hermeneutics*, ed. Hubert L. Dreyfus and Paul Rabinow (Chicago: University of Chicago Press), 221. "Slavery is not a power relationship when man is in chains. (In this case it is a question of a physical relationship of constraint.)"

134. Simone de Beauvoir, *The Second Sex*, trans. and ed. H. M. Parshley (New York: Vintage Books, 1989).

135. Shelby, "Parasites, Pimps, and Capitalists," 15.

136. See ibid., 12–15; Paul Apostolidis, "La Lucha y La Casa: Neopolitics of the Labor Movement," paper presented at the Western Political Science Association Meeting, Oakland, March 2005.

137. Elster, "Exploitation, Freedom, and Justice."

138. Shelby, "Parasites, Pimps, and Capitalists," 15.

The hypothetical freedom that these particular workers possess is not citizenship, nor was it when Marx was writing. Exploited workers were and are disenfranchised (de facto or de jure) to varying degrees. This is the important link between economic exploitation in an era of economic globalization and the exercise of prerogative power in its contemporary form. Behind the coercion of employers are state authorities that facilitate this exploitation through relaxed legal codes for work conditions (deregulation);[139] the arrest of illegal workers (even though employers are rarely fined);[140] the deportation of certain workers for minor legal infractions;[141] the *general* deportation of certain groups;[142] the governmental *encouragement* to hire illegal or temporary workers;[143] the invasion of all immigrants' privacy;[144] indefinite stays in holding cells for those so targeted;[145] police and INS/BCIS violence against the poor (such as poor African American men) and immigrants;[146] societal violence against foreign workers;[147] and

139. See Sassen, *Globalization and Its Discontents.*

140. See Shanks, *Immigration and Politics of American Sovereignty:Arguing Immigration,* ed. Nicolaus Mills; Portes and Rumbaut, *Immigrant America,* 84; among others.

141. See David L. Marcus, "Three Times and Out," *Boston Globe,* October 14, 1998, A1; Kevin Uhrich, "Proposition 187 Rears Its Ugly Head," *Los Angeles Reader,* May 26, 1995, 4.

142. Before September 11, 2001, the group most often deported was Haitians. See Carol J. Williams, "Rapid US Deportation Forces New Route on Haitian Refugees," *Boston Sunday Globe,* July 13, 2003, A11; Associated Press, "US Deportations at Record Level," *Boston Globe,* May 14, 1997, A3; Nancy Gertner and Daniel Kanstroom, "The Recent Spotlight on the INS Failed to Reveal Its Darkside," *Boston Sunday Globe,* May 21, 2000, E1; Teresa Mears, "The Woes of Immigrants Forced to Emigrate," *Boston Globe,* March 26, 2000, A6; David Oliver Relin, "Who Will Stand Up for Them?" *Parade Magazine,* August 4, 2002, 4, 5; William Branigin and Gabriel Escobar, "INS Deportations Rising," *Boston Globe,* April 25, 1999, A19; Judith Graham, "Congressman Wants Deportation of Immigrant Student," *Boston Sunday Globe,* September 29, 2002, A15; Richard Chacon, "California Border Crackdown Puts Migrants in Deadly Territory," *Boston Globe,* April 4, 1999, A3.

143. See Sassen, *Globalization and Its Discontents;* Portes and Rumbaut, *Immigrant America,* 270.

144. Curt Anderson, "Ashcroft Expands FBI Arrest Powers," *Boston Globe,* March 20, 2003, B2; "Thousands of Men from Five Nations Face Fingerprinting," *Boston Globe,* November 7, 2002, A31; Wayne Washington, "INS Rule Will Restrict Family Visits, Critics Say," *Boston Globe,* May 2, 2002, A3; Cindy Rodriguez, "INS Revives Sweeps," *Boston Globe,* April 18, 2002, B1; Robert Schlesinger, "US Defends Plan for Search of Data," *Boston Globe,* November 21, 2002, A1.

145. Editorial, "Secret Trials in America," *Boston Globe,* December 4, 1999, A18; Associated Press, "US Frees Ethiopian Jew Held Nine Years," *Boston Globe,* May 24, 1999, A6; Teresa Mears, "As INS Jails Fill, a Release Plan Surfaces," *Boston Sunday Globe,* February 14, 1999, A16; Jane Wardell, "Amnesty Says Rights Are Casualty in War on Terrorism," *Boston Globe,* May 29, 2003, A20; Will Dunham, "Suicide Attempts by Detainees on Rise," *Boston Globe,* May 29, 2003, A18; Editorial, "No Justice in Guantánamo," *Boston Globe,* March 30, 2003, D10.

146. See, for example, Wilson; Kenneth B. Noble, "Videotape of Beating Jolts Los Angeles," *New York Times,* April 3, 1996, 10; Sebastian Rotella, "Case Highlights Alleged Abuses at Border," *Los Angeles Times,* January 14, 1996, A3.

147. See Jennifer Morita, "Study Finds Increased Risk for Foreign-born Living in California," *Daily Bruin,* February 16, 1996, 2.

the racism of U.S. officials.[148] Similarly, the working poor who were born here can be subject to police surveillance, welfare inquiries, the scrutiny of housing authorities, racial profiling,[149] the "War on Drugs" (which has resulted in high incarceration rates for African American males in the prime of their life), and increased crime. In this way, the law targets the worker but not the employer and prerogative goes far beyond the scope of employment to proliferate at all levels of daily life in ways that mainstream or middle-class citizens do not experience.[150] Clearly, the exercise of prerogative power is not limited to an elite group in one area; rather, given a rationalized and yet disperse political system and the globalization of the economy (which decentralizes workplaces), prerogative is exercised in and through the social body of the working poor. To put it differently, bureaucratic mechanisms and the law paradoxically bring about the suspension of law in these cases.

Another important point that Shelby makes is that exploitation is "self-sustaining" or ongoing. In the context of these particular workers, the relationship of exploitation can be maintained by wages that are below a "living wage"[151] and often below minimum wage. In addition, laws that are meant to protect workers can be subverted by designating certain jobs as temporary or casual; and workers can even be forbidden to organize unions, bargain collectively, or take employers to court. Even when wages are relatively decent, the precariousness of temporary and casual employment makes blue-collar workers more vulnerable than in the past. For example, in states that have "at will" employment, it is legal to terminate a worker with no notice; in this way, job precariousness evolves into government

148. See "Alleged Remarks Land Judge on Leave," *Patriot Ledger* (Massachusetts), August 5, 2003, 13.

149. See Executive Summary, "Wrong Then, Wrong Now: Racial Profiling Before and After September 11, 2001," http://www.civilrights.org/publications/reports/racial_profiling; for updated information, see Amnesty International's website, http://www.amnestyusa.org. See also Deborah Ramirez, Jack McDevitt, and Amy Farrell, "A Resource Guide on Racial Profiling Data Collection Systems: Promising Practices and Lessons Learned," monograph sponsored by the U.S. Department of Justice (Wheaton: Northwestern University, November 2000); Mikal Muharrar, "Media Blackface: 'Racial Profiling' in News Reporting," http://www.fair.org/extra/9809/media-blackface.html; Institute on Race and Justice, Executive Summary: "Massachusetts Racial and Gender Profiling Final Report" (Boston: Northeastern University, IRJ, May 4, 2004); American Civil Liberties Union (ACLU), "Racial Equality: Racial Profiling—Press Releases," http://www.aclu.org/RacialEquality/RacialEqualitylist.cfm?c=133.

150. See Arnold, *Homelessness, Citizenship, and Identity,* for further elaboration of these power dynamics.

151. As argued by the Living Wage Campaign, which contends that in most U.S. cities even the minimum wage is insufficient for subsistence. This group suggests that wages from $8 upward are more realistic for subsistence and for just remuneration.

policy. More generally, poor school systems, inefficient training programs, decaying urban infrastructures, and even walls that seal off certain high-crime urban neighborhoods all contribute to limited mobility, whether that mobility is interpreted literally or as social mobility.

It can be argued that low-wage policies are a key to exploitation, in that poverty-level wages prevent workers from changing their circumstances. For certain, such policies help *maintain* exploitation. Low wages are now tolerated for various reasons. As Wilson has demonstrated, the United States has pursued a "low-wage strategy" in the face of international global competition. Companies succeed in this market either by "improving productivity and quality or by reducing workers' income."[152] In contrast, European countries have allowed for pay raises and benefits, arguably at the cost of higher unemployment.[153] Companies use the euphemism of "flexibility" to impose precarious work contracts with no benefits and low wages.

Exploitation is self-sustaining in the United States because of its low-wage strategy and deregulated workspaces and work conditions. Low wages are possible because of the feminization, racialization, and "immigrantization" of labor since the 1970s. All three processes have split the labor market, thus maintaining low pay while obscuring exploitative conditions and labor relations. Bonacich's well-known argument that split labor markets explain ethnic and other antagonisms illuminates how exploitation can occur even while masked. First, she believes that low wages are not assigned to certain groups owing to racism, sexism, or xenophobia per se but rather "from differences in resources and motives which are often correlates of ethnicity."[154] Her main argument is that various types of antagonism begin in a split labor market—that is, the presence of two groups of workers who are paid differently for the same job. These groups can include women, immigrants, prison labor, child labor, or any other group that enters the job market at a lower pay rate (or threatens to do so).[155] This argument challenges the notion that certain minorities who are American born simply feel that they are entitled to higher pay than immigrants.[156] Instead, employers may pitch their labor

152. Wilson, *When Work Disappears*, 152.
153. Ibid., 153.
154. Bonacich, "A Theory of Ethnic Antagonism," 547. Bonacich uses the word *antagonism* because it includes "all levels of intergroup conflict, including ideologies and beliefs (such as racism and prejudice), behaviors (such as discrimination, lynchings, riots), and institutions (such as laws perpetuating segregation)," 549.
155. Ibid., 552.
156. This notion is reflected in the commonplace assertion that immigrants do jobs that others (such as African Americans) will not.

recruitment at different levels depending on the standard of living of each group. Most significant for her analysis is the idea that the lower-paid group is lacking in political resources. For example, certain governments have historically protected their émigrés when they arrive in the host polity.[157] I would argue that the most exploited groups in the United States today are often those whose governments reject them or will not help them in any way. A prime example of this is Haitians, who are the group most often scrutinized and deported by the INS/BCIS and whose country very often locks them up when they arrive "home."[158] For her part, Bonacich cites Mexican migrant workers as having "received little protection from their government."[159] In the United States, women who have transferred from welfare to workfare or other low-paid jobs have historically been treated as "dependents" or as social leeches who are finally moving from parasitism to production. In this way, exploitation is obscured and the emphasis is on this individual having been saved from sloth and moral turpitude. At the same time, for low-skilled or unskilled African American males filling service positions, casual construction jobs, or temporary industrial jobs, the threat of police surveillance or even prison serves as a form of social control rather than support.[160]

The declining influence of unions (for example, guest workers and other immigrant laborers are not allowed to unionize or strike) contributes to lower wages and more dangerous conditions. So does the lack of incentive to join a union, now that so much work is treated as temporary (by either the government or the employer).[161] This argument can be extended to poor women and minorities who are temporary workers, and to service workers who are employed under short-term contracts; there is not only a great deal of resistance to unionization among employers but also less incentive for it among these workers. The long hours and low pay contribute to a downward spiral of isolation and limited information as well as to the blocking of political activism. This is not to deny the important work that immigrant groups have done to fight for unionization and

---

157. See Klaus Bade, *Migration Past, Migration Future: Germany and the United States* (Providence: Berghahn Books, 1997), regarding Germany doing this.

158. See Richard Chacón, "Imprisoned by Policy," *Boston Globe*, October 19, 2000, A1; Charles A. Radin, "Fears of Deportation Bias," *Boston Globe*, June 26, 2000, A1; "Haitians Decry Unequal Treatment by US," *Boston Globe*, January 13, 2000, A7. Guatemalans are another group who can be exploited owing to their own government's policies. See Jennifer Harbury's work on CIA abuses in Guatemala.

159. Bonacich, "A Theory of Ethnic Antagonism," 550.

160. On incarceration, see Bauman, *Globalization*.

161. Bonacich, "A Theory of Ethnic Antagonism," 550, 551.

collective bargaining rights, but to argue that the relative decline in the influence of unions has negatively affected wages.

In any case, the interests of employers and employees are obviously at odds. Employers want "as cheap and docile a labor force as possible to compete effectively with other businesses."[162] If this labor is unavailable, the firm can relocate abroad or to another state. The group that is paid more fears that the lower-paid group will place downward pressure on their wages. When the labor market is split along ethnic lines, this economic conflict is then projected outward as ethnic antagonism even though it is material factors that are at stake. In the context of this chapter, one could argue that African Americans and other American-born racial minorities and immigrants often turn on one another rather than on their employers. This was evident during the Los Angeles riots (or uprising) of 1992 and in many other struggles and conflicts.[163] A similar dynamic could be held to exist with the increasing feminization of labor among immigrants and African American women: gender roles and traditional family structures are being fundamentally altered as a result.[164] Clearly, these antagonisms can be framed politically rather than individually.

The threat of offshore production, outsourcing, and capital flight ensures that no group gains an advantage for too long. This is precisely why exploitation can occur not only as extraction of labor but in the form of physical possession (or what Colette Guillaumin calls the "appropriation of bodies," discussed in the next chapter). This can involve preventing employees from leaving a worksite or permanently compromising their physical health (for example, garment workers, and others who do delicate, refined work can eventually lose their eyesight).[165]

In sum, exploitation as it pertains to workers in a global economy involves the following: (1) workers are exploited both politically and economically, in that differentials in power and economic inequality are mutually reinforcing; (2) workers may benefit from and be complicit in a relationship of subordination and yet still be coerced and exploited; as noted earlier, in a liberal capitalist state, physical coercion or violence is not a

162. Ibid., 553.

163. See Davis, *City of Quartz*; Richard Rothstein, "Immigration Dilemmas," in *Arguing Immigration*, ed. Nicolaus Mills; John Cassidy, "The Melting-Pot Myth," *The New Yorker*, July 14, 1997, 40–43.

164. See Sassen, *Globalization and Its Dicontents*, regarding immigrants. See also Wilson, *When Work Disappears*, regarding marriage rates among African Americans in poor urban communities, given changes in the economy.

165. For example, sugar cane cutters in Florida and sheepherders in the southwest; see also Sassen, *Globalization and Its Discontents*, 119, regarding women in manufacturing.

necessary condition of exploitation, but other forms of coercion are; (3) those who are being exploited make regular sacrifices in terms of time, health, and mobility in situations where being deprived of this work will "prevent her from satisfaction of some *vital* need";[166] (4) workers are disenfranchised—they are not only subject to a separate set of laws but are policed and subject to arbitrary power rather than to the rule of law; to put it differently, *the law is used to effect a suspension of law;* as a corollary, this has a disciplinary effect on legal workers; and (5) the system is self-sustaining in the United States as a result of low-wage strategies, the deregulation of workplaces and work conditions, and—as I will discuss briefly below—the introduction of workfare. Bonacich's theory also illuminates why ethnic and racial antagonisms arise and why gender relations are transformed as well, and why "flexible" labor has become acceptable for so many different groups and for so long. In turn, ethnic, racial, and gender splits obscure exploitation and create diversions that perpetuate the political disenfranchisement or statelessness of these groups.

Class?

Having discussed how exploitation manifests itself, I now reintroduce the idea of class, which I consider important to any analysis of exploitation.[167] In a more globalized economy, the groups now performing low-tier labor are not recognized as working class, not only because class itself is denied the same status as race and gender in Supreme Court decisions and public policy, but also—as I have argued earlier—because the work performed does not fit the same criteria that working-class jobs did in the past. As labor becomes more "flexible," the meaning of class can come to be defined by income alone in ways that ignore labor relations, the historical context of those relations, and the current global dynamics. In fact, "the substitution of bureaucratic for sociological conceptions of class reveals the essence of Wohlfahrtsstaatsräson: bureaucratic classification defined by abstract criteria is used to accentuate attributes deemed systematically useful rather than to accommodate differences created by historical practices, institutions and values." For this reason, "bureaucracy signifies, not as Weber thought the antithesis of Staatsräson, but its ritualization."[168] In this way, the arbitrary quality of bureaucratic classifications

---

166. Shelby, "Parasites, Pimps, and Capitalists," conference paper, 15.
167. See Žižek, "Why We All Love to Haite Haider."
168. Wolin, "Democracy and the Welfare State," 178.

synchronizes with the "flexibility" of labor in ways that allow for the deployment of prerogative power. As discussed in Chapter 2, this marks the transition from Staatsräson to Wohlfahrtsstaatsräson: the latter allows for a suspension of the law based on notions of the common good that in the end evade all accountability.

Class is the basis of liberal inclusion; it also does much to decide who wins and who loses in the capitalist marketplace. To emphasize individuals over groups, as John Roemer does,[169] is to disregard historical, political, and economic contexts and to reinforce the primacy of the individual in liberal capitalist ideational structures. What is ignored is the relations of production as a result of which workers voluntarily accept employment but regularly make sacrifices that benefit their employers in ways that illuminate (as well as fortify) the power differentials between the two agents. Employees are *forced* to make sacrifices for the other's benefit. Again, "the key feature of exploitation is control, not consumption."[170]

A common view is that everyone profits from labor flexibility because it leads to full employment and greater competitiveness in the global economy. Actually, low-wage policies only ensure the greater polarization of incomes and increased poverty. The poor do not gain from this relationship, as a consequence of which they exist at a bare minimum and sacrifice their health and long-term security. Those who benefit are the employers and the lawmakers. The police, the BCIS, and housing and welfare/workfare workers reinforce power and Wohlfahrtsstaatsräson, not to mention the bond between state and economic sectors. In fact, this lack of political freedom among groups that are monitored by these agencies is what ensures economic exploitation: the asymmetry of power is built into the relationship.

Conclusion

Once the new types of employment are recognized as blue-collar work, despite their increasing casualization, deregulation, and even illegality, and once the new workforce is recognized as a working class, it becomes easier to see how exploitation can occur. In this sense, Marx's ideas are relevant not only as a broad critique of capitalism but also in examining

169. John Roemer, *Free to Lose*, cited in Himmelweit, "Exploitation."
170. Shelby, "Parasites, Pimps and Capitalists," conference paper, 25.

the linkages among political disenfranchisement, state interests, and the economy. The hyperexploitation that is now occurring—an exploitation that goes beyond extracting surplus-value—is facilitated by the state and is made possible by the global economy. While it may seem paradoxical that a more international economy would strengthen certain elements of the state, it is important to note that state power has indeed changed and is certainly not all-powerful. Transnational firms not only challenge state power but also shape its interests. Motivated to fight against its own obsolescence, the state allies itself with capital and provides it with indispensable goods: legal and military backing as well as the conditions for a compliant labor force. Low-wage policies go unchallenged because the labor force is rendered "docile" through disenfranchisement and disempowerment. (This is not to argue that resistance does not occur at all levels—from acts of microresistance, to unionization efforts, to mass protest; my point is that all of these acts are now treated politically and economically as illicit, traitorous, and abnormal in ways that they were not when unions were stronger and manufacturing jobs were the paradigm of work.)

Yet the state is not simply an adjunct to the economy; it has its own logic that is in both harmony and tension with the economy. As noted in previous chapters, capital is global while the state is rigidly territorial. Nationalist movements and interests can undercut capital while supporting the state. And the more democratic elements of the modern nation-state are often in total opposition to the low wages, poor work conditions, and general instability that global work now generates. Nevertheless, as I argued in Chapters 1 and 2, ascetic values form a crucial nexus between prerogative power and economic interests. In a more global economy, this nexus is strengthened. Ascetic values shape which sorts of employment are officially recognized as valid or legal as well as which are not, thus allowing for exploitation to remain hidden. Ascetic criteria also determine which groups are considered working class and which are not, thus allowing for the nonrecognition of the new working class.

Finally, asceticism articulates with biopower in defining bare life. In this context, bare life is constituted by workers who are not subject to the same laws as mainstream workers. As a consequence, in the context of the global economy and the strengthening of prerogative power, the new working class is exploited both politically and economically. Political exploitation takes the form of ethnic antagonism—for example, where one group (such as immigrants) serves as the exemplar of the Protestant ethic and another (such as inner-city African Americans) as its antithesis, yet both are scrutinized, policed, and viewed as criminal. In other words, ascetic criteria justify even while they obscure the political coercion and economic exploitation of those who are considered bare life. We tell ourselves that immigrants create sweatshops and form underground economies, that they are criminal and stealing jobs. Yet at the same time, poor inner-city minorities who work two jobs or for less than the minimum wage are largely viewed as unemployed and thus parasites (on the welfare system) or criminal. That is why it is so broadly perceived that these groups will never be comparable to the traditional working class, nor will it ever be possible to exploit them. Thus we see a parallel between bare life (the subject who has been stripped of legal status) and the exploited subject (the individual who is stripped of economic status), with the two dynamics reinforcing each other.

The global economy generates strong anxiety at nearly all levels of employment and income (witness the proliferation of articles debating how many jobs will be outsourced in the coming years). It is supposed that instability and "flexibility" are the price of freedom. In response to these tensions, we feel justified in calling for greater order and stability as manifested in the War on Terror and the War on Drugs. This is why the racial profiling of immigrants is more open now and can then be used to justify further racial profiling, be it against other immigrants or inner-city residents (the "underclass"). This, combined with ascetic ideals, explains why charitable giving went down after 9/11, except for the victims of 9/11: only "pure" victims deserve charity; all others deserve to be policed, criminalized, and exploited.

In the next chapter, I examine the "immigrantization," racialization, and feminization of labor. I explain how government policies have enabled these changes in the workforce even while fostering rhetoric against all three trends. I will also discuss various popular beliefs that reinforce and legitimize these state policies. While these appear to be contradictory tendencies, the power dynamics they generate reflect concerns with sovereignty and also illuminate the role of asceticism. These processes, furthermore, are ideological manifestations of biopower.

4

ANTAGONISM AND EXPLOITATION: THE IMPORTANCE OF BIOPOWER

Ascetic values[1] have led to the devaluation of the work performed in the global economy as well as to "job slotting," which links certain groups (those considered more natural or biological and less intelligent or rational) to specific jobs (service work and physical labor). Ascetic values are a form of ideational "glue": they not only justify the increasingly economic focus of sovereign power, but also, for some individuals, further the processes of dehumanization by making pseudoscientific claims about intelligence, the work ethic, and assimilability. In this chapter I examine the histories of the groups that constitute the ideal type for the new working class in today's global economy. I also consider the power dynamics affecting each of these groups, including anti-immigrant sentiments, the re-emergence of biological racism[2] toward African Americans and immigrants of color, and the active promotion of docility and submissiveness as labor becomes more feminized. These power dynamics are visible in the conventional distinctions so often made between these groups, whose members are variously identified as welfare-to-workfare mothers, the African American

1. Which importantly rest on the distinction between bare life—subsistence work and the idea that those who perform it are less than fully human—and work and wealth that contribute to society, that go beyond the self and demonstrate a secular form of election.

2. Or, as Robert Miles and Malcolm Brown put it, it is racism in "a pseudoscientific form with a biological referent"; Miles and Brown, *Racism*, 2nd ed. (London: Routledge, 2000), 65.

"underclass," or immigrant workers. All three groups are construed as absolutely different from one another; yet their histories are tightly intertwined. What links them is the political treatment they have received in American history, their de facto or de jure disenfranchisement, and their integration into the low-tier workforce. The consequences for European American (white) workers are several: they are constantly devalued as "white trash," and poor white men confront the added charge that they are gender transgressors because they lack economic independence.[3] In this chapter I show that reactions to all of these groups are biologizing in nature, which not only deflects attention from exploitative work conditions but also obscures the antagonism—be it economic, gendered, racial, or ethnic—that elite or dominant groups feel toward those who comprise the new working class.

Ascetic values and neoliberal discourse have come to reinforce each other, and to powerful effect, yet the political forces unleashed on workers by this convergence have worked in subtle ways. This apparent depoliticization obscures even further how the working class is not only exploited but also politically disenfranchised. First, as politics ostensibly becomes more economic in focus, biological and genetic claims become increasingly important, marking the difference between bare life and citizen (which should be viewed as epistemological rather than ontological categories).[4] That is, in a global economy, the economics of subsistence and mere living are contrasted with material excess, financial "success," and truly being human. Second, material well-being and the preservation of life and the species (the common good) have increasingly become the chief political ends, and for this reason, administrative authority has gained increasing importance.

As I have argued, the sovereignty exerted through administrative authority mirrors our current military interventions, demonstrating how prerogative power is exercised not only in relation to foreign affairs but also on poorer populations in the United States. Because the perceived domestic threats are thought to be vague and shadowy, they justify surveillance techniques that are increasingly invasive. These techniques include DNA fingerprinting, electronic ankle bracelets (which are used on asylum applicants), the monitoring of e-mail correspondence, sneak–and-peak

---

3. See Matt Wray and Annalee Newitz, eds., *White Trash* (New York: Routledge, 1997); Kurt Borchard, *The Word on the Street: Homeless Men in Las Vegas* (Reno: University of Nevada Press, 2005).

4. See Antonio Vázquez-Arroyo, "Agamben, Derrida, and the Genres of Political Theory," *Theory and Event* 8, no. 1 (2005): 11.

laws, and the government organization and oversight of guest workers and of low-wage work in the form of workfare. The War on Drugs, War on Terror, and the criminalization of poverty are not a casting out of society's undesirable groups; rather, their purpose is to ensure the formation of a new working class that can be exploited economically and politically. These wars articulate with ethnic, racial, and gender antagonism—the ideological and discursive underpinnings of biopower—to obscure exploitation.

Contemporary ethnic and racial antagonism, perhaps most evident at the mass level in the Los Angeles riots of 1992,[5] can be linked to two major changes in the United States. First, while ethnic antagonism is not new in and of itself,[6] it has increased as a consequence of the 1965 Immigration and Nationality Act, which has changed the demographic makeup of urban areas. Second, economic globalization caused radical transformations in the labor market and labor conditions in the 1980s and more recently has meant greater participation of immigrants, minorities, and women in the labor market. These changes in the workforce were occurring at the same time it was being claimed that racism and sexism were over. It is noteworthy that access to the workforce for these groups has been increasing at precisely the same time that genetic racism has resurfaced, that ethnic antagonism is being promoted openly by academics and elites, and that a paradigm of femininity that is docile and submissive is manifesting itself in the attitudes and behaviors demanded of women in low-tier employment. These different forms of prejudice are facilitating and obscuring political and economic exploitation. At a deeper level, these dynamics reflect the greater influence of ascetic and biopolitical criteria in a transformed labor market. The growing participation in the workforce of poor women, inner-city minorities, and immigrants transforms their protests against exploitation, their efforts at unionization, and their calls for group identity into "separatism," "ethnic enclaves," and "entitlement"

---

5. They lasted roughly from April 29 to May 4. I will call them riots but would point out that they have also been called an uprising; I choose "riots" for the sake of convention, not partisanship.

6. It is quite evident from the Civil War era onward. The most salient ethnic split at this time was between the Irish and African Americans, whether the latter were free or enslaved. Furthermore, the Irish were often used as strikebreakers, which led to an ethnic split between "white" workers and the "black" Irish. See James MacPherson's work as well as primary sources at this time, especially New York newspaper editorials; see also Jacqueline Jones, *American Work* (New York: W. W. Norton, 1998), 282–83, 290, 292, 326; Robert Miles, *Racism* (New York: Routledge, 1999), 58. This split also occurred along class lines, with yeoman farmers in the Confederate South constantly being reminded that they were free and independent in contrast to slaves. See Paul D. Escott, *After Secession* (Baton Rouge: Louisiana State University Press, 1978).

or "uppity behavior." Both politically and economically, these groups are conceived of in terms of their race, ethnicity, or gender rather than the work they do; and their political activities are devalued or criminalized. Indeed, the work performed in a global economy often "looks" criminal or leads to falling wages and thus is devalued twice over. Correspondingly, at the level of policy, low wages can be justified not only in terms of the work done but also because these groups do not have the political power to consistently protest their conditions. That is, their protests are viewed as criminal or otherwise invalid because, as I argued in Chapter 3, they are not seen as a working class.[7]

The conceptual separation of the new working class into immigrants, welfare/workfare recipients, and the "underclass" conceals how these groups have far more in common than is ordinarily thought in academic analyses, media accounts, and popular opinion. These distinctions are not incidental; indeed, they illuminate gender, racial, and ethnic antagonisms as well as, at their heart, a politics of bare life. That is, these groups are defined according to their race, gender, or ethnicity first and foremost (and again, this includes white workers who are negatively evaluated against this new ideal type). At the same time, the commonalities among these groups not only demonstrate how they serve as the new working class but also—significantly—point to the link between foreign policy (the War on Terror and immigration, refugee, and guest-worker policies) and domestic policies (the War on Drugs, the criminalization of the homeless, and welfare-to-workfare policies). This link exposes how foreign policy considerations affect domestic politics and economic relations in important ways; in addition, it demonstrates how neoliberal policies are hastening the predominance of a politics of bare life.

In this chapter, I begin by examining the recent history of immigration law to explain the dynamics of recent ethnic antagonism in the context of a globalizing economy. I also discuss the recent backlash against immigration. Then I investigate how the changes brought about by the 1965 immigration law have affected African American blue-collar workers, arguing that they and immigrants are constantly being pitted against each other culturally, politically, and economically. In the third section, I explain how the feminization of labor corresponds to these other two trends and discuss how antagonism is generated between dominating and

7. As Gayatri Chakravorty Spivak would argue, the "silence" of the subaltern is not a result of the apathy of marginalized individuals; it is explained by dominant groups' refusal to listen to or acknowledge protest. Spivak, "The Silence of the Subaltern? Speculations on Widow Sacrifice," *Wedge* 7–8 (Winter–Spring 1985): 120–30.

dominated groups as well as among individuals within the exploited groups. Each of these sections demonstrates how the new working class is viewed in biological terms and serves as cheap labor even as their contributions to the economy are ignored and forgotten.

Immigration Policy, Globalization, and the New Ethnic Antagonism

In this section, I will be referring to three levels of racial or ethnic thinking. (1) *Ethnic antagonism* as developed by Edna Bonacich and explicated in Chapter 3. In brief, she argues that antagonisms arise—be they gender, ethnic, racial, or free labor versus unfree—when one group undercuts another in the labor market by accepting lower wages or worse conditions or by acting as strikebreakers. This is only possible when public policy allows undercutting; clearly, the government at such times plays a role in fostering these conditions. (2) The raising of *racial and ethnic barriers*. Exclusionary practices may not be racist but they do demonstrate race thinking. (3) *Racism*. When I use that word, it is in the same way that Robert Miles defines it—that is, to include motive and intention. Thus, exclusionary practices that unintentionally affect certain racial groups negatively do not fall under this definition. Nor is racism merely identifying race above other somatic factors (which is "race thinking," according to Hannah Arendt and Colette Guillaumin, or "racialization" according to Miles). Racism should be defined less in terms of function and more in terms of ideological content, as Miles argues:

> The distinguishing content of racism as an ideology is, first, its signification of some biological characteristic(s) as the criterion by which a collectivity may be identified. In this way, the collectivity is represented as having a natural, unchanging origin and status, and therefore as being inherently different. In other words, a process of racialisation must be occurring. Second, the group so identified must be attributed with additional, negatively evaluated characteristics and/or must be represented as inducing negative consequences for any other. Those characteristics may be either biological or cultural. Thus, all the people considered to make up a natural, biological collectivity are represented as possessing a range of (negatively evaluated) biological and/or cultural characteristics. It follows that such a naturally defined

collectivity constitutes a problematic presence: it is represented
ideologically [and discursively] as a threat.[8]

Ultimately, I want to link the re-emergence of biological racism to the
growing importance of biopower as sovereign concerns have increasingly
become economically focused.

Despite claims to the contrary, the United States has a long history of
political inclusion and exclusion based on *ius sanguinis*. The significance
of this history is that until recent times, the government defined citizenship along racial and ethnic lines and in this way (so it can be argued)
helped foster the racism and ignorance that have characterized much of
the backlash against immigration since the 1990s,[9] not to mention
ethnic antagonism. It is not controversial to say that from the turn of the
century until 1952, U.S. immigration policy was openly racist. Like many
other countries, the United States in the early twentieth century became
increasingly concerned about questions of race[10] and intelligence and the
negative consequences of the presence of supposedly inferior races. As
concerns with race grew in importance, "dire consequences were predicted,
and the Johnson-Lodge Immigration Act of 1924 was passed with the
intention of preventing 'race deterioration.'"[11] This act was the first *general*
immigration law in that it synthesized the increasing number of restrictions into one act.[12] The McCarran–Walter Immigration and Nationality
Act of 1952 eliminated racial barriers to naturalization and immigration.
However, it also retained most quota preferences and was prejudiced against
the Japanese and Chinese in particular.[13] Through the quota system, racial
barriers could continue in practice, albeit more covertly. Then in 1965,
quotas for all countries were equalized by the Immigration and Nationality Act.[14] Finally—so it was thought—immigration policy would become
nonracial in intention and implementation.

8. Miles, *Racism*, 79.
9. For a similar account of how government has shaped racism through immigration
policy, see Kathleen Paul, *Whitewashing Britain* (Ithaca: Cornell University Press, 1997).
10. I do not think that race is real; I am referring to it only as a social fact. See Barbara
Fields, "Slavery, Race, and Ideology in the United States of America," *New Left Review* 18
(May–June 1990): 95–118.
11. Miles, *Racism*, 58.
12. Saskia Sassen, *Globalization and Its Discontents: Essays on the New Mobility of People
and Money* (New York: New Press, 1998), 50n1.
13. For example, see Nicolaus Mills, "Introduction," in *Arguing Immigration*, ed. Nicolaus
Mills (New York: Touchstone, 1994.
14. This act is known formally as the Hart-Celler Act, or the Immigration and Nationality
Act Amendments of 1965. Cheryl Shanks, *Immigration and Politics of American Sovereignty,
1890–1990* (Ann Arbor: University of Michigan Press, 2001), 182.

Because the 1965 Act permitted immigration from each country equally, it included formerly excluded groups such as Asians and Africans. However, the law did not allow for greater numbers of entrants, and in this way it was "profoundly conservative"[15]—in fact, it was considered more restrictive than the 1952 law. The changes in this act reflected two sets of factors. One was pressure from the civil rights movements, which extended to the decolonization movements of the time, including protests against the Vietnam War; the other addressed Cold War issues and how to present the United States as a global leader. As Cheryl Shanks remarks: "Immigration policy made great propaganda, the currency of the cold war."[16] To put it differently, in the context of the postcolonial movements and civil rights activism, Cold War interests needed to be reformulated to suit the times. The United States did not want to appear racist in its war of ideas with the Soviet Union.

So at the heart of the debates leading up to this legislation was the question of whether immigration policy should continue to be used as a Cold War weapon.[17] Eliminating racial quotas would improve the image of the United States internationally and thereby attract newly emerging nation-states to its side rather than the Soviet Union's. However, because racial quotas were being eliminated, an implicit goal was to control the characteristics of future immigrants through the stipulation that there be a 74 percent preference for family members. The aim was to replicate the racial or ethnic makeup of citizens already present in the United States.[18] As Sassen remarks, "there was a generalized expectation it would bring in more of the nationalities already present in the country, that is, Europeans, given its emphasis on family reunion."[19] No one foresaw what would actually happen: a radical alteration of the ethnicity of immigrants and, as a result, significant changes in the demographic composition of U.S. cities. The family reunification scheme was racial in intent, yet it led to an explosion of precisely the groups the United States had been trying to exclude for the past century. And these changes were accompanied by a wave of illegal immigration, mostly from Mexico—a logical result of family reunification and a greater "Third World" presence.

The unexpected effects of the 1965 act were stated by Senator Edward Kennedy as "two unintended consequences of this revision: a few countries

---

15. Ibid., 144.
16. Ibid., 145.
17. See ibid., chap. 6, for these debates.
18. Ibid., 180–81.
19. Sassen, *Globalization and Its Discontents*, 12, and see also 32–33.

of the world have come to dominate the legal immigration system, and the level of immigration has risen dramatically. Neither result was intended and both have occurred because of the emphasis on family connections."[20] Nicolaus Mills clarifies the unforeseen outcome: "The 1965 law contained a major loophole as a result of its family reunification policy, which allowed the parents, spouses, and minor children of any adult American citizen to enter the country *without* being subject to numerical restrictions." For this reason, the number of Asian and Latino immigrants greatly increased: "the result has been a national backlash against immigration."[21] In this way an attempt to maintain the nation's ethnic or racial integrity through the back door resulted in precisely the opposite.

Radical demographic changes were glaringly visible by the 1980s: the numbers of Asians in the United States had increased by 107 percent, the number of Latinos by 53 percent.[22] There was also greater female immigration, and thus the possibility for the feminization of labor—which has in fact occurred—along with a change in work skills possessed by immigrants compared to the past (although I will problematize this view below).[23] These recent developments have also led to the formation of ethnic neighborhoods, which are not new except in terms of their demographic and economic composition. The 1965 policy failed not only to control legal entrants but also to stem the tide of illegal immigration. In the 1980s this led to demands for further reforms to immigration laws. It is not an exaggeration to say that the immigration policy enacted in 1965 transformed the United States: a history of racial exclusion ended, and a much more diverse population began to develop; the labor supply correspondingly changed and allowed for the feminization of labor as well as greater use of immigrant labor in general; and the backlash against these immigrants resulted in more open racial rhetoric, especially in the new millennium.

The unforeseen consequences of the 1965 act, combined with a change in how the United States viewed itself toward the end of the Cold

20. Kennedy quoted in Shanks, *Immigration and Politics*, 202.

21. Mills, "Introduction," 17.

22. Ibid.. 22. For more specific numbers, see Sassen, *Globalization and Its Discontents*, 35–37. See also Sonia Shah, "Introduction: Slaying the Dragon Lady," in *Dragon Ladies: Asian American Feminists Breathe Fire*, ed. Sonia Shah (Boston: South End Press, 1997). It should be noted that "Asian" and "Latino" are problematic, homogenizing terms yet much of the research I have done has drawn from these categories.

23. See Sassen, *Globalization and Its Discontents*, 35–37, as well as the entire book. This pattern is logical and occurred throughout Europe; given the push for family reunification, many women joined their spouses, who had been recruited as guest workers.

War, led to a greater focus on economic strategies and increased concerns about economic hegemony; as well, immigrants came to be viewed more and more in economic terms.[24] For a brief time, the United States perceived that it was losing economic dominance, and as a consequence, foreign policy thinking changed in such a way that democracy was thought to be achievable in economic rather than ideological terms. The issues of the early 1970s—"the death of the dollar standard and the oil price shocks"—led to negative trends in "inflation, the balance of manufacturing and service jobs, the U.S. balance of payments, and its fiscal balance."[25] With Japan and Germany seemingly faring better than the United States, economic competition became as important as military or ideological competition.

There was a corresponding change in perceptions of immigrants. The growth in illegal (Mexican) immigration was seen as an "invasion,"[26] the implication being, as Portes and Rumbaut note, that unauthorized workers were arriving uninvited and with no encouragement.[27] As a result, the political and military factors underlying immigration were downplayed. This new lens through which people viewed immigrants—an economic one—would have important implications for how they are viewed today: "*Economic* signified frivolous, unserious grounds for admission and was a label applied to groups that administrations did not want to accept."[28] Soon enough, typologies were drawn up describing how both policymakers and the public were coming to group (that is, "stereotype") immigrants along economic lines.[29] Shanks aptly characterizes the change in view: "Immigrants became primarily factors of production."[30] "Labor migrants" (Portes and Rumbaut's term) are now thought to constitute the bulk of immigrants to the United States and are often believed to be distinguished from immigrants of the past by their poor education and low

24. As Shanks notes, this shift was surprising: Cold War tensions were at a new height, yet politicians were more concerned about immigrants in terms of "whether they could compete economically with the Germans and Japanese at an intensity sufficient to salvage American power and authority." Shanks, *Immigration and Politics*, 187.

25. Ibid., 195.

26. See ibid., 190.

27. Alejandro Portes and Rubén Rumbaut, *Immigrant America* (Berkeley and Los Angeles: University of California Press, 1996), 17.

28. Shanks, *Immigration and Politics*, 197.

29. See, for example, Bonnie Honig, *Democracy and the Foreigner* (Princeton: Princeton University Press, 2001); Portes and Rumbaut, *Immigrant America*.

30. Shanks, *Immigration and Politics*, 202.

skill levels. Portes and Rumbaut note that it is "labor migrants" who are most often associated with negative views of immigrants.[31]

The debates over immigration—both popular and among policymakers—reflected these new concerns. There was a greater preoccupation with how much immigrants were costing the nation;[32] paradoxically, immigrants were viewed as both stealing jobs and burdening the welfare, health, and educational systems.[33] This was not new in American history—much of the dialogue reproduced rhetoric about Irish immigrants in the Civil War era; even so, it signaled a change in focus for this generation and pointed to major transformations in the way Americans perceived immigrants. Furthermore, because of technological advances, the costs and benefits of immigration could be calculated with greater exactitude than before. Add to this the fact that economic thinking predominates today as it never did in the past: neoliberal policies have become increasingly popular, apparently subordinating political to economic interests and affecting domestic as well as foreign policy.[34]

U.S. sovereignty was significantly tied to these economic considerations. The question of sovereignty was important in the context of economic globalization and the growing presence of unauthorized workers on U.S. soil. Thus, "sovereignty returned as a central concern when the Western alliance no longer protected the country from its most serious threat, economic competition from within the Western alliance."[35] As debates developed about how immigration related to foreign policy, "three convictions—that ideological exclusions were misplaced, economic exclusions were wrongly ignored, and sovereignty was therefore being placed in jeopardy—came to undergird an increasingly popular alternative policy."[36] The economic focus of questions of sovereignty was (and is) largely unquestioned; the debate now was over *how* the United States could become or remain competitive in international markets. But even as economic logic increasingly dominated questions of sovereignty, sovereignty trumped economics in the end. Economic arguments could logically lead to the

---

31. See Portes and Rumbaut, *Immigrant America*, 14.

32. See Shanks, *Immigration and Politics*, 197–98; see also Section II, "Costs and Benefits," in Mills, "Introduction."

33. For an insightful analysis of contradictory views of immigrants (xenophobia and xenophilia), see Honig, *Democracy and the Foreigner*. Borjas argues that there is an alarming welfare dependency among poor immigrants. Borjas, "Tired, Poor, On Welfare," in Mills, ed., *Arguing Immigration* (New York: Touchstone, 1994).

34. One positive gain from this economic focus was that homosexuals were removed from the list of exclusions. Shanks, *Immigration and Politics*, 198.

35. Ibid., 201.

36. Ibid., 202.

promotion of more open borders, especially for wealthier immigrants who could invest in the economy or for immigrants with special skills;[37] but at the same time, more open borders left the United States vulnerable in several ways.

More open borders would encourage both legal and illegal immigration. They would also heighten this country's dependence on other countries, making the United States one among equals rather than a global hegemon.[38] For example, if a military dictator expelled a group of people from his country, the expectation that the United States would pick up the slack would in fact place it in a subordinate position, subject to that dictator's whims. Moreover, weaker territorial boundaries would erode the country as a nation-state and undermine the possibility of nationalism. Finally, a more liberal policy would transform the United States' military position and possibly render it impotent and defenseless. It followed that control over *who* entered and *how many* was logically the main concern of sovereignty, which was now being viewed primarily in economic terms. Overall, then, in this neoliberal era, the demands of nation-state sovereignty are much more closely aligned with those of capital than before, but they are also in tension with these economic interests.

These concerns were easier to encapsulate for the general public, given the numbers of illegal immigrants that had come since the 1960s. According to the popular wisdom, unauthorized immigration threatened the sovereignty of borders, increased the population numbers without government control, and added a supposedly criminal element to the population that undermined a true American community.[39] It was further argued that immigrants, be they legal or not, took away jobs and welfare benefits, depressed wages, and undermined the integrity of national citizenship. Borders were meant to protect Americans, and a greater influx of immigrants threatened this.[40] In this way, sovereignty and economic interests were closely linked. These same interests combined to create a view of "labor immigrants" that maintained racial exclusion and prejudices of the past, notwithstanding the elimination of racial quotas from public policy. In 1982, for example, the INS (Immigration and Naturalization Service) conducted sweeps throughout the Southwest that were labeled "Operation Jobs." Several political leaders of the time noted that the sweeps

37. See ibid., 203.
38. Ibid., 207. The United States "needed asymmetry. Symmetry involved feedback, and feedback threatened sovereignty."
39. See, in particular, articles from *The National Review*.
40. See Shanks, *Immigration and Politics*, 201–12, regarding all of these argument.

were not only economic in intention but also racial, in the sense that the INS was not stopping European Americans to check their papers.[41]

The ensuing changes in immigration policy reflected all of these developments and were designed to correct the mistakes of the 1965 act. The 1986 Immigration Reform and Control Act (IRCA) pertained only to individuals already in the United States. This act had three important components: first, it addressed the legal status of foreigners' residence by providing an amnesty for some undocumented workers; second, it provided for sanctions against employers who repeatedly hired unauthorized immigrants; and third, it expanded the guest-worker program so as to ensure a cheap supply of agricultural labor. This third stipulation had been established in the 1965 Act, which had provided for temporary workers when a shortage of laborers could be proven; it was this program that was liberalized in the 1986 IRCA.[42] The sugar cane industry regularly uses H-2 (visa) workers; also, guest workers are employed in the fruit and tobacco industries, and sheepherders have been brought in from Spain (and more recently Peru). Added to this was a special provision to the amnesty program that legalized "special agricultural workers" (SAWS) who had been working illegally for a minimum of ninety days between May 1985 and May 1986.[43]

The 1986 bill reflected concerns about sovereignty and about regaining control of U.S. borders. The amnesty would not only legalize some residents' status but also facilitate more rapid deportation of other foreigners. Moreover, allowing for guest workers would ensure a temporary labor supply that could then disappear once it was no longer needed. These three new provisions would—so it was hoped—allow for more legal immigration while stemming the tide of unauthorized immigration. In sum, the IRCA was designed to stem the tide of illegal immigration while helping employers "by liberalizing access to legal temporary workers."[44]

Alternatively, it was envisioned that employer sanctions would discourage illegal hiring practices, but this element of the law was in effect worthless. Employers could only be sanctioned for *knowingly* hiring unauthorized immigrants and were not required to verify the authenticity of documents.

41. Ibid., 222.
42. Portes and Rumbaut, *Immigrant America*, 15–16.
43. See the following websites for more information regarding agricultural workers and the hiring of H-2A workers: U.S. Department of Labor, Bureau of Labor and Statistics, "Agricultural Workers," http://www.bls.gov; U.S. Department of Labor, Office of the Assistant Secretary for Policy, "Temporary Agricultural Workers (H-2A Visas)," http://www.dol.gov/asp.
44. Portes and Rumbaut, *Immigrant America*, 14.

Moreover, the economic and political power of the groups who hired urban and agricultural workers was not seen for what it was: their influence could not easily be broken, and as a result of the weak legislation, illegal recruitment of workers has continued to this day. The flawed legislation, the power of employers, and the desire for work on the part of immigrants has led to a stronger influx of workers rather than a weaker one. What is more, any risks incurred in entering illegally or overstaying a permit or visa have fallen on the individual worker rather than the employer. This reinforces the notion that it is "they" who are criminal rather than "us," despite evidence of heavy recruiting as well as tacit government encouragement of this recruitment.[45]

Furthermore, the amnesty, which did allow certain immigrants to legalize their status in the United States, caused problems within immigrant communities because it was conceived of individually. Very often, only certain members of a family were accepted under the amnesty program while others were not. While this dilemma was partly resolved in the 1990 Immigration Act,[46] it was viewed as "punitive" and "family-busting." It forced immigrants to make hard choices and increasingly criminalized their status. As Mike Davis recounts in *City of Quartz*, the law also divided the Catholic Church in the Los Angeles area (the area with the most significant Mexican immigration): some of the Church leaders allied themselves with the INS while others, led by Father Olivares, offered sanctuary to the undocumented at places like La Placita, a mission in the Los Angeles area. Olivares openly opposed the 1986 IRCA: "When laws trample human rights, they must not be obeyed . . . to the extent that we openly aid, abet and harbor the undocumented, we indeed are breaking the law. The gospel would have us do no other."[47]

Finally, the desire to stem immigration also led to greater IMF and World Bank intervention in poorer countries as well as the formation of economic alliances such as NAFTA in the late 1980s and early 1990s. The logic—which prevails today—of these sorts of alliances and conditional aid was that as countries became more self-sufficient, fewer individuals would want to leave.[48] As Sassen shows, however, these strategies do not

45. Ibid., 279. See Robert Kuttner for an argument regarding immigrants' parasitism on the United States as well as the charge that many use false documents. Kuttner, "Illegal Immigration: Would a National ID Card Help?" in *Arguing Immigration*, ed. Nicolaus Mills.

46. See Portes and Rumbaut, *Immigrant America*, 280.

47. Olivares, quoted in *In These Times* (Chicago, November 9–15, 1988), in Mike Davis, *City of Quartz* (New York: Vintage Books, 1992), 355.

48. For this argument, see Richard Rothstein, "Immigration Dilemmas," in *Arguing Immigration*, ed. Nicolaus Mills.

work; in fact, the contrary of the desired reaction occurs: "Paradoxically, the very measures commonly thought to deter immigration—foreign investment and the promotion of export-oriented growth in developing countries—seem to have had precisely the opposite effect."[49] She notes that the countries with the highest growth rates are in fact significant generators of migration to the United States. Sassen's bridge or linkages theory helps explain why migrations occur for reasons besides individual economic interest. The military, political, cultural, and economic linkages that the U.S. government, American corporations, international regulatory groups (IMF, World Bank), and cultural industries have established build bridges for potential immigrants, introducing them to the language and culture of the United States.[50] They create points of contact that facilitate emigration instead of discouraging it.

In addition, the globalization of markets has altered economic and social relations in these countries in such a way that traditional economies are lost, urbanization accelerates, skill levels change, and gender relations are altered. With these radical changes and the possibility of capital flight when the workers become less "competitive" with workers in other markets, these individuals often have no choice but to seek work elsewhere.[51] In the case of Mexico, it can be argued that the push for agribusiness and export-led growth has produced such a migration. Also, deregulated factories and the absence of worker protections are contributing to the formation of a migrant labor pool; as workers begin to deteriorate physically, they are replaced by younger ones.[52] Finally, U.S. protection of its own markets also attracts workers from other areas when their countries' markets can no longer compete with American products.

Note also that the conditionality imposed by Bretton Woods institutions on former colonies has led to unequal conditions and, often, migration. The requirement that these countries drop their trade barriers, establish free-trade zones, and cut subsidies for their domestic producers (among other things) has damaged local industries; meanwhile, the United States and Europe continue to subsidize many of their own enterprises. Thus,

49. Sassen, *Globalization and Its Discontents*, 34. For a similar argument, see the conclusions of Portes and Rumbaut in *Immigrant America*.

50. Sassen, *Globalization and Its Discontents*, 34, but see also her entire book.

51. Ibid., 43: "People uprooted from their traditional ways of life, then left unemployed and unemployable as export firms hire younger workers or move production to other countries, may see few options but emigration, especially if an export-led growth strategy has weakened the country's domestic market oriented economy."

52. See ibid., 43; William Adler, *Mollie's Job: A Story of Life and Work on the Global Assembly Line* (New York: Touchstone, 2000).

the sugar cane industry in the Caribbean has been undermined by U.S. corn and corn syrup production;[53] the dairy industry in Jamaica has been in effect destroyed by U.S. agricultural subsidies and by demands that the island country open its market to U.S. imports; and grain and cattle subsidies in Europe have hurt African farmers and dairy owners. Clearly, then, neoliberal conditions have been imposed unequally internationally, just as ascetic values are hypocritically being forced on the poor. This inequality inevitably spurs migration as local economies are destroyed and export-led growth benefits political and economic elites.[54] Those who lose out—the workers—may well see no alternative but to migrate.

Economic globalization and a much stronger emphasis on economic interests, combined with a focus on sovereignty given these developments, began to influence immigration policy in the 1990s. The 1990 Immigration Act placed restrictions on all immigrants "regardless of place of birth, reason for emigrating, or relation to a U.S. citizen."[55] After the 1990 act, approximately thirty-six bills relating to the act were approved by Congress. In 1996, the Antiterrorism and Effective Death Penalty Act and the Illegal Immigration Reform and Immigration Responsibility Act of 1996 (IIRIRA) were passed. As a district court judge and immigration researcher have remarked: "These laws . . . contained a wide range of exceptionally harsh mechanisms aimed at noncitizens, many of whom are legal permanent residents of the United States. Judicial review of certain types of deportation orders has been completely eliminated. Thousands of noncitizens seeking to enter the country are summarily excluded by INS agents operating with virtually unreviewable discretion."[56] Secret evidence was allowed during these proceedings, and well over 150,000 individuals per year were detained permanently because their countries did not have deportation agreements with the United States.[57] Renewed efforts to monitor immigrants and to enable open racial profiling emerged after 9/11. To date, Haitians and Mexicans have been the groups most discriminated against; they have

53. See Michael Hiscox's work on this subject, for example, "Partisan Rancor and Trade Politics in the New Century," chap. 11, http://www.petersoninstitute.org/publications/chapters_ preview/3829/11iie3829.pdf.

54. For more general arguments about these inequalities, among many others, see the film *Life Is Debt*, narrated by Jamaica Kincaid, on Jamaica; Michael Hiscox's work on U.S. trade; and Joseph Stiglitz, *Globalization and Its Discontents* (New York: W. W. Norton, 2003).

55. Shanks, *Immigration and Politics*, 227. See ibid., 226–27, regarding both acts.

56. Nancy Gertner and Daniel Kanstroom, "The Recent Spotlight on the INS Failed to Reveal Its Dark Side," *Boston Globe*, May 21, 2000, E1.

57. See ibid.; Patrick J. McDonnell, "Judges Rule Against Indefinite INS Jailings," *Boston Globe*, July 12, 1999, A4; Editorial, "Secret Trials in America," *Boston Globe*, December 4, 1999, A18.

been subject to the greatest number of deportations, and Haitians have been the only group forced to pay back welfare. Jamaicans, Mexicans and Cape Verdeans have also been subject to discriminatory treatment.[58]

To add to this, in 1997 a former Foreign Service officer accused the State Department of "racial and ethnic discrimination." The screening of visa applicants was supposedly weeding out the poor, yet it seemed that race and class were equally important in these processes. Certain ethnicities were variously being labeled RK ("Rich Kid"), LP ("Looks Poor"), TP ("Talks Poor"), and LR ("Looks Rough"). Because the State Department refused to gather information about which embassies and consulates were conducting profiling, it is difficult to ascertain whether there has been systematic racism.[59] Still, it can be argued that these examples demonstrate that racial considerations are by no means absent from immigration policy and, it follows, concerns about the demographic composition of the American citizenry.

Changes in the economy, changes in how immigrants were viewed, and the unintended consequences of immigration policy together demonstrate the important links among state sovereignty, "race," and economic matters. The portrayal of poor and/or unauthorized immigrants—especially of color—as criminal and as a hidden, uncountable, shadowy threat is much like the portrayal of terrorists. The state alone is not responsible for fostering racism, ethnic antagonism, and xenophobia; nevertheless, state policies frame the issues and have a strong impact on public perceptions. And as noted earlier, the arguments are often contradictory: "But the dream of national home, helped along by the symbolic foreigner, in turn animates a suspicion of immigrant foreignness at the same time. 'Their' admirable hard work and boundless acquisition puts 'us' out of jobs. 'Their' good, reinvigorative communities also look like fragmentary ethnic enclaves. 'Their' traditional family values threaten to overturn our still new and fragile gains in gender equality. 'Their' voluntarist embrace

58. See Nicolaus Mills, ed., "The Era of the *Golden Venture*," introduction to *Arguing Immigration*, 24; Charles A. Radin, "Fears of Deportation Bias," *Boston Globe*, June 26, 2000, A1; Mark Babineck, "Agents Indicted in Death of Mexican Immigrant," *Boston Globe*, September 26, 2002, A9; Teresa Mears, "Immigrants Are Told to Pay Back Aid," *Boston Globe*, October 19, 1997, A18; Knight-Ridder Service, "Case Spotlights Use of Codes to Label US Visa Applicants," *Boston Sunday Globe*, June 8, 1997, A28; David Bacon, "INS Declares War on Labor," *The Nation*, October 25, 1999; Richard Chacon, "Imprisoned by Policy Convicts Deported by US Languish in Haitian Jails," *Boston Globe*, October 19, 2000, A1; Agnes Blum, "Helping Those Who Get One-Way Tickets to Haiti," *Boston Globe*, June 9, 2002, 5; "Haitians Decry Unequal Treatment," *Boston Globe*, January 13, 2000, A7.

59. Knight-Ridder, "Case Spotlights Use of Codes."

of America, effective only to the extent that they come from elsewhere, works to reaffirm but also endangers 'our' way of life."[60] The general public's schizophrenic attitude toward immigrants is mirrored in policies that restrict immigration and criminalize many residents' status yet at the same time encourage (or neglect to prosecute) unauthorized work recruitment, sweatshop labor, and worker exploitation.

As U.S. policy unintentionally changed the demographics of major cities, it also provided a cheap labor pool that, with the internationalization of the economy, conveniently arrived as the need was growing for lower-skilled docile and/or vulnerable workers. The covert racism of the 1965 act did not result in a homogeneous population but rather the opposite, and since that year, racial rhetoric has been fueling antagonism toward these others, who conveniently are taking jobs "no one else wants" even while being accused of depressing wages, creating illegal work sites, and milking the welfare system.[61] Besides all the racial and ethnic typing, the popular assumption is that the United States is taking in the "losers" from other countries—the poorest, those who could not survive in their own country. Yet Portes and Rumbaut (among others) argue that it is not the poorest or the least skilled who emigrate: even "unauthorized immigrants tend to have above-average levels of education and occupational skills in comparison with their homeland populations. More important, they are positively self-selected in terms of ambition and willingness to work."[62] Furthermore, few of these individuals were unemployed in their home country,[63] which challenges the notion that the poorest of the poor enter this country. Sassen notes that the economic perspective has led to the conclusion that immigration is not related to U.S. economic needs or to military, economic, cultural, and political linkages that are established in the country of origin. Policy, in turn, has thus been perceived as an issue of how generous and humane the United States is rather than the extent to which it owes other countries a debt.[64] Immigration law is thus conceived around the individual migrant's *choice* to emigrate from his or her country and does not include an analysis of broader economic, military, and political trends (among others) that might influence immigration to the United States.

---

60. Honig, *Democracy and the Foreigner*, 76.
61. See, for example, Kuttner, "Illegal Immigration."
62. Portes and Rumbaut, *Immigrant America*, 10.
63. Ibid., 11.
64. Sassen, *Globalization and Its Discontents*, 31.

This is why individuals and families who would be considered refugees according to the UN Charter's definition are now very often perceived as merely fleeing poverty.[65] Of course there are economic reasons to migrate—obviously, economic globalization has accelerated international migration. Even so, people migrate for a host of other reasons. The point here is that shifting perceptions of immigrants have intersected with race in such a way that it is now assumed that certain groups are (for example) criminal, or lacking skills, or carriers of social or religious pathologies. And typically, such labeled groups are darker skinned and from poorer countries.. The treatment of Haitians is especially illustrative of this point.[66] To put it differently, the predominance of economic interests when immigration policy is being determined has enabled ascetic and biopolitical concerns to strongly influence immigration.

These changes—economic, demographic, and perceptual—have led to the resurgence of anti-immigration sentiment, reminiscent of reactions to Italians, Poles, and Irish at the beginning of the twentieth century. The hostile reaction continues to this day and has allowed more overt racism toward African Americans to develop (see below), despite Samuel Huntington's confidence that race and ethnicity have "virtually disappeared as a defining component of national identity" since 1965.[67] This racist response has been fostered by academics and policymakers just as much as it is a popular reaction to the flood of new immigrants.

First, reinforcing ethnic/racial and gender splits, the passage of the Patriot Act and the transformation of the INS into the BCIS (Bureau of Citizenship and Immigration Services) have led to open, publicly supported racial profiling.[68] Although racial profiling is apparently aimed at those

---

65. See, for example, Nicholas Xenos, "Refugees: The Modern Political Condition," *Alternatives* 18 (1993): 419–30.

66. See Paul Farmer, *The Uses of Haiti* (San Francisco: Common Courage Press, 2003).

67. Samuel Huntington, "The Hispanic Challenge," *Foreign Policy* (March–April 2004).

68. See Executive Summary, "Wrong Then, Wrong Now: Racial Profiling Before and After September 11, 2001," http://www.civilrights.org/publications/reports/racial_profiling; Amnesty International's website for updated information, http://www.amnestyusa.org; Deborah Ramirez, Jack McDevitt, and Amy Farrell, monograph, "A Resource Guide on Racial Profiling Data Collection Systems: Promising Practices and Lessons Learned," sponsored by the U.S. Department of Justice (Wheaton: Northwestern University, November 2000); Mikal Muharrar, "Media Blackface: 'Racial Profiling' in News Reporting," September–October, 1998, http://www.fair.org/extra/9809/media-blackface.html; Amy Farrell, Dean Jack McDevitt, Lisa Bailey, Carsten Andresen, and Erica Pierce, Institute on Race and Justice, Executive Summary: "Massachusetts Racial and Gender Profiling Final Report" (Boston: Northeastern University,

who are Muslim and/or of Middle Eastern descent, the door has been opened for racial profiling of all immigrants; combined with the tacit racial policies that were already operating, race is certainly an important consideration for questions of sovereignty and economic interest. As well, the quest for national security after 9/11 has increased public support for harsher treatment of immigrants, closer screening of visa applications, and the extension of policing powers over immigrants. There has also been more rapid deportation, as well as questionable procedures in the detention of some immigrants.[69] Additionally, asylum applicants in eight major cities are now required to wear an electronic ankle bracelet—a device once used only for some convicted criminals on parole.[70]

Anti-immigration rhetoric—especially elite racism and ethnic antagonism—against all immigrants is has come to be more permissible in this context. Huntington's recent arguments that Mexicans who immigrate here are fundamentally different from American-born citizens and that they are "invading" the United States are paradigmatic of ethnic and/or cultural splits. Huntington is not alone in arguing that Mexicans pose a serious danger to our national identity, besides threatening our national security. The traits that Huntington claims Mexicans have—"mistrust of people outside the family; lack of initiative, self-reliance, and ambition; little use for education; and acceptance of poverty as a virtue necessary for entrance in to heaven"—could not be defined as racist, yet they certainly foster ethnic antagonism and negative stereotyping.[71] When he describes these differences as cultural, he is telling his readers that they are fixed and unchanging and that they apply to most Mexicans (and thus are biological or otherwise inherent qualities). What is significant is that Huntington is not merely a professor, influencing students who will have

IRJ, May 4, 2004); American Civil Liberties Union, "Racial Equality: Racial Profiling—Press Releases," http://www.aclu.org/RacialEquality/RacialEqualitylist.cfm?c=133.

69. See, for example, Amy Bach, "Deported . . . Disappeared," *The Nation*, December 24, 2001, http://www.thenation.com/docmhtml?i=20011224&s=bach; Bruce Shapiro, "Alien's Law," December 17, 2001, http://www.thenation.com/doc.mhtml?i=20011217&s=shapiro; Bach, "Vigilante Justice," June 3, 2002, http://www.thenation.com/doc.mhtml?i=20020603&s=bach; David Cole, "Enemy Aliens and American Freedoms," September 23, 2002, http://www.the nation.com/doc.mhtml?i=20020923&c=1&s=cole.

70. Daniel Zwerdling, "Electronic Anklets Track Asylum Seekers in U.S.," NPR, March 2, 2005, http://www.npr.org/templates/story/story.php?storyId=4519090.

71. Huntington, "The Hispanic Challenge," 11. See also Deborah Solomon, "Three Cheers for Assimilation," *New York Times Magazine*, May 2, 2004, 21. For a critique of Huntington's assertions about Latinos, see Louis Menand, "Patriot Games," *The New Yorker*, May 17, 2004, 92–98; Dan Glaister, "On the Border of Disaster?" *The Observer*, March 14, 2004.

greater access to power and jobs than others; he also serves as an advisor to President George Bush on matters of immigration.[72]

Christopher Jencks[73] and many others have similar concerns.[74] Their worries can be summarized as follows (although this is not an exclusive list): lack of assimilation (with regard to language and ethnic neighborhoods), criminality (both in terms of illegal entry and in terms of activities once in the United States), resentment or ungratefulness (exemplified by poor assimilation, ethnic enclaves, and so on), the idea that immigrants send all earnings back to their home country, have low naturalization rates and cause overpopulation, cultural breakdown, an altered racial composition of the United States, and the idea that skill levels have fallen. Hence, while immigrants may work harder than the average citizen, it is supposed that they use false documents to get their jobs, receive welfare under false pretenses, sleep in public (which is illegal), and drain school systems of funds.

An important point here is that immigrants to the United States are often perceived as both criminal and ungrateful. Criminal activity attributed to immigrants tends to be civil in nature rather than violent; the implication, however, is that the former kind underlies the latter. If immigrants enter the country illegally, the argument goes, what will stop them from committing other, more serious crimes? In this way, they are viewed as inherently criminal. This is why political acts—such as organizing communities, unionizing workers, and establishing cultural or self-help groups— are so often viewed as creating ethnic enclaves and undermining the law. These perceptions grow stronger as dissent and unionization are tolerated less and less. These immigrant groups are also perceived as ungrateful or resentful, which only provides further "evidence" that they do not fit in. Portes and Rumbaut propose an alternative view: groups like MAPA (Mexican American Political Association), United Mexican American Students, La Raza, and MECHA (Chicano Student Movement of Aztlán) enact democratic self-organization, as have other marginalized groups throughout U.S. history.[75] Because of these groups, "presidential candidates

---

72. See Maribel Hernandez, "A Citizenship of Aliens: The Case of Undocumented Mexican Immigrants in Los Angeles" (Senior thesis, Committee on Degrees in Social Studies, Harvard University, March 2004).

73. See Christopher Jencks, "Who Should Get In?" *New York Review of Books* XLVIII (November 29, 2001); "Who Should Get In?" Part II, *New York Review of Books* XLVIII (December 20, 2001).

74. See Mills, ed., *Arguing Immigration,* for an overview of debates about immigration in the 1990s.

75. The story of AIWA's battle against Jessica McClintock is a particularly amazing example of transcending hardship and enacting political power. See Shah, ed., *Dragon Ladies.*

[are] increasingly compelled to court the Mexican vote";[76] for example, the Republicans have solicited Mexican votes during elections and have appointed Latinos to administrative posts.[77] In other words, this "new" group has followed the same trajectory as other immigrant groups: "Like downtrodden European minorities, Mexicans suffered much poverty and oppression, underwent subsequent reactive processes of ethnic affirmation and radicalization, and gained eventual entry into the mainstream through the electoral system. Their experiences both confirm lessons drawn from European immigrant history and offer a blueprint for the likely political course of recently arrived minorities."[78]

Yasemin Soysal is correct to argue that immigrants assimilate in ways that correspond to how a particular government is organized (for example, the liberal/individual model in the United States and United Kingdom, the corporatist model in Sweden).[79] As Portes and Rumbaut point out, Latino groups' democratic activities mirror those which have historically been evident among immigrants in the United States. Clearly, then, the choices that immigrants make in this regard are about considerably more than the experiences they brought with them from their country of birth; their activities also reflect practices of assimilation that are typically found in any liberal country. More simply, immigrant organizing in any country usually reflects how political power is constituted in that country. The assimilation/criminalization binary in which immigrants are embedded reduces the complexity of many issues and also oversimplifies immigrants' realities. Significantly, that same binary constantly reinforces differences between "us" and "them." It fosters ethnic antagonism at many levels, and this is exacerbated during times of uncertainty regarding job stability and national security. This ethnic antagonism pits European Americans who have lost jobs against immigrant labor; it also pits African Americans against immigrants.

In contrast to Huntington, Frances Fukuyama contends that Latinos and other immigrant groups are *not* a threat to our culture; he argues, in fact, that they have better family values than average Americans, are more religious, and are more obedient workers. They also have a stronger work ethic. To him, the key question is this: *Which* ethnic groups promote core

76. Portes and Rumbaut, *Immigrant America,* 127.

77. Ibid., 128.

78. Ibid., 129.

79. Yasemin Soysal, *Limits of Citizenship: Migrants and Postnational Membership in Europe* (Chicago: University of Chicago Press, 1994), chap. 6.

cultural values, and which do not?[80] This of course presupposes that distinctions must be made along ethnic and racial lines, that there are strict ethnic or racial boundaries between groups, and that key characteristics can be identified for each. With this logic, Fukuyama contends that "Puerto Ricans have reexported social pathologies like crack-cocaine use" and that those who came from the Mariel boat lift from Cuba increased crime in the United States[81] (the huge Mariel boat lift was launched when Fidel Castro decided to expel from Cuba various imprisoned dissenters, artists, and homosexuals, as well as many others who did not fit in). On Fukuyama's account, others who have experienced war in their own country—particularly Salvadorans—have also increased crime rates.[82] Our economic perspective on immigration enables Fukuyama to make these claims; except for this, Salvadorans and other Central Americans would be recognized for what they are, which is political refugees. Fukuyama's assertion that every ethnic group either promotes or takes away from cultural values is an attack on America's purported growing immorality.

Yet the group that Fukuyama identifies as truly lying outside of all assimilation to American values and ways of life is African Americans. Whereas even illegal Mexican workers have an admirable work ethic and are devoted to their families, "it is much less common to see African Americans doing this sort of thing."[83] In fact, he charges, multiculturalism—the origins of which many attribute to recently arrived immigrants—was the brainchild of African Americans when, after the Civil Rights Movement, "it became clear that integration was not working for blacks. The failure to assimilate was interpreted as an indictment of the old, traditional mainstream Anglo-Saxon culture: 'Wasp' took on a pejorative connotation, and African Americans began to take pride in the separateness of their own traditions. Ironically, the experience of African Americans became the model for subsequent immigrant groups—Latinos, who could have integrated themselves into mainstream society as easily as the Italians or Poles before them."[84] Nevertheless, Fukuyama thinks that while most Latinos are quite devoted to the United States, "multiculturalism is more strongly supported by many other groups—blacks, feminists, gays, Native Americans, etc.—whose ancestors have been in the country from the

80. Frances Fukuyama, "Immigrants and Family Values," in Mills, ed., *Arguing Immigration*, 156.
81. Ibid., 159.
82. Ibid., 159.
83. Ibid., 161.
84. Ibid., 163.

start."[85] The true problem, he argues, is assimilation, but that includes groups who have been in the United States for generations.

The comparison between poor African Americans and poor immigrant groups valorizes an openly racial and ultimately racist public discussion. Fukuyama might be more specific than other authors in making this comparison, but he is not alone in this approach.[86] Moreover, while the Huntington and Fukuyama articles could be viewed as evidence of incoherent approaches to the question of immigration, Bonacich's notion of ethnic antagonism clarifies the differences in attitude. For both Huntington and Fukuyama, ethnicity is the basis on which we should judge who is included in or excluded from the "social contract." Toni Morrison has argued that assimilation of immigrants has historically included repudiating blacks; "Only when the lesson of racial estrangement is learned is assimilation complete."[87] This is why struggles over jobs, affirmative action preferences, or who influences a neighborhood are "persistently framed as struggles between recent arrivals and blacks," to such a degree that it is often concluded that "American blacks are the real aliens."[88] Not surprisingly, this notion is visible in Fukuyama's work, but it is even found in the work of writers who are often viewed as progressive. For example, Jack Miles's account of the racial and economic dynamics of the Los Angeles riots is hardly simplistic, yet even he tells us that "Latinos, even when they are foreign, seem native and safe, while blacks, who are native, seem foreign and dangerous."[89] In *When Work Disappears,* William Julius Wilson provides ample evidence of this bias against African American men as well as ethnic antagonism between African Americans and immigrants.

I contend that the unintended consequences of the 1965 immigration act and the racial motives that subsequent legislation hid opened a space for expressing racism more openly against African Americans than was previously considered acceptable. This law has not only fostered ethnic antagonism but also obscured the political and economic exploitation of both groups. For example, racial thinking is demonstrated in "job slotting," so that certain types of jobs are supposed to naturally conform to certain groups. In *Whitewashing Britain,* Kathleen Paul argues that West Indian

85. Ibid., 164.
86. See Toni Morrison, "On the Backs of Blacks"; Jack Miles, "Blacks vs. Browns"; and Fukuyama, "Immigrants and Family Values," in Mills, ed., *Arguing Immigration.*
87. Morrison, "On the Backs of Blacks," 98.
88. Ibid., 98.
89. Miles, "Blacks vs. Browns," 119.

immigrants, among others, were stereotyped as being low-skilled or unskilled workers; as a result, they not only were slotted for the least skilled jobs but also progressively lost the skills they once had.[90] This continued on to the next generation, so that in the end, slotting established a self-fulfilling prophecy. Similarly, it can be argued that in the United States, strong associations are made between certain types of jobs and particular groups.[91] The fact that many of these jobs are dead end or low-skilled is ignored, so that these qualities are thought to inhere to the groups instead. "Slotting" is applied not only to immigrants but also to African Americans; furthermore, this practice intersects with gender. As a consequence, slotting has created ethnically, racially, and gender-based hierarchies with regard to wealth, the distribution of jobs, and perceptions of intelligence, among other things. More broadly, it is evidence of the confluence of biopower, economic globalization, and exploitation.

The Racialization of Labor
and the Re-emergence of Biological Racism

The greater integration of African Americans into the workforce was facilitated by civil rights legislation and by the fact that several Supreme Court decisions in the early 1970s went beyond the Civil Rights Act to play a "more energetic role in rectifying the effects of historic patterns of discrimination."[92] Changes in the demographics of the manufacturing labor force were most evident in the South at first, as African Americans gradually replaced white workers. This change was largely the result of civil rights legislation; but another factor was the increasing internationalization of competition, in the sense that "black workers served to keep the shaky low-wage industry competitive in the world marketplace."[93] As well, more and more black workers were hired by hotels and the service industries. Job creation and political activism further encouraged the hiring of African American workers; however, because of job slotting, racism, and economic recessions, these employees were often the first to lose their jobs in times of economic instability.[94] To summarize, African Americans

90. See Kathleen Paul, *Whitewashing Britain: Race and Citizenship in the Postwar Era* (Ithaca: Cornell University Press, 1997).
91. See Portes and Rumbaut, *Immigrant America*, 85–86; Jerry Ackerman, "Easing Immigrants' Culture Shock," *Boston Sunday Globe*, May 30, 2004, G1, G7.
92. Jones, *American Work*, 362.
93. Ibid., 363.
94. See ibid., 365–68.

began to occupy positions from which they had long been barred, but they often faced discriminatory practices in relation to hiring, job allocation, and so on.[95]

Moreover, for the poorest African Americans, civil rights legislation allowed for greater integration into manufacturing and other low-skilled jobs at a time (the 1970s and 1980s) when these jobs were beginning to disappear. The splits between skilled, unionized work and unskilled, nonunion work became more significant in the 1980s, with the result that wages were no higher for African Americans who finally were able to work in integrated workplaces. These divisions were due to the changing nature of work (a result of economic globalization), but they were also a consequence of racial exclusion by unions, "slotting" in the sense that whites were often hired over African Americans for skilled labor and other discriminatory practices that undermined colorblind employment policies.[96] Discriminatory practices could continue partly because employers resorted to tactics that subverted antidiscrimination laws and partly because affirmative action programs were never on stable ground: charges of reverse discrimination began soon after these programs were in place in the 1970s.[97] This is not to deny that real progress was now possible for certain African Americans; rather, it is to point out that the poorest, those perceived as the least skilled—those who were blue-collar workers—did not benefit to the same degree as others. This was true of African American women as well as men: as more and more African American women entered the workforce, most of the women who worked blue-collar jobs were placed in the "least desirable positions."[98]

By the 1980s and early 1990s, the internationalization of industry that had allowed greater entry of African Americans into all types of employment was leading to their exclusion, especially at the blue-collar level. At the same time, the discourse arose that African Americans were "lazy, irresponsible, and sexually promiscuous"; the subtext was that their unemployment or underemployment was by choice and individual pathology, not a result of broader circumstances.[99] Yet no empirical evidence was offered to substantiate these claims. As Wilson has shown, African

95. See for example, Adler, *Mollie's Job.*
96. Ibid., 355–68. See Deborah King, "Multiple Jeopardy, Multiple Consciousness: The Context of a Black Feminist Ideology," in *Feminist Social Thought: A Reader,* ed. Diane Tietje-Meyers (New York: Routledge, 1997).
97. See Jones, *American Work,* 362.
98. Ibid., 363.
99. Linda Faye Williams, *The Constraint of Race* (University Park: Penn State University Press, 2004), 184–92.

American workers take jobs when they are available, but increasingly they have not been.[100] Thus, Wilson notes, "the impact of industrial restructuring on inner-city employment is clearly apparent to urban blacks."[101] One major study, conducted in Chicago, found that African American employment in industrial jobs dropped from 52 percent in the 1970s to 28 percent by 1987: "No other male ethnic group in the inner city experienced such an overall precipitous drop in manufacturing employment . . . As a result, young black males have turned increasingly to the low-wage service sector and unskilled laboring jobs for employment, or have gone jobless."[102] These patterns hold across the United States[103] and have led to depressed wages, reduced skill levels, and bleak possibility of advancement.

Additionally, because affirmative action in the employment sector has largely been dismantled and the idea that racism is prevalent has been dismissed (see below), there has been no *systematic* effort to hire any particular group for reasons of equity, fairness, or justice. And when African Americans do hold the new types of jobs in the globalized economy, the instability of those jobs is such that their work is not recognized as blue-collar (that is, "real") work. In the 1940s and 1950s, the easy availability of manufacturing jobs helped define the working class and in that way served as a model of citizenship. That definition no longer fits the demographics or work conditions of the global economy. In many ways, work has gone underground and these disenfranchised workers do not fit the model of citizenship that has evolved more recently. Add to these dynamics the increasing polarization of wealth, which has led to a cultural rift between the rich and the poor.

The lowest tier of jobs—employment that is labor-intensive and poorly paid and that generates minimal profits—has always been occupied by African Americans to some degree, but now ethnic and racial slotting have provided competition for jobs that are increasingly exploitative and inhuman—that verge, in fact, on slave labor.[104] Jones notes: "Now reliant

100. See, for example, Wilson, *When Work Disappears*, 30–42, 44, 53, 72, 78, 82, 105, 109, 143, 144.

101. Ibid., 35.

102. Ibid., 30.

103. Ibid., 31. Steven Amberg's (Associate Professor, University of Texas, San Antonio) recent work problematizes this assertion. He has found that states differ in their policies toward workers and firms. Nevertheless, I believe that the overall trends I have analyzed describe the general conditions of low-wage work and signal profound changes, even given regional differences.

104. See Jones, *American Work*, 375. See Alvaro Bedoya, "Captive Labor," *Dollars and Sense* 249 (September–October 2003): 30–34, regarding the agriculture industry; George White, "Workers Held in Near-Slavery, Officials Say," *Los Angeles Times*, August 3, 1995, 1; Molly Gordy, "A Call to Fight Forced Labor," *Parade Magazine*, February 20, 2000, 4–5.

for workers upon Latin American and Southeast Asian refugees as well as African Americans, labor-intensive industries spurred the growth of garment sweatshops, prison workshops, and 'sweatshops in the fields' (migrant labor camps). The exploitation of Chinese seamstresses in New York city, black prisoners in Arizona, and Mexican strawberry pickers in California testified to a never-ending quest for laborers who were at once cheap and lacking in political power."[105] This is especially true in agribusiness, which hires a quarter of a million unauthorized immigrants every year, as well as in meatpacking enterprises,[106] the garment industry, and the service sector. The impact of immigrant labor has become significant: already in 1994, immigrants occupied 9 percent of low-tier positions.[107] The anti-immigration sentiment that emerged in the late 1990s and that continues to this day has focused on the costs of immigration—most specifically, the burden on this country's education and health care systems— yet it has ignored the contributions that low-wage workers have made to the economy.[108] At the same time, the media's excessive attention on immigrants now makes it seem that immigrants are taking all low-tier jobs and that African Americans are refusing to accept the same wages or conditions. Yet African Americans continue to occupy many of these low-tier positions, and one major study found that they actually receive less in wages than Mexicans or Puerto Ricans.[109] Again, the terms of these jobs have changed,[110] the willingness to work has not.

Perhaps this focus on immigrants, coupled with the lack of recognition that service work and casual manufacturing are now the predominant forms of blue-collar employment, explains why conventional wisdom would have it that all poor African Americans are on welfare, or that they are unemployed either by choice[111] or because they are criminals. Wilson

105. Jones, *American Work*, 370–71.

106. See David Bacon, "INS Declares War on Labor," *The Nation*, October 25, 1999; Human Rights Watch, "Human Rights Watch Welcomes U.S. Government Meat and Poultry Study," http://hrw.org/English/docs/2005/02/03/usdom10117_txt.htm; "Abusive Child Labor Found in U.S. Agriculture," June 1, 2000, http://hrw.org/English/docs/2000/06/20/usdom 580_txt.thm; and National Catholic Rural Life Conference, "U.S. Agricultural Workers," http://www.ncrlc.com/AgriculturalWorkers.html.

107. Jones, *American Work*, 375.

108. See ibid., 376. And perhaps, that they keep consumer prices down, granted that antisweatshop activists would argue that if a living wage were paid to these workers, consumer prices would remain the same (if cuts were made elsewhere).

109. Wilson, *When Work Disappears*, 140.

110. For a discussion of what is recognized as formal work versus informal work, see ibid., 74–75.

111. For a discussion of why it is rational to turn down some jobs—particularly those in the suburbs—see ibid., 42.

points out that formal work demands from workers more reliability, consistency, and self-discipline.[112] Because this type of work is disappearing, and/or because African Americans are apparently participating less in formal work, the characteristics of more casual or informal work are being attributed to the workers rather than the workplace. For these reasons, African American employees performing low-tier work are not recognized as doing so.

Instead, nowadays it is often noted—for example, in Zygmunt Bauman's work on globalization—that more and more African American men are being incarcerated.[113] Bauman asserts that this signals how useless these individuals have become to an economy stripped of the Protestant work ethic; prisons house the detritus of globalization, and this, he contends, is why there is less impetus to get prisoners to learn to work. In that sense, he contends, imprisonment is *"an alternative to employment"*[114] and signals the push to *"dismantle* the habits of permanent, round-the-clock, steady and regular work; what else may the slogan of 'flexible labour' mean?"[115] But it could also be argued that prisoners' labor has simply not been recognized as real work. In fact, "the modern equivalent of bound labor found its most dramatic expression in the incarceration of increasing numbers of men—particularly black men—throughout the country"[116] at this time, because of the War on Drugs. To put it differently, the War on Drugs is today articulated[117] with neoliberal concerns about security and the availability of cheap labor. In this way, sovereignty and economic interests have been united.

Indeed, prison labor has changed with the globalization of the economy and is a site of "outsourcing," as it is now legal for private employers to contract prison work.[118] Prison workers test blood for medical firms, take hotel reservations, perform data entry, pack boxes, and so on. These prisoners are paid, but they receive less than the minimum wage and obviously

112. Ibid., 75.

113. See Glenn C. Loury, "The Conservative Line on Race," *The Atlantic*, November 1997, 10, http://www.theatlantic.com/issues/97nov/race.htm.

114. Zygmunt Bauman, *Globalization* (New York: Columbia University Press, 1998), 111.

115. Ibid., 112.

116. Jones, *American Work*, 377.

117. For a definition of the word *articulation*, see, for example, Chantal Mouffe, or Stuart Hall's discussion of this term.

118. Jones, *American Work*, 377. See Adam Nossiter, "With Jobs to Do, Louisiana Parish Turns to Inmates," *New York Times*, July 5, 2006. (Thanks to Brent Floyd for sending this article to me.)

have no bargaining power.[119] The terms of this labor cannot be called racist; however, the fact that certain crimes are marked as "black" and are punishable by longer prison sentences (most notable here is the crack/cocaine dichotomy, where crack dealers receive longer sentences than coke dealers) has resulted in a disproportionate number of African American workers in prisons.[120] In this way, asceticism and biopower work in conjunction with the prerogative power of the War on Drugs.

In sum, African American workers faced years of open discrimination until the implementation of the Civil Rights Act, Supreme Court decisions that went beyond the act, and Great Society programs. As a result, the greater integration of African Americans into the labor market occurred; then later, for the poorest African Americans, the disappearance of traditional manufacturing jobs was devastating. In recent years, many more African American males in their prime are unemployed. Viewed historically, the greater integration of this group was a positive development at many levels. However, owing to changes in the economy (especially the loss of traditional manufacturing jobs),[121] the influx of low-skilled immigrants into the inner cities from the 1960s on, the feminization of labor, and the decreasing recognition that racism exists, many of these individuals are now unemployed or sporadically employed, and even worse, they themselves are blamed for it.[122] Moreover, the depression of wages[123] and the withdrawal of government funding to inner cities has led to new poverty neighborhoods (see Chapter 3), and this is reinforcing social isolation and disaffection. Add to this bleak scenario the progressive dismantling of affirmative action and the defunding of jobs programs, community organizations, and educational projects.

All of this has led to contemporary notions that African Americans do not work by choice, are all on welfare, and so on; and that they constitute

119. Jones, *American Work*, 377–78. Although, as Chris Sturr (editor, *Dollars 'n Sense*) has noted, not all prisoners are put to work. The split between "old school" treatment of prisoners, including the revival of chain gangs, and the new use of their labor in the low-tier economy is discussed in David Garland, *Culture of Control* (Chicago: University of Chicago Press, 2001).

120. Jones, *American Work*, 378. See Loury, "The Conservative Line on Race." Although it appears that the pendulum may be swinging the other way in mid-2004, with even conservative lawmakers now realizing that prisons are overpopulated and that the prison population is not being "rehabilitated."

121. Regarding the disappearance of work, see Wilson, *When Work Disappears*, xiii, xix, 16, 17, 19, 22, 25–29, 52–54.

122. See Adler, *Mollie's Job*.

123. Regarding the transformations in wage structures, see Wilson, *When Work Disappears*, 30, 34, 140, 151–54.

an *underclass* rather than an unemployed working class. To interpret job-lessness in this way—as a choice based on an inherent moral or biological character—is to analyze job loss and economic change in a vacuum. Many authors have remarked that the re-emergence of pseudoscientific racism—during a time when affirmative action is being dismantled, welfare is being overhauled, and lower-tier work is becoming increasingly exploitative—has served as a highly convenient excuse for radical structural transfor-mations and for the increasing disenfranchisement of working-class African Americans.

Rac*ism* toward African Americans manifests itself in invidious com-parisons with immigrants. It is implied that African Americans lack a work ethic, have poor family values, are violent (in the case of men), and perhaps do not really belong here (that is, they never "assimilated"). These arguments are clearly ascetic in nature in that they classify people according to their work status. They also reflect biopower—that is, they identify qualities of a group as inherent to that group and then politicize those qualities (for example, through the War on Drugs, and the racial rhetoric that has helped end welfare and some parts of affirmative action). Racism is also evident in the recurring naturalization of race despite all the available proof that there is no such thing.[124] Similarly, it has become acceptable to argue that real estate segregation is natural and that African Americans are not naturally intelligent and are failing miserably at school.

These arguments are more striking in an era that is thought to be post–Civil Rights, postracism, and relatively egalitarian in terms of the law. Racial theories and policies before World War II were clearly racist according to Robert Miles's definition (given above). African Americans were identified according to somatic characteristics that portrayed them as inferior and that *intentionally* allowed for great political and economic inequality. After the war and especially from the Civil Rights Movement on, racial thinking changed so that it was now argued that structural factors were far more important in determining one's life chances. In other words, the inferior political and economic position of African Americans was linked not to biological inferiority but rather to unequal circumstances. These historical differences were reflected in the emphasis on IQ: low IQs were attributed to genetic inferiority before World War II; then after-wards, they were blamed instead on unequal education, differences in

124. That race is not real is claimed on the genetic front (see Colette Guillaumin, *Racism, Sexism, Power, and Ideology* [New York: Routledge, 1995]) and in investigating the history of "races"; see Spivak, "Race Before Racism: The Disappearance of the American," *boundary 2* 25 (Summer 1998): 35–53.

income levels, and so on. This change in perspective was partly due to the exposure of problems with the tests themselves—that is, with the ways they were administered and interpreted.[125] It was also due to the fear of any type of scientific racism of the sort the Nazis had practiced. This postwar attitude was challenged in 1969, when a Berkeley psychologist named Arthur Jensen argued that IQ is largely genetic. Jensen released his "bombshell,"[126] contending that "black students' poor academic performance was due to irreversible genetic deficiencies, so programs like Head Start were useless and should be replaced by vocational education."[127] While this argument initially fueled right-wing rhetoric ("the effect of Jensen's work on fascist groups throughout the world was immediate and electric"),[128] it gained widespread popularity in the 1990s.[129]

The "new" racism of the 1990s was not new in the sense that it was genetic or biologically based, that it essentialized race and emphasized IQ;[130] rather, it was new in that in the post-Holocaust era, it had not been acceptable to claim that one "race" was inferior to another. Moreover, these arguments conveniently arose at a time when affirmative action, welfare, and unions were being dismantled and jobs were increasingly changing from traditional to global in character—precisely when these changes could be justified by positing the inferiority of people whom the changes would affect. The historical context was one of greater economic instability for all: "In the midst of social dislocation caused by rapid technological change and large-scale immigration, it was no wonder that the race-baiting rhetoric of antebellum New England echoed in late twentieth-century pronouncements about the place of African Americans in the national labor market. Desperate to avoid a forced relocation to the end of the employment queue, whites would assert their claim to a moral and intellectual superiority over blacks, unknowingly imitating the political strategies of anxious tradesmen and mechanics a century and a half before."[131] Significantly, this superiority emerged with the book *The Bell Curve* by Richard Herrnstein and Charles Murray.

125. See Barry Alan Mehler, "Race-Science Returns," http://www.ferris.edu/isar/archives/billig/chapter2.htm.

126. Ibid., 2.

127. Adam Miller, "Professors of Hate," *Rolling Stone* 693 (October 20, 1994), 7.

128. Mehler, "Race-Science Returns," 3.

129. See Mehler regarding Jensen's effect on the scientific community.

130. See Guillaumin, *Racism*, 83, 96n, 212, 214, 282n, for a critique of the social construction of intelligence as natural, as well as its racist, classist, and sexist consequences; see Wilson, *When Work Disappears*, xiv–xvi.

131. Jones, *American Work*, 371.

Herrnstein and Murray changed the terms of the racial debate by arguing not that structural forces led to low IQ scores but the reverse: low genetic capability led to many social problems.[132] What was disturbing was that academics, television talk show hosts (including Charlie Rose), authors, and many others took these findings at face value. Some critics explained the popularity of this book as reflecting the feeling on the part of European Americans (whites) that affirmative action programs are a form of punishment; in other words, this book vindicated whites' latent racism as well as their feelings of being assaulted by civil rights legislation. For example, Michael Levin declared, "I'm interested in innocence for whites and the genetic hypothesis is evidence for the defense. It undercuts affirmative action, the basis for which is the great black claim to the American consciousness that 'We're down, and you owe us for what you did to us with slavery and Jim Crow.' Race differences show whites aren't at fault for Macks being down, and making whites pay for something they're not responsible for is a terrible injustice. Eliminating affirmative action is the first step. Next—please, yes, if only—eliminate the Civil Rights Act.'"[133] Similarly, Murray has written that "there is 'a huge number of well-meaning whites who fear that they are closet racists, and this book tells them they are not. It's going to make them feel better about things they already think but do not know how to say.'"[134]

It also comes at time when all Americans feel that their jobs are more unstable: "Indeed, *The Bell Curve* is at its core a polemic about the structure of the American labor force; by ranking in one long queue all potential workers according to their 'IQ,' the authors seek to reserve the best jobs for people who score well on standardized intelligence tests."[135] Indeed, the authors seem to have written the book for political rather than scientific reasons. In this way, they could avoid accusations of scientific racism and their findings could take on the guise of science with a "biological referent."[136] To put it differently, Herrnstein and Murray were not objective by Max Weber's standards[137] because they were conducting research based

132. See Wilson, *When Work Disappears*, xv–xvii.

133. Miller, "Professors of Hate," 2.

134. Murray, quoted in *New York Times Magazine* (October 9, 1994), quoted in Jim Naureckas, "Racism Resurgent: How Media Let *The Bell Curve's* Pseudo-Science Define the Agenda on Race," http://www.fair.org/extra/9501/bell.html, 5.

135. Jones, *American Work*, 388.

136. Miles and Brown, *Racism*, 65.

137. Max Weber, "Objectivity in the Social Sciences," in *The Methodology of the Social Sciences*, ed. and trans. Edward A. Shils and Henry A. Finch (New York: Free Press, 1969).

on circular reasoning.[138] They were also criticized for misinterpreting their data and for the sources of their data.[139] Nevertheless, they denied that their tests were faulty or biased.[140]

The political beliefs espoused in *The Bell Curve* can be traced back to eugenic arguments dating to before World War II. In addition, the authors were using data originating with the Pioneer Fund and with sources associated with that fund. The study and promotion of eugenics and biological racism had gone underground after World War II, only to reappear in the 1960s with decolonization, the end of Jim Crow, and the beginning of desegregation. The Pioneer Fund and similar groups were instrumental in barring Asians from the United States, on the grounds that their intelligence and superior work ethic would give them an unfair advantage over whites in the labor market; in forcing the sterilization of "tens of thousands" of Americans; in creating obstacles for Jews fleeing Russian pogroms and Nazi repression who tried to come to the United States; and in eugenic policies toward African Americans and immigrants in more recent times.[141] The Pioneer Fund was also influential after World War II, variously influencing restrictive immigration policies and taking the side of segregationists in *Brown v. Board of Education* and other regressive causes.[142] The fund's recent grant recipients "have lobbied for restrictive immigration policies and promoted various forms of segregation. To rid the world of 'undesirables'—and their potential offspring—some grant recipients have suggested sterilization or even extermination."[143]

Murray and Herrnstein also intended their findings to influence the immigration debate of the 1990s. They suggested that East Asians have a genetically higher IQ than either blacks or whites—which, of course, reinforces notions of race and biological inferiority and superiority. Their methodology in this area has been criticized for a multitude of reasons.[144] The authors also claim that Latinos have a mean IQ of 91, although for

138. See Fields, "Slavery, Race, and Ideology," on the propensity of historians and other academics to analyze race tautologically.

139. See Wilson, *When Work Disappears,* xv–xvii; Miller, "Professors of Hate," 2; Naureckas, "Racism Resurgent," 4; Charles Lane, "The Tainted Sources of 'The Bell Curve,'" *New York Review of Books* XIV (December 1, 1994).

140. See Lane, "The Tainted Sources"; Charles Murray, "The Inequality Taboo," *Commentary* 120 (September 2005): 13–22.

141. See Pioneer Fund, http://www.pioneerfund.org; Miller, "Professors of Hate," 6; Mehler, "Race-Science Returns"; Naureckas, "Racism Resurgent."

142. Miller, "Professors of Hate," 7.

143. Ibid., 2.

144. Ibid., 7, 8.

this, they offer no data or proof whatsoever[145] (furthermore, the information they do rely on does not account for language proficiency).[146] Nevertheless, they conclude that "fifty seven percent of legal immigrants in the 1980s [thus] came from ethnic groups with average IQs less than that of American whites, and therefore the mean for all immigrants is probably below that of all native-born Americans."[147] They then recommend a "more eugenically minded—and, hence, restrictive—US immigration policy."[148]

As various critics have pointed out, Murray and Herrnstein have not been totally up front about their sources, and this is perhaps why their claims have so often been taken at face value. I would suggest that given the history in this country of racist laws (including exclusionary immigration laws) and a racist or racially oriented culture, recent debates over their findings have been welcome and timely. They have given a "scientific" gloss to the eugenic elements of their arguments, so as to make them sound neutral; the question, then, is what to do about this reality rather than challenge its premises. Regrettably, Murray and Herrnstein have not been not alone in their public pronouncements and publications. In 1990, Michael Levin made a speech at a New York university during which he declared that blacks are less intelligent than whites and have higher crime rates: "Blackness is a sign of danger." He added that racial profiling by the police is in whites' best interests.[149] He has also called for public policies regarding housing, welfare, education, and affirmative action on the basis of his claims.[150]

Levin's pronouncements indicate that at stake here is not a desire to deny that the category of race has meaning or to make blacks equal, but rather a desire on the part of dominant groups to "win" in what appears to be a zero sum game. His logic would hold that affirmative action and other programs punish whites and discriminate against them. And Levin is not afraid to connect his recommendations to eugenics. In an interview with *Rolling Stone* reporter Adam Miller, when asked what ending welfare would do, he replied: "'The country is being overrun by people who don't work and have illegitimate children. [Ending welfare] would simply be ceasing to subsidize them. That would automatically have a very excellent demographic effect." When Miller suggested that this was eugenics, he

145. Ibid., 8
146. Ibid., 9.
147. Ibid., 8.
148. Ibid., 9.
149. Ibid., 1.
150. Ibid., 2.

responded: "There's nothing wrong with eugenics. It's a perfectly respectable idea I think it may be making a comeback."[151] Many other prominent figures have been either funded by Pioneer or influenced by its researchers; in both academe and government policy, that group's influence has been obvious ever since the eugenics movement was launched in the early part of the last century. As various authors have noted, Pioneer's arguments are not scientific and were rejected decades ago by the large majority of geneticists and biological scientists; yet a minority continue to claim that arguments about heredity and genetic patterning are based on sound empirical evidence. And notwithstanding their lack of scientific authority, these claims have been enjoying a resurgence.[152]

The findings of Pioneer Fund researchers have been joined by prominent academics who express similar ideas. For example, Harvey Mansfield has linked grade inflation at Harvard University to the greater enrollment of African American students as a result of Affirmative Action policies (he neglects to mention other groups that have benefited from these policies);[153] and Abigail Thernstrom (along with many others) is questioning the policies that flowed out of *Brown v. Board of Education*.[154] These people may not be connected to their eugenically minded peers, but they do not seem to mind sharing the same opinions with similar policy consequences. These academics are tightly focused on terms such as color blindness and equality, yet they frame all their arguments in racial terms. As a result, like their more eugenically minded colleagues, they extend racial thinking a prominent place in their scholarship, work practices, and policy recommendations.

These arguments not only are convenient politically but also explain how racism is being perpetuated—that is, how it can be declared over yet be more overt than ever (in recent history). Racism is becoming acceptable again in ways that it has not been since the 1920s; the result has been justifications for separate but equal systems (that is, discrimination) in sectors ranging from education to housing to hiring practices. The new racism has also validated the racial profiling of poor immigrants of color and poor African Americans. Indeed, society today approves the

151. Ibid., 3.
152. See Miles and Brown, *Racism;* Guillaumin, *Racism;* and Cornel West, "Race and Social Theory," in *Keeping Faith: Philosophy and Race in America* (New York: Routledge, 1993), 253.
153. See Stanley Kurtz, "Guest Comment: Crimson Truths, Reality Has a Hearing at Harvard," *National Review,* http://www.nationalreview.com/comment/comment-kurtzprint 030201.html.
154. See Adam Shatz, "The Thernstroms in Black and White," *American Prospect* 12, http://www.prospect.org/print/V12/5/shatz-a.html; Loury, "The Conservative Line on Race."

unequal application of the law, and even its suspension, as long as it is used against individuals who (seemingly) do not understand civilized law. Brute force must be met by brute force: such is the logic.

What is most disturbing about racist arguments is their widespread popularity,[155] the lack of questioning regarding their foundations (particularly in relation to eugenics), and the fact that overt racism is acceptable across the board: "Racism, it seems, has not only become respectable again. It is even chic. True, use of what is now known euphemistically as the 'N-word' is still considered to be in execrable taste. . . . But very nearly everything else goes and, more to the American point, sells. Today a racist tract, if impressively footnoted and aggressively marketed, can launch its author into the heady world of flashy cover stories, obsequious television interviews, and lucrative lectures."[156] That is, the alleged scientific accuracy of these arguments lends them a form of acceptability that has not been the case for genetic racism since World War II. As one author notes, the "data" concerning African American genetic inadequacy are not being questioned; rather, the key debate centers on what to do about these findings. In fact, Murray and Herrnstein as well as others, such as Dinesh D'Souza, have been called "courageous" and "heroic" for releasing these data during a time of racial sensitivity.[157] As Wilson remarks, *The Bell Curve* has led to the proliferation of discourse on the genetic capabilities of inner-city residents.[158] It also points to a "resurgence of racism in U.S. media and society—a racism that does not want to face up to its own identity."[159]

Most of these arguments have been taken at face value. As a consequence, even to this day the general public listens closely to them and many academics express their approval of them. Because these ideas are arising from elite sources, they are influencing not only public opinion but also policy formation and academic analyses. Whether there is a direct link between racist ideas and the dismantling of certain programs or only an elective affinity is up for debate, but it is clear that these arguments have bolstered the dismantling of affirmative action programs and the

155. See Naureckas, "Racism Resurgent," on the book's popular reception.

156. Joseph Barnes, "Book Review: *The End of Racism,* by Dinesh D'Souza," *Zmagazine,* http://wwzmagorg/zmag/articles/dec95reviews.htm, 1.

157. See Naureckas, "Racism Resurgent"; Barnes, "Book Review: *The End of Racism*"; Miller, "Professors of Hate"; Lane, "The Tainted Sources"; Mehler, chap. 2, "Race-Science Returns," and chap. 3, "Mankind Quarterly." For all of above, http://www.ferris.edu/isar/archives/billig/chapter2.htm.

158. Wilson, *When Work Disappears,* xv.

159. Naureckas, *Racism Resurgent,* 5.

end of welfare "as we know it," as well as recent notions that desegre-gated schools are a bad idea.[160] Racism is also clearly affecting hiring policies as well as gender typing between African American men and women; hiring is becoming linked to negative stereotyping.[161] At the very least, the re-emergence of biological racism is articulating with the political and economic context in which it is again emerging—that is, in the context of neoliberal politics and economic policies that emphasize individual achievement and that downplay broader social, economic, and other trends.

For those academics and policymakers who want to avoid being labeled racist, there is the option to use the culture argument, which ends up replicating the "right to difference" slogans of neoconservatives in Europe and which is the intellectual relative of American racism (or its twin, given that this argument involves the same normative assumptions, policy recommendations, and consequences as racist ones). The culture argument can be applied to poor immigrants and African Americans equally, as evidenced earlier in the quotes from Huntington and Fukuyama, and this illuminates the importance of the intersection of economic class with race.[162] Paul Gilroy notes that cultural arguments are not always inseparable from biological ones and that this is especially true from the perspective of those who are the objects of these claims.[163] Racism can also be discerned in its historical context: these arguments fit the trajectory of racisms and the racialization of Others, be they immigrants or American-born minorities; thus it can be "demonstrate[d] that prior to silence, racist discourse was articulated."[164] One of the most prominent examples of this, by Dinesh D'Souza, not only proclaims the *end* of racism but also argues that discriminatory practices against African Americans are merely practical, borne of experience. Because it has been demonstrated that African Americans are naturally violent, promiscuous, and financially insolvent—so he claims—it is reasonable to discriminate against them according to market logic.[165]

Yet D'Souza also contends that if African Americans sense racism, it is only a matter of perception. In other words, racism is a problem that they feel—like adult children who are mad at their parents years later—

160. See the Thernstroms' work; see Jones, *American Work*, 388.

161. See Wilson, *When Work Disappears*, esp. 111–17, 118, 119, 122, 123, 126, 143, 144.

162. See also a review of the Thernstrom's book, *No Excuses: Closing the Racial Gap in Learning*, by Jennifer L. Hochschild, "Minding the Gap," *Harvard Magazine*, March–April 2004, 23–28.

163. Gilroy, discussed in Miles and Brown, *Racism*, 65.

164. Miles and Brown, *Racism*, 110.

165. See Barnes, "Book Review: *The End of Racism*," 6–7.

rather than actually experience. Put another way, individual blacks can choose to perceive racism or not, and meanwhile, whites need to get over their "guilt."[166] To argue that culture is the issue is to (attempt to) depoliticize racial divisions[167] and reduce racism to a matter of personal emotions. D'Souza, like Huntington and Fukuyama, also contends that multiculturalism and charges of racism are ways for African Americans to assert their culture, gain respect for it, and hide the fact that they simply can't assimilate. Of course, this very charge *effects* a cultural division by positing strict boundaries between mainstream, civilized culture and marginal, criminal, unassimilated, and ultimately barbarian culture(s). As D'Souza aptly puts it: "For many whites the criminal and irresponsible black underclass represents a revival of barbarism in the midst of Western civilization. . . . If blacks can close the civilization gap, the race problem in this country is likely to become insignificant."[168] But D'Souza says he is not racist and that racism itself has ended.

These arguments, of course, presuppose that there is such a thing as race[169] and that it can be pure. They involve the biologizing of whoever is being targeted—a list that in the past has included women, Irish, and blacks—as well as claims that these groups represent nature. That is, they represent reproduction, fornication, violence, sex in general—the antithesis of civilization (that is, intelligence or rationality). In this way, images and representations are made to be real, and science is then based on them. As Collette Guillaumin argues: "The notion of race is a scientific invention of this sort; and theories of racial relationships may perhaps be accounted for in the same way, for some of them assert that there is a 'natural' element in certain social processes—in short, that some human groups are more natural than others."[170] Writ large, species thinking is not racist per se but does prepare the intellectual and political ground for it. In effect, this is a step toward the greater influence of biopower in political and economic structures, institutions, and practices.

This logic indicates a mixing of the "natural" and legal. Laws have normally reflected social practices, "but with racial laws, the legal criterion became overlaid by the ideological one of 'natural' affiliation. The alleged 'fact' is

---

166. See ibid., 1–7.

167. See ibid., 7.

168. Jones, *American Work*, 385n4; Dinesh D'Souza, *The End of Racism; Principles for a Multiracial Society* (New York: Free Press, 1995), 527.

169. See Miles, *Racism*; Guillaumin, *Racism*; Oliver Cromwell Cox, *Race: A Study in Social Dynamics* (New York: Monthly Review Press, 2000).

170. Guillaumin, *Racism*, 79–80.

always related to a mythical past."[171] In this way, the idea that women are naturally suited to service work and "like to clean up shit" or the notion that African Americans do not like to work is "an intentionally purely subjective critique of their states of mind. On the other hand, that which refers to the effective experiences of the groups of 'women' and 'blacks' (cleaning up, unemployment), that which refers to the facts is correct: women do clean up the shit, and being black condemns one to unemployment—but *the relationship between the facts is false*."[172] Importantly, racial and gender typologies are linked to reproductive, unproductive, and/or subsistence labor as natural extensions of their existence.

Racism is re-emerging at a time of significant dismantling of certain key political and economic institutions aimed at fostering equal opportunity. Also in this era, workfare has been replacing welfare, neoliberal policies have been gaining ever greater popularity and influence, and working-class jobs have become increasingly exploitative. In this context, it is worthwhile to explore the relationship between capital and race (on the assumption that class must be highly significant, since I am discussing poor workers). The Marxist literature on race[173] challenges claims that racism is biological or otherwise inherent and out of a person's control. Instead, it argues that racial ideology serves to justify the commodification and exploitation of labor. This is not to say that European Americans cannot also be exploited; the point here is that race and gender articulate with exploitation, which is why denigrated European Americans are *white* trash—the racial signifier remains. The history and actual reality of political disenfranchisement or second-class citizenship serves as a better foundation for economic exploitation.

To put it differently, the immobility (social, spatial, and so on) of certain groups renders them potentially highly exploitative subjects in ways that European Americans are not, even if the latter suffer from these dynamics as disciplinary effects. If one accepts this premise, the question is which came first in this relationship—racism or exploitation? Oliver Cromwell Cox's work, which has recently been revived, shows that the dehumanizing element of buying and selling labor power—the commodification of labor power—requires that workers be viewed as "inanimate

171. Ibid., 77.
172. Ibid., 143.
173. See, for example, Cox, *Race*; Barbara Fields, "Slavery, Race, and Ideology"; Edna Bonacich, "A Theory of Ethnic Antagonism: The Split Labor Market," *American Sociological Review* 37 (1972); Miles, *Racism*.

or subhuman." In contrast to slavery, which was characterized by personal relations, capitalist relations are necessarily impersonal—that is, inhuman. For this reason, "the capitalists proceed in a normal way; that is to say, they develop and exploit ethnocentrism and show by any irrational or logical means available that the working class [is] of their own race or whole peoples of other races, whose labor they are bent upon exploiting are something apart: (a) not human at all, (b) only part human, (c) inferior humans, and so on."[174] The biopolitical aims of sovereignty can then be seen as articulating with the logic of capitalism, and racial ideology serves as a crucial nexus in this dehumanization. Bare life is more than a basis for acquiring and maintaining power; in the neoliberal context, it unites the various strategies and mechanisms of power. This explains why racial profiling and the incarceration of poor African Americans have been increasingly justified as biological racism becomes more acceptable.

Connected to the new racism, the end of Cold War thinking and policies in the 1980s not only brought about changes in immigration policy and the way we view immigrants but also raised a supposedly new threat with the war that accompanied their arrival: the War on Drugs.[175] This war took "a devastating toll on the demographic integrity of black families and communities"[176] so that "the number of black males in this country's prisons and jails has more than tripled since 1980."[177] That is, "the growth of drug imprisonment accounted for more than a third of the increase in black incarceration from 1985 to 1990, making it [the War on Drugs] in all likelihood the single most important factor [in higher incarceration rates]."[178] In addition to this (or because of it, depending on one's point of view), national debate began to focus on racial profiling by the police, and an act was proposed to stop it. However, Congress failed to pass the End Racial Profiling Act of 2001 in its 107th Session—most likely because of 9/11—and has in fact allowed for greater profiling of African Americans as well as poorer immigrants and men of Arab descent.[179] When viewed in combination with the ascetic prescriptions of welfare, workfare programs, and public housing policies, the surveillance and control of poor minorities

174. Cox, Race, 181.
175. See Jones, American Work, 377–78.
176. Ibid., 377.
177. Loury, "The Conservative Line on Race," 9.
178. Ibid., 10.
179. See Executive Summary, "Wrong Then, Wrong Now"; Amnesty International, http://www.amnestyusa.org; Ramirez, McDevitt, and Farrell, "Resource Guide on Racial Profiling"; Muharrar, "Media Blackface"; Executive Summary, "Massachusetts Racial and Gender Profiling Final Report"; ACLU, "Racial Equality: Racial Profiling—Press Releases."

reveals biopolitical considerations in the deployment of sovereignty as well as the exercise of prerogative power at local levels.

Ethnic Antagonism

Racial theorizing and anti-immigration sentiment create distinctions between the groups affected, despite obvious commonalities in how they are portrayed and in their economic and political circumstances. The term "underclass" is one such example; often applied to African Americans, it implies that this group in particular is below any line of normalcy. The term gained national prominence in 1977 and became accepted as a description of the hardcore (black) poor.[180] This expression is even employed by authors who view themselves as liberals. Clearly, they are unaware of the consequences of this term,[181] which serves to differentiate this "group" from the working poor and immigrant workers and to isolate them from mainstream American values. Although the term "culture of poverty" grew out of the concept of the "underclass," the latter expression continues to be heard often in current debates about social welfare policies.[182] The conceptual separation of "underclass" African Americans from the working poor, and of poor African Americans from poor immigrants, obscures the permeability among all these "groups" as they slip into and out of joblessness, compete for the same low-paid employment, go on and off welfare, and live in close proximity to one another (not to mention intermarry).

In fact, poor African Americans and poor immigrants are subject to the same rhetoric and contradictions.[183] Immigrants are accused of creating sweatshops, entering the country illegally, and taking jobs from others, as if they were solely to blame for these things. Similarly, African Americans are accused of cultural degeneracy and criminality even though they have long suffered from policies that divide families and that increase the possibility of criminality. Immigrants who form political, cultural, or unionizing groups are accused of ingratitude and of creating ethnic enclaves. Similarly, African Americans who refuse to be mistreated on the job, who insist on bargaining for wages, or who attempt to form unions

---

180. See Wilson, *When Work Disappears*, 174–75.

181. See, for example, Isabelle V. Barker, "Theorizing Citizenship in an Era of Labor Migration and Inequality," paper presented at the Association for Political Theory, Grand Rapids, October 2003, 15.

182. See Wilson, *When Work Disappears*, 174–75.

183. See John Cassidy, "The Melting-Pot Myth," *The New Yorker*, July 14, 1997.

are viewed as "uppity," ungrateful, or demanding entitlements.[184] Rarely are these activities viewed as free speech, political mobilization, or dissent, the rights to which are supposedly the bedrock of American values. Immigrants are excoriated for exploiting public benefits (most obviously, welfare) while at the same time "stealing" jobs; in the same vein, African Americans are accused of taking jobs through affirmative action and, in the same breath, of not wanting to work:[185] "From a historical perspective, the dual charge that blacks as a group are both lay (as welfare recipients) and predatory job seekers (as beneficiaries of affirmative action policies) recapitulates the defensive and confused rhetoric of early nineteenth-century white workers."[186] The supposed criminality of both groups is believed to extend to all their practices and beliefs. In both cases, these workers are not recognized as a working class, deserving of the benefits that historically accrued to the working classes of 1950s and 1960s America. Instead, job slotting reinforces associations of race or ethnicity with work done at subsistence levels, which further places this work outside of the realm of "real" work.

Just like immigrants, African Americans end up working the crappiest jobs, often for less pay than immigrants. And they frequently needed to hold down two jobs. They also put up with insecure labor contracts and have little say in wages or who they work for. Even so, they are portrayed as lazy, parasitical, criminal, and violent. They are also faced with a gender split, which has some positive aspects, but even so, reinforces the focus on biological notions of identity and the importance of that identity for political and economic inclusion. Inequalities based on biology are now openly accepted and are viewed as inherent, unchanging characteristics beyond the control of the individual; yet at the same time, these individuals are held responsible for their poverty.

In this way, political and economic exploitation is inverted. It is charged that these groups embrace multiculturalism and separatism and that they milk benefits and jobs to their own advantage. In other words, they cannot be exploited because they *are* the exploiters. But these inversions and conceptual distinctions are also evidence of an important fact: European Americans and some wealthier minorities are antagonistic toward

184. As Jones states: "Like the anxious native-born workers of the early nineteenth century, these observers interpret black demands for employment opportunity and political representation as a threat to civic order—a loud, insistent, and ultimately impolite assault upon the sensibilities of the privileged." *American Work*, 388.

185. See ibid., 380, regarding the stereotype that African Americans won't take jobs.

186. Ibid., 385.

both groups. The constant comparisons between poor African Americans and poor immigrants hide the speaker, the origin of the "gaze": the political and economic elites. As Guillaumin notes, whites do not identify themselves as a race: "Dominant groups never quite believe that they themselves belong to a race, even today."[187] Ascetic arguments also serve to hide the "whiteness" or privileged status of the observer. Authors debate the family values of each group, their work ethic, their intelligence, and their assimilability to the American national identity; rarely is there a parallel examination of those who consider themselves mainstream or the dominant race. This explains why double standards can operate: only one part of the equation is presented.

Further obscuring exploitation is the ascetic framework of public policy and economic practices, a framework that serves to divide the groups: immigrants supposedly have a better work ethic than African Americans as well as stronger family values, greater integrity, and so on. African Americans are viewed as lazy, immigrants are not; African Americans do not accept jobs that immigrants will accept (there is hardly any discussion of whether Anglos will take these jobs, and if not, why not). What is not recognized is that the differences between these groups may stem from the same internalization of the Protestant ethic that Americans cannot avoid but that they interpret and act upon differently.[188] Mexicans may have a strong sense of family values; but so do many poor African Americans, who do not consider it responsible to get married when their employment prospects are so bleak.[189] And while first-generation immigrants may not complain about poor treatment on the job or politically, by the second generation they mirror the political and economic behavior of poorer African Americans.[190] Wilson has argued that when mistreated, African Americans perhaps complain more than immigrants. He and I would both argue that this hardly makes them uppity or unassimilable. This notion of worker's rights and of feeling wronged if exploited is precisely

---

187. Guillaumin, *Race*, 76. Hochschild, in "Minding the Gap," her review of the Thernstroms' 2004 book on education, notes that the authors do not examine Anglo culture, for example, but rather cultures of other races; in this way they illustrate Guillaumin's precise point—dominant "races" do not view themselves as belonging to a race.

188. See Wilson, *American Work*, on why ghetto behavior is not necessarily a rejection of ascetic norms (69–71); on ascetic values applied to the poor (72, 78, chap. 3, 67, 109, 159, 160, 161, 162, 164, 169, 171); on whether ascetic values are internalized (69); and on evidence that ghetto residents share ascetic values (178–82).

189. See ibid., 88–107.

190. See Dowell Myers et al., "The Changing Immigrants of Southern California," study (Los Angeles: University of Southern California School of Urban and Regional Planning, October 25, 1995); Portes and Rumbaut, *Immigrant America;* Wilson, *When Work Disappears*, 141.

democratic (if not liberal); it is *not* democratic to submit to exploitation.[191] In fact, the positing of differences between immigrants and African Americans has more to do with the elites' antagonism toward African Americans and a desire to encourage tensions between immigrants and blacks. It also pertains to a knee-jerk association of poverty with race as well as to the behaviors and values that supposedly inhere to the poor.[192]

The Los Angeles riots symbolized all of these concerns. They were portrayed as senseless destruction and as evidence of antagonism that was seemingly biological.[193] In fact, the riots were a release of the tensions generated by globalization; they were fueled largely by economic circumstances.[194] The antagonisms that surfaced during those riots had their own logic: "Recent immigrants living in ethnic clusters and laboring within larger, diverse metropolitan areas could locate seemingly few reasons to view African Americans other than as rivals apart from themselves a group, African Americans retained a heightened political self-consciousness that allowed little room for alliances with newcomers who were in the process of asserting their claim to the American workplace. And native-born whites throughout the workforce—in good jobs as well as bad—persisted in seeing black co-workers as interlopers and as a threat to their own job security and economic well-being."[195] Tensions have been noted between Latinos and African Americans[196] as well as between Koreans and African Americans,[197] not to mention between European Americans and African Americans.[198] The idea that there is only one race—black—perhaps explains why there is more hostility to African Americans, as well as why some African Americans can move into positions of power that Latinos, for example, need years to reach. On the other hand, perhaps because Latinos are now the largest minority, there is increasing

191. Wilson, *When Work Disappears*, 141.
192. See ibid., 162, 166, 167, 172.
193. Miles, in *Arguing Immigration*, notes this portrayal yet argues that the riots had no political content. Nevertheless, his own analysis demonstrates many of the politico-economic underpinnings of the riots.
194. See Wilson, *When Work Disappears*, 17, 66, 78, 98, 99, 140, 141, 144.
195. Jones, *American Work*, 382; and see 387.
196. Wilson, *When Work Disappears*, 188–89.
197. Ibid., 190–91. See Yuri Kochiyama, "Preface: Trailblazing in a White World," in *Dragon Ladies*, viii.
198. Wilson, *When Work Disappears*, xx, 202. See David Roediger, *The Wages of Whiteness: Race and the Making of the American Working Class* (New York: Verso, 1999); Jones, *American Work*, 391. A 1995 poll demonstrated that whites overestimated the number of African Americans in the population and, thus, their economic threat; Jones, 377.

attention and negative stereotyping toward them; the Ku Klux Klan's recent focus on Mexicans[199] signals this change of the times.

Biological and cultural racism has resurfaced at the same time that unions are declining, workplaces are being increasingly deregulated, and globalization is altering employment structures. In the circumstances, it provides an ideological tool for obscuring exploitation. Racism today, be it biological or cultural, makes open racial antagonism acceptable. And it has become just as acceptable to compare African Americans to other ethnic groups and thereby deflect attention from black–white relations (as historically constructed, not biologically given). Today's racism also obscures political and economic subordination as race and culture seemingly supersede these considerations. Finally, racism is actually encouraging conflict between blacks and other minority groups under the guise of "natural" difference, be it racial (they naturally abhor one another) or cultural (one group has a better work ethic, or one group can assimilate better). In this way, the origins of these comparisons are suppressed, and so are their underlying assumptions. To put it differently, the racialization and immigrantization of labor has come to articulate with economic and political exploitation, thus revealing biopolitical concerns that permeate all spheres. The white working class is positioned in the middle: on the one hand, racially denigrated themselves and at key times forming alliances with other oppressed groups; on the other, engaging in antagonistic politics and workplace behavior. Regardless, they are faced with the demands of a new ideal type of worker: docile, compliant, politically vulnerable, and marginalized.

Feminization of Labor

The feminization of labor was a logical outgrowth of the greater presence of female immigrants, the increasing power of racism—which was directed in particular toward African American males in the labor market—and the nature of the jobs available in the global economy, which either corresponded to women's "natures" (service work) or their sphere (the home or casual factories). The greater entry of poor women into the labor market has also been due to the radical restructuring of welfare, with its increasing emphasis on workfare. This greater participation of women in labor markets

199. See Jones, *American Work*, 377.

has altered relations between men and women in immigrant and African American communities.

First, the shift from welfare to workfare has led to a feminization of low-tier positions and has also created an industrial reserve army for the new economy.[200] Before the 1996 changes in welfare, the decision about whether to stay on welfare rather than work a low-wage job had been viewed as a practical one, in that low-wage jobs often pay badly and do not offer day care or health insurance.[201] That welfare is actually a better deal than a low-wage job is a rather significant point to make, in that welfare payments themselves are below the poverty line.[202] Many observers have noted that women on welfare are often forced to supplement their welfare payments with informal or under-the-table work, which then bolsters perceptions that they are cheats or criminals. However, since the 1996 changes, poor women can no longer make this decision. As I discussed in Chapter 1, welfare is now limited to two years, and several morality-based restrictions have been established that can lead to cut-off for non-compliance. In essence, the push is for poor women to work in workfare or other low-paid positions. In fact, it could be said that workfare, as it has been introduced, amounts to a tradeoff for low-tier employers: "Public and private employers alike prepared to reduce their unionized labor forces through attrition in order to make way for 'workfare' employees."[203] This inducement to work corresponds both to the needs of global capital and to the increasing influence of ascetic ideas in political decisions.[204]

Having to choose between a low-paid job and welfare benefits does not help an individual or family rise above the poverty line. A welfare state that is accessible to all—as in Europe—not only destigmatizes poverty but also ensures better child welfare and health. Europeans believe—at least, they generally used to—that social welfare is a right as well as a key component of citizenship (as T. H. Marshall is famous for arguing); in contrast, in the United States, welfare compels those who receive it to renounce their rights and citizenship, given their dependent status. The

200. See Wendy Brown regarding this point before the 1996 changes. Brown, *States of Injury: Power and Freedom in Late Modernity* (Princeton: Princeton University Press, 1995), 185n34.

201. See Wilson, *When Work Disappears*, 79–86.

202. See ibid., 80, 165; Kathleen Arnold, *Homelessness, Citizenship, and Identity* (Albany: SUNY Press, 2004), chap. 4; Deborah Connolly, *Homeless Mothers* (Minneapolis: University of Minnesota Press, 2000).

203. Jones, *American Work*, 381.

204. See Wilson, *When Work Disappears*, 209, on the misguided nature of the dismantling of welfare; see Jones, *American Work*, on the relation between workfare and the needs of global capital, 387.

connection made in this country between welfare and moral degeneracy forms a dialectical relationship with citizenship; that is, one is formulated as the opposite of the other. As well, participation in workfare does not transform former welfare recipients into citizens—they still fall under the state's surveillance; they still lack the bargaining power enjoyed by other workers; and poverty-level wages and the lack of benefits consign these individuals to continued poverty. Ascetic values have stigmatized welfare *as well as* certain forms of work, and as a result, these individuals pass from one form of exploitation (political) to another (politico-economic).

The transformation of welfare to workfare, then, has contributed to the feminization of labor in low-tier positions; it has also reinforced the imposition on the poor of the Protestant ethic, which demands hard work, long hours, and sexual abstention, among other things. The change from welfare to workfare is not only ascetic in nature but also a sign of racial antagonism and sexism (which points to the strengthening of bio-politics). As Wilson points out, there is a "positive relationship between hostile feelings toward blacks and opposition to welfare."[205] In particular there is hostility toward "welfare mothers," who are assumed to be over-whelmingly black.[206] As a consequence, poverty is often associated with race (even though most poor people are white) and welfare is closely correlated with gender. To summarize, hostility toward welfare is often paired with negative stereotyping in terms of race, gender, and class.[207]

Mirroring the new acceptability of racial thinking, and in tandem with the change in emphasis from cultural factors to individual and biological ones, there has been a shift toward compelling all able-bodied individuals to work and treating as outcasts those who do not. To put it differently, there is in effect a campaign—particularly in terms of workfare—to get individuals to accept any job they can.[208] This is part of the more general trend toward the feminization of labor: "The devolution of federal respon-sibility for the poor to the states [in the dismantling of welfare] was matched by an expanding power among individual corporations to seek out and hire the most tractable workforces possible, and to extract from those workers the highest rates of productivity at the lowest possible wages."[209]

205. Wilson, *When Work Disappears*, 203.

206. Ibid., 171. See Connolly, *Homeless Mothers*; Frances Fox Piven, "Poorhouse Politics," *The Progressive* 59, no. 2 (1995), on racialized images of welfare recipients and hostility toward African American single mothers.

207. See Wilson, *When Work Disappears*, 155–60, 166.

208. Ibid., 79, 164, 168, 169, 170.

209. Jones, *American Work*, 382.

In this way, the feminization of welfare[210] is linked to the feminization of the global workforce.

As noted earlier, this feminization occurs not only because of the greater availability of poor, low-skilled women for these jobs but also because this work is *associated* with women.[211] For example, many low-paying jobs are in the service sector and social services.[212] As a result, "unlike lower-educated men, lower-educated women are working more, not less, than in previous years,"[213] and women in general are occupying most of the new jobs in the service sector.[214] It is worth noting that African American women are being hired more often than African American men. As Wilson has demonstrated, the reasons why have to do with racial typing—which brings to light the prevalence of racial antagonism in the low-tier labor market, as well as the foundations for gender estrangement or antagonism.[215] Regarding the first point, he has found that there is a specific hostility to hiring African American men.[216] For example, one study found that employers view black women as "more responsible and determined or hav[ing] better attitudes and a better work ethic."[217] African American women are also viewed as less threatening and as *needing* to work because of the correlation between being poor and black and being a single mother (even though there are more single white mothers).[218]

Furthermore, there has been a marked decline in marriage rates. National data indicate no correlation between falling marriage rates and unemployment. Wilson, though, *has* found a correspondence in the inner cities,[219] and according to his account, it has been accompanied by a growing distrust between African American men and women. Correlation or no, there is less pressure to marry in this community than in some immigrant communities.[220] Marriage rates are also falling in non-black communities, but this does not stop family values rhetoric from targeting African Americans, and that rhetoric blames them for the decline of the nuclear family even though the decline is obviously a national issue (and, as noted

210. On this point, see Carole Pateman, *The Disorder of Women* (Stanford: Stanford University Press, 1992), chap. 8.
211. See Jones, *American Work,* 379.
212. See Wilson, *When Work Disappears,* 27–28, 32–33.
213. Ibid., 27.
214. Ibid., 154.
215. See ibid., 117–19.
216. See ibid., chap. 5.
217. Ibid., 123.
218. Ibid., 87. See also Piven.
219. Ibid., 95–105.
220. Ibid., 99–105.

earlier, is likely related to an internalization of the Protestant ethic rather than a rejection of it).[221]

Not only are African American women and men compared during hiring processes, but so also are immigrant women and African Americans. "Attitude" has been a key factor in hiring in the service economy; as a consequence, negative assumptions about African American women as "too poor, uneducated, and temperamentally ill-suited for the rigors of modern office work"[222] have entered into hiring decisions.[223] The growth in the female immigrant labor force has allowed these comparisons to be made, besides contributing to the feminization of labor more generally.

The greater entry of immigrant women into the labor market has obviously been a product of the 1965 changes in immigration policy—in particular the family reunification provision—but it also mirrors global trends toward the feminization of labor.[224] In fact, it can be argued—as Sassen does—that there is a clear correlation between the feminization of labor and the growth of export production in less industrialized countries, growth that in turn stimulates migrations. Even so, as Sassen notes, these three trends are rarely linked. She points out that "immigration and offshore production are ways of securing a low-wage labor force and of fighting the demands of organized workers in developed countries."[225] Obviously, when employment—in particular, service-sector employment—cannot be outsourced, it can be filled by immigrant labor. Jobs that are transferred to other countries are filled by low-wage workers in those countries. However, as discussed in Chapter 3, global processes are making it possible to keep these lower-tier, nonunion jobs in the United States, further linking the two developments.

But at the same time (also discussed in Chapter 3), low-paying factory work overseas can create bridges to the United States, thus spurring immigration from less industrialized countries. Significantly, both export manufacturing and export agriculture displace workers and small farmers, thus inducing migration to other countries. In fact, in certain regions (such as Latin America, Asia, and Africa), these processes are interconnected:

221. See ibid. Regarding family values (chap. 4, and 91, 93, 94, and 177) and regarding the idea that changes in family values reflect a broad U.S. trend and are not particular to the black community.

222. Jones, *American Work*, 380.

223. See Cornel West on this point.

224. See Shah regarding Asian immigrant women after 1965 and their work in the global economy.

225. Sassen, *Globalization and Its Discontents*, 111.

export agriculture has led to male emigration and the feminization of farming. Then, either later (in Asia, Africa) or around the same time (Latin America), export manufacturing leads to urban migration from rural areas when those farms can no longer compete in the global economy.[226] Most often, there has been an increase in hiring women in these areas, even as industries modernize: "The growth of labor-intensive manufacturing plants in several Third World countries, as well as the growing use of sweatshops and industrial homework via subcontracting both in the Third World and in highly industrialized countries, all point to the viability of these forms in 'modern' contexts."[227] The fact remains, however, that women are preferred to men when hiring is done—ostensibly, because certain jobs come to be associated with female labor. These trends also spur the migration of unemployed men in developing countries to the United States. In all these ways, the 1965 changes and the effects of export manufacturing and agriculture have combined to accelerate migration to the United States.[228]

Like other poor groups in the United States, immigrant women are often the lowest paid; they can function as a labor reserve.[229] Because of shifts in the supply of jobs and the growth of service positions, it should be no surprise that more and more immigrant women are participating in the labor market. However, as Sassen remarks, the word *feminization* does not simply imply greater participation of women; it also points to job slotting, with certain jobs being strongly correlated with women.[230] These changes have been transpiring in the context of the transformation in work conditions that I have discussed in terms of the impact of globalization on low-tier jobs in the United States. This does not mean that immigrant women are the predominant workforce for all low-tier jobs in the United States; in fact, their "occupational concentration" is far greater than for other groups. In other words, as immigrant women fill certain types of jobs in manufacturing and services, these types of employment become more and more prevalent among them.[231] Immigrant women are concentrated in operative and service employment, and this varies by nationality.[232] These trends challenge the individual view

226. Ibid., 112–13.
227. Ibid., 115.
228. Ibid., 118–20.
229. Ibid., 115–16.
230. Ibid., 120–21.
231. See ibid., 126, although this is not quite her argument.
232. See ibid., 127–29. Operative jobs include factory and warehouse work. The term designates unskilled work that is low-paid and involves miscellaneous tasks.

of immigration—the one which holds that immigrants themselves create these job opportunities (such as sweatshops and under-the-table day care) and thus evidence criminality. To summarize, the greater informalization of work, the downgrading of manufacturing, the increasing prevalence of service jobs, and the feminization of labor are all related.[233]

Nevertheless, relative to the deeper isolation that African American women in inner cities can experience, the feminization of labor for immigrants is perhaps more positive, in that it has led to increased autonomy and greater access to community organizations. Because they are earning an income, they have greater control over household economic decisions and are in direct contact with public services. In the context of the traditional roles so many of them had been filling in their countries of origin, this can only result in a change in gender relations and an increase in these women's autonomy.[234] In contrast to African Americans, marriage rates are not declining among poorer immigrants. The altered gender relations these immigrant women are undergoing may be antagonistic, but not in the same ways as they are for African Americans. This is not to idealize one situation over the other; nor is it to deny that these experiences overlap with intermarriage; rather, I am pointing out that circumstances may be different in the context of a group that still has high marriage and fertility rates.

With regard to both African American women and immigrant women, hiring poor women is convenient for a few reasons. First, they are paid less than poorer men. Low wages then increase dependence on men or the state, besides preventing unionization as workers are forced to work long hours to make a decent salary.[235] Second, they are considered more docile (although this perceived docility may be relative to the men to whom they are correlated), which is arguably true, though if it is, it is because of circumstances rather than biology. For example, paying women less than men increases women's dependence on both the state and the employer at the same that it impoverishes them.[236] For immigrant women, poor language skills can heighten perceptions that they are vulnerable and that they are filling roles that their cultural traditions expect them to fill.[237]

233. Ibid., 131.
234. See ibid., 91.
235. Wilson, *When Work Disappears*, 27. See Brown's discussion of the consequences of this in *States of Injury*, 184. See Sassen, *Globalization and Its Discontents*, 121–26.
236. This point was made by Simone de Beauvoir, *The Second Sex*, trans. and ed. H. M. Parshley (New York: Vintage Books, 1989), chap. 8, and more recently by Wendy Brown, 185.
237. See Honig's discussion of the perceived vulnerability of Russian "mail order" brides, who, once they begin to speak English better and learn to assert their rights, are then viewed as predatory and dangerous. Honig, *Democracy and the Foreigner*, chap. 4.

Also, the social isolation that single mothers experience can increase their feelings of powerlessness and, in this way, maintain exploitative labor relations. What is more, low-tier work by its very nature is located in marginal areas—in sweatshops, *maquiladoras,* or homes, or along national borders, for example. Or, in the case of service work, labor is not necessarily performed in any one location (for example, a janitorial company will contract out with various employers). The marginality of these locations strongly suggests why it is that so many women who cross the Mexican border to work in *maquiladoras* have been murdered in recent years.[238] As a result of deregulation, these workspaces constitute a space not only of exploitation but also of bare life.

Third, the greater feminization of labor reinforces the sexual division of labor at the same time that it creates gender antagonism. This dynamic is buttressed by government policies, even though it would appear that the state has absented itself by deregulating the economy and by establishing workfare programs, which supposedly are designed to foster independence. As Brown states: "The state's role in these arrangements lies in securing, though private property rights, capitalist relations of production in the first place; buttressing and mediating—through production subsidies, contracts, bailouts, and fiscal regulation—these relations of production; maintaining—through legal and political regulation of marriage, sexuality, contraception and abortion—control of women's reproductive work; and perpetuating, through a gendered welfare and unemployment benefits system and the absence of quality public day care, the specifically capitalist sexual division of labor."[239] In this way, state power is strengthened even as its relations with capital can lead to the loss of sovereignty in other ways. Meanwhile, the move to workfare alters relations between women and the state, uniting the political and economic more closely even as certain forms of surveillance are no longer possible.

The perceived docility of poor women, combined with their social isolation and dependence, often leads to highly exploitative conditions. As Sassen describes, conditions in casual factories abroad often lead to deteriorating health. In new industrial zones, female workers are often fired after a brief amount of time because "after three to five years of assembling components under microscopes, these workers typically suffer from headaches and deteriorating eyesight. In order to keep wage levels

---

238. See, for example, Mark Stevenson, "Border Slayings Fuel Anger at US," *Boston Globe,* April 4, 1999, A8; but many more women have been killed since then—mostly in Ciudad Juárez.
239. Brown, *States of Injury,* 185–86.

low and replace workers whose health begins to fail, firms continually fire their older workers and hire young, healthier, and more compliant cohorts of women."[240] Sweatshops and *maquiladoras* in the United States and along the Mexican border are often exposed as having similar conditions, which are possible in an economy that is increasingly deregulated and where unions are weak.[241] Simone de Beauvoir's description of women's exploitation during the Industrial Revolution reads like a page out of Sassen. As needlework, lacemaking, and other activities moved from households to factories, women began to work long hours in unhygienic conditions, often becoming too sick to work. As with employment conditions now, the lack of unionization allowed for women's greater exploitation as well as gender antagonism: "It is understandable that male workers at first saw a formidable danger in this cut-rate competition and that they exhibited hostility to it."[242] The proliferation of industrial homework and casual factories mirrors these conditions of the nineteenth century and, furthermore, erodes the division between public and private.[243]

That women continue to perform household duties and care for children unremunerated, more so than men, increases the likelihood that they will be exploited in that they are often not free to pursue training programs or to participate in activities that would increase their competitiveness in the labor market. Guillaumin calls this the "appropriation of women," which is the consequence of reducing women to material objects and of wholly appropriating their labor in the home *and* as wage laborers. This process includes the appropriation of women's time as potentially limitless; the appropriation of the products of the body; sexual obligations; and the normative expectation that it is women who will care for children, the elderly, and their sexual partners. In this way, a material appropriation of the body is brought about.[244] For similar reasons, Spivak calls the feminization of labor "pimping" and remarks (as I quoted in Chapter 1) that "now women all over the world are absorbing many of the costs of management, of health care, of workplace safety and the like by working at home."[245]

At first glance, the feminization of labor would seem to be improving the situation of women. This case could in fact be made because immigrant

240. Sassen, *Globalization and Its Discontents*,43.
241. See, for example, Adler, *Mollie's Job*.
242. See Beauvoir, *The Second Sex*, 117.
243. See Brown, *States of Injury*, 194.
244. Guillaumin, *Racism*, 179, 180.
245. Spivak, "Race before Racism," 336, 341.

women were becoming more politically active and more autonomous. For all women workers, it could be held that they were becoming more economically independent and that they were engaging in spheres outside the home. Gender relations *are* being altered so that women are becoming less subordinate. Finally, these workers are making possible the existence of services needed by low-income residents in the inner cities.

Nevertheless, poor African American women in the inner cities have been found to be especially socially isolated, and informal or casual work conditions can worsen this isolation as well as prevent any upward mobility in labor participation.[246] Moreover, this situation has led to the greater impoverishment of these communities as well as increased child poverty.[247] Real wages have not improved in recent years; the feminization of labor has been accompanied by lower overall income levels, longer hours of work, and greater physical deterioration or danger.[248] These trends signal the greater exploitation of workers in blue-collar work and the growing immiseration of the poor. Finally, women's gains are not happening in a bubble; they are being made because poorer men are losing their blue-collar jobs and themselves are being increasingly marginalized, socially, economically, and politically. Specifically, less educated men's employment rates and incomes have been falling as women have been moving into the labor force.[249]

In another vein, the three processes I have described—the "immigrantization," racialization, and feminization of labor—demonstrate that whatever conceptual separations have been foisted on these groups, their labor histories are tightly intertwined. That immigrants, blacks, and women are portrayed more often than not as distinct reveals ethnic, gender, and class antagonisms rather than social realities. And just as "immigrantization" and racialization have been occurring at the same time as a backlash against immigration and the emergence of a new racism, the feminization of labor displays sexism and antagonism toward poor women. For example, African American women are especially being targeted in family values campaigns and antiwelfare rhetoric, yet they are also held responsible if they are single mothers or if they leave their children at home in order to work. The portrayal of poor immigrant women as

246. Wilson, *When Work Disappears,* 144, for example.

247. See ibid., 91–93, 106, 109.

248. See Jones, *American Work,* 386, for example.

249. Paul J. Devereux, "Changes in Male Labor Supply and Wages," *Industrial and Labor Relations Review* 56 (April 2003): 409–27.

docile is equally problematic, in that this trait is valued in women and is viewed as a positive attribute when workers are being hired in the new economy. Poor language skills, economic vulnerability, and the "proclivity" to fill traditional gender roles ensure women's subordination and exploitation and yet are precisely the characteristics that employers find desirable. In fact, immigrant women themselves may perceive that accepting exploitation and sexism is an "ethical choice" if they are to be "good women."[250]

On the one hand, poor African American women are made out to be the paradigm of all that is wrong with American family values, the degeneration of intelligence, and the decline of the work ethic. On the other hand, poor and vulnerable immigrant women are viewed as the paradigm of what is desirable in women: docile, willing to work for low pay, and accepting of exploitative work without complaint. The posing of these two paradigms against each other not only demonstrates ethnic, racial, and gender antagonism between economic elites and these poorer women but also fosters antagonism between these two groups of poorer workers. In turn, the relative docility of African American workers and immigrant women is juxtaposed to African American and Latino men's intractability and criminality. These paradigms are not merely economic outcomes; they are *generated* by the partnership of global capital and the state (which is why they serve as ideology *and* discourse) and in this way serve to create a new and highly contradictory ideal type of worker.

It would appear that these developments have been occurring at the same time that the government has become increasingly absent or weak. For example, faulty legislation has resulted in greater waves of immigration and the dismantling of welfare and affirmative action, which seemingly has allowed the market to choose which groups to hire. However, the supposed absence of government responsibility for these trends is deceitful in several ways. First: "Just as microelectronics assembly plants in Third World Free Trade Zones do not simply employ women workers but produce them—their bodies, social relations, sexualities, life conditions, genders, psyches, consciousnesses—the state does not simply handle clients or employ staff but produces state subjects, as bureaucratized, dependent, disciplined, and gendered."[251] Second: "Free market purists decry the interference of the federal government in hiring practices, but ignore the myriad ways that federal policies have always shaped, and continue to

250. See Spivak, "Race before Racism," 342.
251. Brown, *States of Inquiry*, 195.

shape, the composition and size of the domestic labor market." For example, it is the government that sets interest rates, awards defense contracts, establishes workfare programs, and offers tax breaks for certain companies. "Therefore, calls for the cessation of 'government interference' in hiring practices have a disingenuous ring about them; employers object to such 'interference' only when they perceive it to hinder their own economic interests."[252] In fact, though deregulation may well "deterritorialize national territory" in many ways, as Sassen argues, it also strengthens state sovereignty and the *need* for prerogative in the United States. Blue-collar workers are no longer the paradigm of citizenship. They are now truly or historically disenfranchised; viewed as marginal, illegal, and immoral; and denigrated along racial and cultural lines. Activities such as unionization, political protest, and simply refusing to accept exploitative work are not viewed as forms of valid political dissent or group empowerment but rather as threatening, separatist, and—most importantly—criminal.[253]

This is how state power can be linked today to the greater exploitation of blue-collar work. For example, workfare, guest-worker policies, prison labor, and breaks for international companies as a consequence of deregulation have all increased state policing and state encouragement of dismal labor conditions instead of allowing for a purely free market. Incarcerated labor shares certain similarities with that of guest workers; both are monitored by the state so that wages and terms of employment are fixed, unionization is forbidden, freedom of mobility has been lost, and the labor is not recognized as contributing to the economy. Slavelike conditions for poor immigrants of color, prison labor, and low-tier labor in deteriorating inner cities have combined with racial profiling of African Americans and immigrants of color; this supports my contention that the state is increasing its prerogative power. And ascetic criteria are not only strengthening that power but also obscuring economic and political exploitation.

To summarize, all three histories intertwine and help explain one another. First, the United States' racial policies, both domestic (in relation to African Americans) and foreign (in relation to immigration policy), have helped depoliticize and thereby naturalize ethnic and racial antagonisms. Second, the influx of immigrants has resulted in radical demographic changes in urban areas and created a supply of low-wage workers at a convenient time, that is, while economic restructuring has been going on. The depression

252. Jones, *American Work*, 387.
253. Although it should be noted that major unions are now recruiting immigrants, which is a reversal of a historically anti-immigration stance.

of wages has ignited ethnic antagonisms in two ways: poor, urban African Americans are being forced to compete with immigrants; and recent waves of immigration have enabled the feminization of labor. The War on Drugs and racism directed against African American males has also encouraged the feminization of labor by exacerbating gender splits, effecting changes in the nuclear family, and altering gender roles culturally and economically and—it follows—politically. In times of economic instability—times that supposedly increase "freedom" through "flexibility" and "open" markets—elite European Americans feel threatened by these groups yet focus on *their* antagonism.

Conclusion

This chapter has demonstrated, first of all, that the history of these groups is intertwined in ways that highlight how conventional distinctions are inaccurate and misleading. Racism is able to flourish today because of the greater presence of immigrants, which makes it possible to generate divisions between the two "groups" even though they share many of the same circumstances and experiences. Similarly, the feminization of labor is a logical outcome of the greater participation of immigrants and African Americans in low-tier positions. At the same time, and fostering both these developments, political control is being directed toward male workers, and fears of uprisings or protests are encouraging the hiring of the most docile (powerless) workers. In all of this, species thinking and thus bio-power are at work. Racial, gendered, and ethnic thinking, prejudice, and antagonisms are the ideological and discursive effects of biopower, as sovereign power and capitalist values increasingly intersect.

The notion that the state and the economy occupy separate spheres is no longer tenable. For example, the changes in labor demographics and the accompanying ideational obscuring of those changes have not occurred solely in the economic sphere; they have been actively promoted by the state. Additionally, sovereignty now focuses on economic issues rather than those of Cold War politics; as a result, open markets and deregulation are shoring up state power instead of depleting it. At first glance, one might think that sovereignty loses its reason to exist as market logic takes over; what has actually happened is that neoliberals have reconceived sovereignty so that it continues to operate but in a more dispersed manner, in such a way that it has in fact benefited from the contingencies of the new political and economic contexts.

Whatever the transformations in nation-states given the internationalization of the economy, prerogative power is being strengthened. What *are* disappearing are democratic practices and spaces for those practices. This is partly because those who are most affected by economic changes and who face the most instability therefrom are viewed as criminal, unassimilated, or ungrateful. Prerogative power today is justified against those who are "outside"—whether that word is applied in terms of geographic borders or social and cultural assimilation. It is significant that all of us are being affected by the convergence of job insecurity and fears of terrorism. When these two factors combine, the suspension of law becomes defensible on all fronts even though this never quite alleviates anxiety and instability. Also, the view that poverty and insecurity inhere to only a few groups allows those who are not of those groups to deny their own fragility in the new economy.[254] In this sort of climate, immigrants are easily viewed as terrorists, and other minorities (especially African American men) are perceived as outsiders, as a violent "underclass." The biological nature of the new racism and sexism has created a divide between those who are civilized and those who are "natural"; this justifies the application of force against the latter groups.

Groups are being increasingly dehumanized—viewed as biological life—precisely at a time when both economic instability and the threat of terrorism seem long-term. The enemy is being generalized; thus it is becoming more difficult to pin down; as a consequence, fears of terrorism and economic instability are being projected onto those within our borders who are perceived as "others"; as a final step, this justifies the normalization of the state of exception.

In Chapters 3 and 4, I have analyzed how exploitation occurs today and who is being exploited and thus treated as bare life. In the next chapter, I consider prerogative power in its more concrete manifestations as well as possible approaches to addressing the debilitated political status of the new working class. I turn to Simone de Beauvoir's notion of authentic love to propose a new view of the problem of bare life that Giorgio Agamben has posed. Changes in power relations need not require that biopower be removed from questions of sovereignty in order to make certain groups "human." Such changes will, however, require a rejection of the human–bare life hierarchy in favor of a dialectical tension between immanence (bare life) and transcendence (life beyond bare life).

---

254. See Wilson, *When Work Disappears*, 220, 232, 235.

5

WAR AND "LOVE"

So far in this book I have analyzed ascetic values based on the Protestant ethic that have justified treating certain groups as less than citizens. The very morality that ostensibly signals an increasing humanitarianism in politics is precisely dehumanizing in this regard. I have also examined the liberal roots of prerogative power in Locke to suggest that liberal democracy does not preclude the domestic exercise of prerogative. In fact, as a result of the dominance of neoliberal policies, the exercise of prerogative has increased. I have linked these ideas to the notions of political and economic exploitation and to the increasing dominance of biopower. In particular, the new racism, the anti-immigration sentiments that took root in the 1990s, and the resurgence of normative demands that female workers be docile and submissive have all been ideological effects of the dynamics explored in earlier chapters. These dynamics have created a new paradigm of the ideal flexible worker, whoever is doing the work.

Thus far, I have underscored the notion that prerogative power is a crucial part of modern citizenship and liberal power. In this chapter, I elaborate on this theory of prerogative in order to examine how "war" is being waged against low-tier workers. In suggesting this, I am not claiming that prerogative power is the only operative modality of late-modern power; I *am* saying that its exercise has become regular and systematic, as will be evidenced by the cases I investigate below. Similar to my critique of asceticism in the first chapter, I will be questioning the wars that are being waged today in the name of humanity and good (for example, "infinite justice"), as well as how they are linked to the ascetic ideational system that justifies prerogative. Ascetic policies—especially neoliberal ones—seemingly depoliticize discourses and deployments of power by portraying them as moral and private, and as interventions rather than prerogative acts; in much the same way, the wars on terror, drugs, and narcoterrorism are being framed in moral terms, as police interventions, and are thereby depoliticized.[1] These wars not only efface political processes and exercises of sovereignty, but also the linkages between these and the construction of bare life domestically and internationally.

I do not want to suggest that a politics of bare life is the only political process operating; I will however, be evaluating the consequences of neo-liberal politics and economics for poor workers in the present day. Even if this power is "absolute" in many ways, its deployment in dispersed sites and through a variety of agents makes it porous, allowing for pockets of resistance. I believe that my arguments suggest a way to explain how low-tier work is both politically and economically exploitative. In examining the problems set forth in this book, I will be offering theoretical approaches that bring together Simone de Beauvoir's notion of truly mutual relation-ships as a call to hold immanence (bare life) and transcendence (life beyond bare life) in healthy tension; Michel Foucault's concepts of power and resistance; and Giorgio Agamben's call for extraterritoriality and potentiality as the focal points of a new politics. Their writings suggest that the many acts of resistance already being carried out are challenging the sovereignty of the state on a daily basis; and furthermore, that the context of reception—that is, in institutions and entrenched political processes—needs to be systematically opened to democratic possibilities in order to ensure that democracy can flourish better than it has been. By looking at those who have been treated as bare life, we can deduce concrete solutions—greater unionization, a living wage, political power for temporary workers, the elimination of guest-worker programs as they currently exist, the free movement of people equal to the free movement of capital, and more abstractly, a radical challenge to discourses and policies that hierarchize public/private, full-time/part-time, native-born/immigrant, rational/irrational, assimilated/unassimilated, and reproductive/

---

1. See Slavoj Žižek, "Are We in a War? Do We Have an Enemy?" *London Review of Books* 24, May 23, 2002, http://www.lrb.co.uk; Michael Hardt and Antonio Negri, *Empire* (Cam-bridge, Mass.: Harvard University Press, 2000), 34–38.

productive work. This is not a call to rehumanize citizenship[2] or to revitalize rights discourse but to recognize that the *stateless* should be guiding our notions of political inclusion rather than the model of the citizen on which we have been relying.[3] This does not mean that the marginalized should be privileged over the mainstream; it *does* mean considering what has heretofore been viewed as anomalous as a guide for future political and economic decisions and alliances.

War

April 2, 1996: The FBI opened a civil rights investigation Tuesday into the video-taped clubbing of two illegal immigrants. Sheriff's deputies clubbed the immigrants Monday after chasing a battered pickup crammed with people suspected of sneaking across the border. TV news helicopters captured the beating on video in broad daylight. One deputy, holding his baton two-handed like a baseball bat, was videotaped clubbing the driver on the back and shoulders, even as the driver fell to the ground. When a woman got out of the cab, the same deputy beat her in the back with the baton, then grabbed her by the hair and pulled her to the ground. At least one other deputy struck her with his baton. Neither of the two Mexican citizens appeared to resist or attempt to get away from the white officers.[4]
—"FBI TO PROBE BEATING OF ILLEGAL IMMIGRANTS," *DAILY BRUIN*, APRIL 3, 1996, 6

It would be honest and, above all, more useful to investigate carefully the juridical procedures and deployments of power by which human beings could be so completely deprived of their rights and prerogatives that no act committed against them could appear any longer as a crime. (At this point, in fact, everything had truly become possible.)
—GIORGIO AGAMBEN, *HOMO SACER*[5]

---

2. As some contemporary authors want to do—see Bryan S. Turner and Chris Rojek, *Society and Culture: Principles of Scarcity and Solidarity* (London: Sage Publications, 2001), 120–23.

3. As Giorgio Agamben suggests in "We Refugees," trans. Michael Rocke, n.d., http://www.egs.edu/faculty/agamben/agamben-we-refugees.html.

4. "FBI to Probe Beating of Illegal Immigrants," *Daily Bruin*, April 3, 1996, 6. See "ACLU of Southern California Settles Mexican Immigrant Beating Case," June 20, 1997, http://archive.aclu.org/news/n062097d.html; "Deputies Suspended After Caught Beating Suspected Illegal Immigrants," April 2, 1996, http://www.cnn.com/US/9604/02/ immigrant.beating/index2.html; "Woman Beaten by Deputies Released from Custody," April 3, 1996, http://www.cnn.com/US/9604/03/police_beating/index.html..

5. Agamben, *Homo Sacer: Sovereign Power and Bare Life*, trans. Daniel Heller-Roazen (Stanford: Stanford University Press, 1998), 171.

As I argued in Chapter 2, prerogative power has been conceived of as a part of liberal democracy rather than as antithetical to it. The deployment of sovereignty is considered legitimate in that it is exercised on behalf of the common good rather than reflecting a monarch's personal whims or interests.[6] Hence, consent is not necessary but the preconditions— wisdom, and the common good (or national interest, in modern parlance)— characterize the difference between what John Locke would call arbitrary power and prerogative.[7] Nevertheless, prerogative power is still arbitrary in that it is exercised outside of the law and, in its fullest expression, can include total violence and war making. Prerogative is deployed in the State of Nature where reason is possible but consent is not. Furthermore, according to Locke, prerogative can be exercised domestically but is under the purview of federative power, which deals with foreign affairs. In this way, "the internal/external distinction serves to create a domestic domain for *Staatsräson* while lodging it in the same constitutional hands as power over foreign affairs."[8] Thus, Western political theorists of the modern state have never really conceived of the absence of prerogative within state boundaries. Rather, in a modern nation-state, the rule of law can be used to suspend the law; in this way, prerogative power is not outside the rule of law but inextricably bound to it.[9] Moreover, the exercise of prerogative is not dictatorial per se but must be considered in terms of its "democratic" context.[10]

Prerogative is rational in that it refers to the law and some legislative or juridical procedures are often required in order to suspend the law. But this suspension can nevertheless be unpredictable (for example, in the degree or type of violence exerted), and the agents are not hindered by law as they would be in other contexts. There are examples of the

6. See Sheldon Wolin, "Democracy and the Welfare State: The Political and Theoretical Connections between Staatsräson and Wohlfahrtsstaatsräson," in *The Presence of the Past: Essays on the State and the Constitution* (Baltimore: Johns Hopkins University Press, 1989); as well as Pasquale Pasquino, "Locke on King's Prerogative," *Political Theory* 26 (April 1998), 198–208, on the importance of this point.

7. John Locke, *Second Treatise of Government* (Cambridge: Hackett Publishing, Classics Series, 1980), chap. Xiv; and see Pasquino on this distinction in Locke.

8. Wolin, "Democracy and the Welfare State," 168.

9. Nevertheless, this does not produce a black-and-white situation of within-the-law/ outside-the-law but rather a juridically undecidable situation. See Agamben, *State of Exception* (Chicago: University of Chicago Press, 2005).

10. The mistake that is made is to call this absolute power in Carl Schmitt's sense of a dictator. Both Agamben, in *State of Exception,* and Pasquino discuss how this power can still be called prerogative or the state of exception even though it differs from monarchical prerogative and dictatorship in Schmitt's conception.

positive exercise of prerogative power—most notably, the Emancipation Proclamation decreed by Abraham Lincoln—but the precariousness of this benevolence must be emphasized. The subject of prerogative power, whether treated compassionately, indifferently, or violently, has been stripped of all legal rights, be they de facto or de jure. As I have argued, Agamben's notion of bare life (that is, biological life) captures the idea of a subject who is treated outside of the law, as a wartime enemy might be. Biological racism, sexism, ethnic hatred, and xenophobia are all signs that an individual's status has been reduced to biological life.

The clearest example of the contemporary U.S. exercise of prerogative power domestically is Guantánamo Bay. Technically, the United States can argue that this is not a site of domestic power because the detention center is on foreign ground, but this land is essentially an annex to the United States.[11] Furthermore, it is not in a war zone and therefore is not conceived of as temporary either geographically or temporally. In fact, the suspension of law on the island was first declared when Haitian refugees were housed there in 1991;[12] thus, this suspension was not first conceived of as a requirement of war. The absence of any rule of law in this case is fairly obvious, but more so when Iraqi detainees were designated as enemy combatants rather than as prisoners of war (POWs), who would at least be protected by the Geneva Convention.[13] The justification for this legally blurry geopolitical space has been the threat to national security that these individuals pose.

Correspondingly, the Patriot Act seemingly was passed in exceptional circumstances and is apparently directed at a narrow group—male Arabs and Muslims.[14] The results of that act and the piecemeal adoption of provisions in what has been called the Patriot Act II have been discussed and criticized in the media, in public debate, and in academe, for example. Yet the consequences—the abuses at Abu Ghraib,[15] the tactics used at

11. See Daphne Eviatar, "Nowhere Land," *Boston Globe*, April 18, 2004, E4.

12. Ibid.

13. See Eyal Press, "Tortured Logic," *amnestynow*, Summer 2003; Charlie Savage, "Justices Struggle to Find Balance on Detainee Policy," *Boston Globe*, April 29, 2004, A3; "Rationalizing Torture," *Boston Globe*, June 13, 2004, H10; Dana Priest and Joe Stephens, "Harsh Questioning Methods Were OK'd for Cuba Prison," *Boston Globe*, May 9, 2004, A20.

14. It is interesting to note that a Vietnamese refugee—Viet Dinh—was one of the chief architects of the Patriot Act.

15. See Bryan Bender, "Activists Urge Probe of U.S. Detention Policies," *Boston Globe*, June 17, 2004, A2.

Guantánamo Bay,[16] the use of secret prisons,[17] and the continued surveillance of thousands of residents of the United States[18]—have not brought an end to the continued implementation of these measures.[19] Even amidst criticisms and the exposure of abuses, various parts of "Patriot II" have been passed.[20] It is argued that 9/11 and the War on Terror have forced the American public to accept some hard choices, including the need to suspend some individual liberties for some residents for the time being. The recent renewal of major provisions of the Patriot Act, the signing statement on torture,[21] the ongoing use of free-speech zones and exclusion zones, and President George W. Bush's unprecedented use of signing statements affirm that prerogative power has been expanded.[22]

Thus, the events of 9/11 have seemingly brought about a state of emergency that requires extensive tightening of policing, surveillance, and immigration services at home and abroad. Yet the incident described

16. Including dressing prisoners in red to make them think they will be executed. Scott Higham, "Camp Memos Tell of Detainees' Fear," *Boston Globe*, June 13, 2004, A3. See "Rationalizing Torture," *Boston Globe*, June 13, 2004, H10.

17. See Priest, "CIA Holds Terror Suspects in Secret Prisons," *Washington Post*, November 2, 2005, A1; Jason Burke, "Secret World of U.S. Jails," *The Observer International*, June 13, 2004; CNN, "Bush: CIA Holds Terror Suspects in Secret Prisons," September 7, 2006, http://www.CNN.com/2006/POLITICS/09/06/bush.speech.html.

18. See Beverley Lumpkin, "Patriot Act Redux," February 21, 2003, http://abcnews.go.com/sections/us/HallsOf Justice; Shelley Murphy, "Prosecutors Defend 'Sneak and Peek' Warrant," *Boston Globe*, October 30, 2003, B3.

19. Alternatively, calls to replace John Ashcroft and the move to do so do not indicate the declining significance of raison d'état on domestic terrain. His replacement by Alberto Gonzales, who wrote the legal justification for designating Iraqi detainees as enemy combatants, effectively changed nothing but appeased critics who had called for Ashcroft's resignation after the Iraqi prison scandal. See, for example, "Bush Attorney General Pick Is Alberto Gonzales," November 2004, http://www.cnn.com/2004/ALLPOLITICS/11/10/bush.cabinet/index.html.

20. See David Martin,"With a Whisper, Not a Bang," *San Antonio Current*, December 24, 2003, http://www.sacurrent.com. Measures continue to be passed as of this writing.

21. See Terry M. Neal, "A Dangerous Veto Threat," *Washington Post*, November 15, 2005, http://washingtonpost.com; President's Statement on Signing of H.R. 2863, "Department of Defense, Emergency Supplemental Appropriations to Address Hurricanes in the Gulf of Mexico, and Pandemic Influenza Act, 2006," December 30, 2005, http://www.whitehouse.gov/news/releases/2005/12/20051230-8.html.

22. See American Civil Liberties Union, "Free Speech Zone," September 23, 2003, http://www.aclu.org/FreeSpeech/FreeSpeech.cfm?ID=13699&c=86; Julie Hilden, "Constitutionality of Free Speech Zones," August 4, 2004, http://www.cnn.com/2004/LAW/08/04/hilden.freespeech; Jim Hightower, "Bush Zones Go National," *The Nation*, July 29, 2004, http://www.thenation.com/doc.mhtml?i=20040816&s=hightower; Charlie Savage, "Bush Could Bypass New Torture Ban," *Boston Globe*, January 4, 2006, http://boston.com; John Dean, "The Problem with Presidential Signing Statements: Their Use and Misuse by the Bush Administration," FindLaw, January 13, 2006, http://writ.news.findlaw.com/dean/2006 0113.html.

in the above epigraph indicates that the suspension of law is not exceptional (that is, only called forth during wartime), nor is it aimed at those
suspected of terrorist activities or other violent crimes; rather, it is being
deployed on groups perceived as bare life, to use Agamben's term. Next,
I establish how prerogative power is being exercised domestically (and
not just in wartime or at the international level), regularly (rather than as
a state of exception), and on individuals considered bare life (rather than
on "enemies" per se).[23]

Even before 9/11 the U.S. government had begun jailing and deporting
record numbers of immigrants as a result of the Antiterrorism and
Effective Death Penalty Act and the Illegal Immigration Reform and Immigration Responsibility Act (IIRIRA), both of which were passed in 1996.
But it was not terrorists who were being deported; targeted instead were
individuals with drunken driving records from the 1970s, or who had
written bad checks, or whose visa status was indeterminate. In fact, under
these laws the number-one destination country for deportation was Mexico,
a country that has not been associated with Middle Eastern terrorism.[24]
Haitians are also technically near the top of this list, though they tend to
escape this juridical classification because they are most often intercepted
in the water—a circumstance that denies them the right to an appeal or
hearing and, it follows, the possibility of legal deportation.[25] The incident
described in the epigraph occurred on April 2, 1996, and was remarkable
only because it did not receive the national attention or outrage that the
Rodney King incident had earlier.[26] These immigrants were perceived as

23. As Agamben states: "The originary political relation is marked by this zone of
indistinction in which the life of the exile . . . borders on the life of *homo sacer* who can be
killed but not sacrificed. This relation is more original than the Schmittian opposition
between friend and enemy, fellow citizen and foreigner." *Homo Sacer*, 110.

24. William Branigin and Gabriel Escobar, "INS Deportations Rising," *Boston Globe*, April 25,
1999, A19; John Budris, "Jailed Immigrant a Man Without a Country," *Boston Globe*, May 9,
1999, B6; Nancy Gertner and Daniel Kanstroom, "The Recent Spotlight on the INS Failed to
Reveal Its Dark Side," *Boston Globe*, May 21, 2000, E1, E3; David L. Marcus, "Three Times
and Out," *Boston Globe*, October 14, 1998, A1; Patrick J. McDonnell, "Judges Rule Against
Indefinite INS Jailings," *Boston Globe*, July 12, 1999, A4; Teresa Mears, "As INS Jails Fill, a
Release Plan Surfaces," *Boston Globe*, February 14, 1999, A16; Teresa Mears, "The Woes of
Immigrants Forced to Emigrate," *Boston Globe*, March 26, 2000, A6; "Secret Trials in America,"
Boston Globe, December 4, 1999, A18; "U.S. Deportations at Record Level," *Boston Globe*,
May 14, 1997, A3.

25. See Viet D. Dinh, "Law and Asylum," in *Arguing Immigration*, ed. Nicolaus Mills
(New York: Touchstone, 1994); Jerry Seper, "U.S. Prepares for Haitian Refugees," *Washington
Times*, February 24, 2004, http://www.washingtontimes.com.

26. Rodney King was the African American man whose beating by California police was
videotaped in March 1991. The jury acquittal of four officers involved sparked the Los
Angeles riots or uprising.

lawbreakers by virtue of their status; yet at the same time they were viewed as entirely outside the law. Clearly, the suspension of law is not just for enemy combatants, nor does it occur only on foreign soil.

Would-be refugees and migrants are often detained indefinitely in holding cells, and brutalized while so held, much like the detainees at Guantánamo. These cases receive far less media and political attention even though this is another example of the regular suspension of law. These people, whose range from infants to the elderly, are held without charge and without legal recourse and are often detained in cells with criminals (although this may change in the case of children). Furthermore, they can be detained indefinitely.[27] There are about four thousand such individuals held each year.[28] That the law has been suspended for these people is obvious, and to make things worse, the benevolence of those who are guarding them is entirely arbitrary. In the case of Abner Louima, the Haitian immigrant who was sodomized and beaten by police officers in August 1997, the suspension of law worked against him. Admittedly, these police officers were brought to "justice." The point is that detained immigrants are not citizens and do not receive the same protections; arguably, this is why abuses occur more frequently. Similarly, the prison guards at Abu Ghraib have also been sentenced, but this has not changed the precarious legal status of Iraqi prisoners. In the same vein, immigrants are treated as outside the law when they are deported quickly or are denied the right to appeal decisions made about their residency status.[29]

Since the implementation of the Patriot Act, men of Arab, South Asian, and/or Islamic identity have been detained and subject to surveillance, often being charged with crimes other than terrorism (when charged at all).[30] Not only that, but various other immigrants have been subject to the

27. See Monica Rhor, "Unwelcome Turn," *Boston Globe*, August 7, 2003, B1; Gertner and Kanstroom, "The Recent Spoltlight"; McDonnell, "Judges Rule Against," *Boston Globe*, July 12, 1999, A4; "U.S. Frees Ethiopian Jew Held Nine Years," *Boston Globe*, May 24, 1999, A6; Budris, "Jailed Immigrant."

28. See Rhor, "Unwelcome Turn"; David Oliver Relin, "Who Will Stand Up for Them?" *Parade Magazine*, August 4, 2002.

29. See Lisa Getter and Jonathan Peterson, "Speedier Rate of Deportation Rulings Assailed," *Los Angeles Times*, January 5, 2003, http://www.latimes.com; Carol J. Williams, "Rapid U.S. Deportation Forces New Route on Haitian Refugees," *Boston Globe*, July 13, 2003, A11; Branigin and Escobar, "INS Deportations Rising"; Rachel L. Swarns, "Study Finds Disparities in Judges' Asylum Rulings," *New York Times*, July 31, 2006.

30. See Vickie Chachere, "Fla. School Trustees Back Bid to Fire Palestinian Professor," *Boston Globe*, December 20, 2001, A25; Judith Graham, "Congressman Wants Deportation of Immigrant Student," *Boston Sunday Globe*, September 29, 2002, A15; Jane Wardell, "Amnesty Says Rights Are Casualty in War on Terrorism," *Boston Globe*, May 29, 2003, A20.

same controls even though they are in no way affiliated with terrorism.[31] Indeed, the Patriot Act should be viewed as on a continuum with the 1996 terrorism provisions rather than as an exception too those provisions (or to put it differently, the passage of the Patriot Act indicates that the state of exception has become the rule, as Walter Benjamin would say).[32]

Just as I have argued that the seemingly moral values behind welfare reform are a form of control and a means for exercising prerogative power; so too are the Patriot Act and related laws and deployments of prerogative aimed at greater surveillance and control of *all* immigrants, not just suspected terrorists. One example is the treatment of two individuals as enemy combatants inside the United States; both were held for more than two years, in near total isolation and without access to legal representation.[33] More broadly, the ongoing updates on terror levels, the constant reminders of terrorist threats, and the implication that the mere presence of individuals from certain countries can pose a national security threat all suggest that times are uncertain and that we should limit our own freedoms and police ourselves and others.[34]

As Hannah Arendt, Sheldon Wolin, and Giorgio Agamben have variously argued, the suspension of law in these situations is directly dependent on legislative enactment. For example, the change of status for Iraqi detainees from POWs to enemy combatants was argued and framed in terms of international law; and a legislative act enabled the deployment of prerogative power. It might be objected that these cases, while reprehensible on their own terms, say nothing about U.S. democracy or citizenship; however, that argument can be made only if the prerogative exercised on foreigners is viewed as entirely different from that which is exercised on U.S. citizens (but is not, according to this objection). I do not believe that argument holds.[35]

31. It should also be noted that the United States began using electronic ankle bracelets for asylum claimants in 2005 in major cities.

32. Walter Benjamin, "Theses on the Philosophy of History," in *Illuminations,* ed. Hannah Arendt, trans. Harry Zohn (New York: Schocken Books, 1969), 257.

33. Savage, "Justices Struggle."

34. See Wolin, "Fear Is Being Used as Re-election Tactic," *Common Dreams News Center,* May 10, 2004, http://www.commondreams.org; Adam Green, "Citizen Spies," *The New Yorker,* August 5, 2002, http://www.newyorker.com; Curt Anderson, "Ashcroft Expands FBI Arrest Powers," *Boston Globe,* March 20, 2003, B2; Chachere, "Fla. School Trustees Back Bid to Fire Palestinian Professor," *Boston Globe,* December 20, 2001, A25; Wayne Parry, "Man Freed After Almost 2 Years in Custody," *Boston Globe,* April 15, 2004, A7; Anderson, "Bush Seeks to Broaden U.S. Powers with Special Subpoenas," *Boston Globe,* September 14, 2003, A19; Martin, "With a Whisper, Not a Bang."

35. See Agamben, "Non au tatouage biopolitique," *Le Monde,* October 10, 2004, http://www.lemonde.fr.

Connected to the power dynamics of the War on Terror is the War on Drugs, as a result of which the United States distinguished itself in the 1990s as the country with the highest imprisonment rate in the world.[36] This "war" has led to the highest incarceration of African American males in their prime since Jim Crow; clearly, then, the law is being used to suspend the law and to treat certain groups as inherently criminal and thus posing a biological threat.[37] "Three strikes" laws, recent cutbacks in legal aid, and the courts' indifference as to whether crimes were are violent or non-violent[38] have led to the same arbitrary situation as the one facing the prisoners in Guantánamo and the refugees in holding cells in Miami, Texas, and California. Specifically, the shift in emphasis in drug-law enforcement from dealers to users has led to a shocking increase in the percentage of incarcerated nonviolent offenders.[39]

The strongest growth in prison populations has been among African Americans and women. Most drug users are white, yet between 1986 and 1991, most drug arrests were of African Americans.[40] Over the same years, the incarceration rate for drug offenses among African American women increased by 828 percent. Moreover, a 1994 Justice Department study of federal prisoners found that women were overrepresented among "low level" drug offenders; these women were nonviolent, had little or no prior criminal record, and were not involved in drug trafficking, yet as a result of mandatory sentencing, they were receiving the same sentences as high-level offenders.[41] What is more, as report after report has emphasized, one in three African American males is now somehow involved in the prison system, be it through jail time, parole, or probation. Observers have noted that because of the enormous costs of this war, including the spending of $26.4 billion to increase the number of prison beds,[42] it cannot simply be scaled back. Perhaps even more significant is the disenfranchisement that occurs after the individual has served his or her sentence: in ten states,

36. Harvard Law Review Association, "Note: Winning the War on Drugs: A 'Second Chance' for Nonviolent Offenders," *Harvard Law Review* 113 (April 2000); Holly Sklar, "Reinforcing Racism with the War on Drugs," *ZMagazine*, December 1995, http://zmagazine.com; "Punishment and Prejudice: Racial Disparities in the War on Drugs," *Human Rights Watch* 12 (May 2000), http://www.hrw.org; Neal Pierce, "International Condemnation for Our 'War on Drugs,'" August 28, 2001, http://www.crimelynx.com/intcon.html.

37. See, for example, Glenn Loury, "The Conservative Line on Race," *The Atlantic* (November 1997), http://www.theatlantic.com/issues/97nov/race.htm.

38. See David Garland, *The Culture of Control* (Chicago: University of Chicago Press, 2001).

39. Harvard Law Review Association, "Note: Winning the War on Drugs," *Harvard Law Review* 113 (April 2000).

40. See Harvard Law Review Association.

41. Sklar, "Reinforcing Racism with the War on Drugs."

42. Pierce, "International Condemnation for Our 'War on Drugs.'"

many prisoners are stripped of the right to vote for life; and in many others, for a ten-year time period, they are denied Pell grants and are excluded from a number of government and municipal jobs.[43] The War on Drugs (and the racially biased sentencing that preceded it) has essentially engendered a split among prisoners, rendering some stateless and others as citizens to be rehabilitated. In arguing this, I am challenging Arendt's contention that ironically, prisoners have rights while the stateless do not.[44]

Although the War on Drugs is no longer at the forefront of media and public attention, the changes it has brought about in the justice system—specifically, in the resort to prisons rather than rehabilitation or education programs—cannot easily be undone. Nor can the damage to African American communities, families, and economic well-being. The public rhetoric of a crack epidemic linked to African Americans did not simply disappear after 9/11. Indeed, this war should be seen in the context of the "new" racism.[45] The war on "narcoterrorism," largely aimed at our southern border, connects the War on Drugs to the War on Terror, making all who cross the border potential enemies or terrorists rather than workers or criminals.[46] The founding of the Office of Counternarcotics Enforcement in 2004 under Homeland Security is one example of this linkage between the prerogative exercised on foreigners and inner-city residents.

43. See Paul Street, "Race, Prison, and Poverty," *ZMagazine*, May 2001, http://www.zmag.org; Loïc Wacquant, "From Slavery to Mass Incarceration," *New Left Review* 13 (January–February 2002), http://www.newleftreview.com/NLF24703.shtml.

44. See Hannah Arendt, *The Origins of Totalitarianism* (New York: Harcourt Brace Jovanovich, 1979), 296.

45. See Jim Naureckas, "Racism Resurgent: How Media Let *The Bell Curve's* Pseudo-Science Define the Agenda on Race" (January–February 1995), http://www.fair.org/extra/9501/bell.html; Joseph Barnes, "Book Review: *The End of Racism* by Dinesh D'Souza," *ZMagazine* (December 1995), http://www.zmag.org/zmag/articles/dec95reviews.htm; Adam Miller, "Professors of Hate," *Rolling Stone* 693 (October 20, 1994); Charles Lane, "The Tainted Sources of 'The Bell Curve,'" *New York Review of Books* 41 (December 1, 1994); Executive Summary, "Wrong Then, Wrong Now: Racial Profiling Before and After September 11, 2001," May 10, 1994, http://www.civilrights.org/publications/reports/racial_profiling; Amnesty International's website for updated information, http://www.amnestyusa.org; Deborah Ramirez, Jack McDevitt, and Amy Farrell, monograph, "A Resource Guide on Racial Profiling Data Collection Systems: Promising Practices and Lessons Learned," sponsored by the U.S. Department of Justice (Wheaton: Northwestern University, November 2000); Mikal Muharrar, "Media Blackface: 'Racial Profiling' in News Reporting," September–October 1998, http://www.fair.org/extra/9809/media-blackface.html; Institute on Race and Justice, Executive Summary: "Massachusetts Racial and Gender Profiling Final Report" (Boston: Northeastern University, IRJ, May 4, 2004); American Civil Liberties Union, "Racial Equality: Racial Profiling—Press Releases," http://www.aclu.org/RacialEquality/RacialEqualitylist.cfm?c=133.

46. See, for example, "Fact Sheet: U.S. Customs and Border Protection—Protecting Our Southern Border Against the Terrorist Threat," August 20, 2004, http://www.cbp.gov.

More specifically, as drug activity has increased along the Mexican border and the administration takes steps to ensure that the War on Terror is always present in the average individual's mind, discursive links are made among illegal entrants, drug dealers, and terrorists. A discourse of narco-terrorism beautifully synthesizes all of these concerns, justifying increased surveillance, incursions, and defense, as well as making all entrants possible terrorists rather than mere illegal immigrants. Meanwhile, the free zone between the United States and Mexico (the Border Industrial Program) is marked by lawlessness, the unsolved murders and abductions of hundreds of young female workers, and the legitimate suspension of the law in the case of factory conditions and environmental regulations. All of this points to a strengthening of sovereign power, yet the border has become more malleable; lawlessness is increasing on the border (witness the murders in Ciudad Juárez), but the government is making efforts to fully deploy its sovereignty in patrolling the border, and a new discursive subject—the narcoterrorist—is being fomented as a justification for broadening the war on terror to include individuals from the principal source of immigrants to the United States. As a result of all this, *Homo laborans* has become indistinguishable from the figure of the terrorist.

Similarly, the treatment of the homeless evidences the suspension of law for certain categories of people. The political situation of the homeless is similar to that of foreign nationals, who can be held without legal representation or recourse because of their status rather than any criminal act. This is possible because policies across the United States (and Europe, Australia, and Japan, among others) have in effect criminalized homeless people's very existence.[47] Their mere presence in public areas (including libraries) and in semipublic malls and office parks can lead to arrest. It is illegal for these people to engage in life-sustaining activities, yet people who do have housing are permitted to perform those same activities. Begging permits have placed the homeless in a double bind by demanding high fees or a permanent address. These people are also subject to arrest sweeps, and their possessions are often burned (even though the private property of housed individuals is held to be inviolable). In all of these ways,

---

47. See Leonard Feldman, *Citizens Without Shelter* (Ithaca: Cornell University Press, 2004). As Feldman notes, because vagrancy laws were ruled unconstitutional, contemporary anti-homeless laws ostensibly punish conduct rather than status. Nevertheless, as he demonstrates, these laws actually *create* politically denigrated statuses through the illegalization of certain activities. Thus, these ordinances not only target the homeless as a group rather than just anyone performing the same activities, but also actively constitute marginalized subjects simultaneously. See Feldman, "Status Injustice: the Role of the State," in *Adding Insult to Injury: The Politics of Recognition,* ed. Kevin Olson (London: Verso, forthcoming).

the law is being used to suspend the law and to treat certain individuals as bare (biological) life.[48] These statutes and regulations punish status rather than criminal acts;[49] furthermore, like our immigration laws, they criminalize homelessness and discipline all who are poor.

Shadows and the New Working Class

A case can be made that two domestic "wars" are being conducted in the United States—the War on Terrorism and the War on Drugs—along with many accompanying shadow wars. For example, the increasing detention and deportation of Haitians and Mexicans could be considered a "shadow" of the Patriot Act and the 1996 terrorist act. Supposedly, these two acts have targeted groups suspected of terrorist activities; in practice, though, they have led mainly to the arrest and deportation of Mexicans and Haitians, as noted earlier. The suspension of law is not being applied to special situations, nor is it viewed as temporary; in fact, it amounts to a permanent state of exception. Similarly, it can be argued that the surveillance of welfare recipients and workfare participants is a "shadow" aspect of the overt racial profiling conducted by many police departments as well as by agents of the War on Terror.[50] And the stringent requirements of workfare programs are inextricably linked to the demands for a flexible workforce and flexible employment. Finally, the Patriot Act and the War on Drugs regard racial profiling in similar terms, exceed their purview as originally conceived, and affect some of the same populations, living in the same areas, working in the same jobs.

As I argued in Chapter 1, welfare and workfare are having a strong negative impact on the political status of the homeless, inner-city residents, and poor immigrants (all of the groups that make up the new working class). Between the late 1970s and the 1990s, the problems and power dynamics of the welfare state were implied by Michel Foucault and

---

48. On homelessness and bare life, see Feldman, *Citizens Without Shelter;* on the criminalization of the homeless, see Kathleen Arnold, *Homelessness, Citizenship, and Identity* (Albany: SUNY Press, 2004); National Law Center on Homelessness and Poverty, "Illegal to be Homeless: the Criminalization of Homelessness in the United States," 2001, http://www.nationalhomeless.org/criminalizationrelease.html; U.S. Conference of Mayors, "A Status Report on Hunger and Homelessness in American Cities, 1999" (1999 USCM Report), http://www.usmayorsorg/UCSM/home.asp; Eric Brosch, "No Place Like Home: Orlando's Poor Laws Attempt to Regulate the Homeless Away," *Harper's,* April 1998, 58–59.

49. See Feldman, *Citizens Without Shelter.*

50. See John Gilliom, *Overseers of the Poor: Surveillance, Resistance, and the Limits of Privacy* (Chicago: University of Chicago Press, 2001).

discussed explicitly by authors ranging from Jürgen Habermas to Richard Cloward and Frances Fox Piven. In the 1990s, various authors highlighted the punitive quality of the welfare system—how it perpetuated poverty and was arbitrary in its implementation.[51] Welfare cutbacks resulting from the 1996 Personal Responsibility and Work Opportunity Reconciliation Act, and stricter requirements tied to moral criteria (such as marriage, family caps, and willingness to work), did not end the state's coercive welfare practices; instead, these developments tied those practices more firmly to the labor market.[52] The state's arbitrary attitude toward welfare recipients is evident in the treatment that clients receive from welfare caseworkers—the strict rules, the threats of cut-off, the demands for good behavior in exchange for aid. More broadly, though, that attitude is evident in the constant fluctuation of benefits, the denial of benefits to thousands of eligible people owing to budget cuts and stricter eligibility rules, and the persistent threat that the safety net will disappear at any moment. All of this keeps the poor in a perpetually unstable situation. Welfare benefits and workfare are not considered "entitlements" or job programs or even forms of dependence, yet they determine how (and even whether) the poor will survive. Moreover, they govern how recipients behave by monitoring compliance in their personal lives and their jobs and by constantly threatening that benefits will be cut off. Although subjection to prerogative power can be considered along a spectrum of power, the political status of the homeless, which I believe is one of bare life, provides a hermeneutic framework for explaining the pockets of prerogative that low-tier workers are subjected to (and this is to acknowledge the fact that there is significant overlap between the homeless and poor workers).

Furthermore, unlike the circumstances at Guantánamo Bay (not to idealize conditions there), the ideational system that creates ethnic, racial, and gender antagonisms obscures these power dynamics and often inverts them, positing these groups as the true usurpers or exploiters (of "us": the

51. See, for example, Michel Foucault, *Discipline and Punish: The Birth of the Prison* (New York: Vintage Books, 1979); Jürgen Habermas, *Theory of Communicative Action*, vol. 2, trans. Thomas McCarthy (Boston: Beacon Press, 1985); Richard Cloward and Frances Fox Piven, *The Politics of Turmoil: Essays in Poverty, Race, and the Urban Crisis* (New York: Pantheon Books, 1965); Deborah Connolly, *Homeless Mothers: Face to Face with Women and Poverty* (Minneapolis: University of Minnesota Press, 2000); Frances Fox Piven, "Poorhouse Politics," *The Progressive* 59, no. 2 (1995); Wendy Brown, *States of Injury: Power and Freedom in Late Modernity* (Princeton: Princeton University Press, 1995); Arnold, *Homelessness, Citizenship, and Identity*; William Julius Wilson, *When Work Disappears* (New York: Vintage Books, 1997). These are just a few titles.

52. Frances Fox Piven and Richard Cloward, "Foreword," in *Workfare States*, Jamie Peck (New York: Guilford Press, 2001), 21–24.

welfare system, taxpayers' dollars, our moral sensibility, and so on). While these examples of prerogative may not all be equivalent, the conceptual framework of bare life allows us to understand the status of these individuals as well as the dangerous path down which neoliberal politics is leading everyone—but most significantly, these workers.

Moreover, as discussed in Chapter 4, the alleged threat to national security posed by immigrants simply feeds into extant ethnic and racial antagonisms, allowing for overt racial comparisons to inform debates, rhetoric, and policy. African Americans and immigrant groups are constantly compared to one another and scrutinized based on their capacity to assimilate into mainstream culture and the job market.[53] Men's work is often compared to women's work, in such a way that women are favored as ideal workers for sweatshops, service work, and simple manufacturing tasks.[54] For their part, men may turn to more informal conditions such as day labor (this work is not limited to immigrants; a significant number of very poor American-born men undertake it).[55] All the while these antagonisms are being generated, the dominant groups espouse low pay, effective disenfranchisement, and subjection to relentless police surveillance as a corrective for the subject groups, as "tough love," and as leading to the formation of disciplined individuals, rather than as coercive, racist, or exploitative.

It could be objected that poor workers are not in the same situation as, say, welfare recipients or unauthorized immigrants. But to make this argument, one must separate the poor conceptually into working and nonworking, responsible and irresponsible, housed and homeless, citizen and noncitizen, and so on. The truth is that poor individuals who work in low-tier positions pass in and out of employment, on and off welfare, and are members of families with mixed citizenship or prisoner status. While social scientists often need to categorize groups of people

53. See, among other articles or chapters, Samuel Huntington, "The Hispanic Challenge," *Foreign Policy* (March–April 2004), http://www.foreignpolicy.com; Toni Morrison, "On the Backs of Blacks," 98; Jack Miles, "Blacks vs. Browns," 119–24; Frances Fukuyama, "Immigrants and Family Values," 156, 161, 163 all in *Arguing Immigration*, ed. Nicolaus Mills (New York: Touchstone, 1994); and John Cassidy, "The Melting-Pot Myth," *The New Yorker*, July 14, 1997, 40–43.

54. See Saskia Sassen, *Globalization and Its Discontents: Essays on the New Mobility of People and Money* (New York: New Press, 1998; Sonia Shah, ed., *Dragon Ladies: Asian American Feminists Breathe Fire* (Boston: South End Press, 1997); Patricia Fernandez-Kelly, "Reading the Signs: The Economics of Gender Twenty-Five Years Later," *Signs* 25 (Summer 2000): 1110; Wilson, *When Work Disappears.*

55. See Abel Valenzuela, "Working on the Margins: Immigrant Day Labor Characteristics and Prospects for Employment," Working Paper no. 22, Center for Comparative Immigration Studies, University of California, San Diego, May 2000; Kurt Borchard, *The Word on the Street: Homeless Men in Las Vegas* (Reno: University of Nevada Press, 2005).

in order to conduct empirical research, erroneous distinctions can be made between the hardcore (that is, unemployed) poor and the working-class poor. For example, it might be assumed that members of the latter group are treated fairly by the police, are equal to all before the law, and are viewed as citizens, even when the reality is that there is no clear distinction between them and the hard-core poor.[56] Moreover, as immigration becomes an increasingly salient factor in the demographic makeup of urban areas, it is hard to argue that immigrants' situations are absolutely distinct from those of African Americans or other racial minorities with citizenship status. Once it is conceded how these lines are blurred, it is easier to see how the prerogative power of the War on Terror, the War on Drugs, and the criminalization of the homeless affects all of these groups, even if to varying degrees. When we combine all of this with the biological racism that is increasingly popular among the political and academic elites, the backlash against feminism (partly evident in the preference for allegedly docile groups for low-tier positions),[57] and the blatant ignorance shown toward foreigners of color, the deployment of prerogative domestically and the treatment of these individuals as biological life seems less fantastic.

To put it differently, my argument suggests a way of bridging the apparent gap between the sovereign or warfare state on the one hand and the welfare or democratic state on the other: a gap that liberal theorists often assume.[58] Furthermore, with Foucault and Agamben, it permits us to see how sovereignty can be exercised even when power is more dispersed, both locally and globally.[59] Once we allow that prerogative power can be deployed by bureaucratic institutions (such as police officers charged with acting as immigration agents, or workfare employers who unofficially serve as bureaucratic agents), the apparent gap between state and local authority can be viewed differently.

56. On this point, see Wilson, *When Work Disappears;* Sheila D. Collins and Gertrude Schaffner Goldberg, *Washington's New Poor Law* (New York: Apex Press, Council on International and Public Affairs, 2001), 13–15.

57. See Jacqueline Jones, *American Work* (New York: W. W. Norton, 1998); Bonnie Honig, *Democracy and the Foreigner* (Princeton: Princeton University Press, 2001); Leslie Salzinger, "From High Heels to Swathed Bodies: Gendered Meanings Under Production in Mexico's Export-Processing Industry," *Feminist Studies* 23 (Autumn 1997): 549–74.

58. An example of this distinction can be found in Mary Kaldor, "Reconceptualizing Organized Violence," in *Re-imagining Political Community,* ed. Daniele Archibugi, David Held, and Martin Köhler (Stanford: Stanford University Press, 1998). For a discussion of this distinction, see Carole Pateman, *The Disorder of Women* (Stanford: Stanford University Press, 1992), chap. 8; Wolin, "Democracy and the Welfare State."

59. See Agamben, *Homo Sacer,* 6–7.

The War on Drugs,[60] the ascetic demands of the welfare/workfare state, the criminalization of homelessness, and the War on Terror have converged to reduce state interference in the market; they have also seemingly decreased the role of government in the average citizen's life even while greatly expanding the possibility for and the actual deployment of prerogative power. As David Garland comments, this combination of factors has led to "the often contradictory combination of what came to be known as 'neo-liberalism' (the re-assertion of market disciplines) and 'neo-conservatism' (the re-assertion of moral disciplines), the commitment to 'rolling back the state' while simultaneously building a state apparatus that is stronger and more authoritarian than before."[61] The only way to allow these contradictory tendencies to coexist, however, is to target certain parts of the population even while spouting all-inclusive rhetoric.

Furthermore, all of these programs show that a war mentality has defined domestic policy since at least the 1980s and is becoming increasingly prevalent.[62] Legally, this has created a highly ambivalent situation, both domestically and internationally: "The attacks of September 11 have been described as an act of war. While the label may have political potency, it is unhelpful within the legal framework of terrorism. The war power being a prerogative of Congress, the formal definition of war is a matter of positive law."[63] Nevertheless, the response has been entirely military, not criminal. At the same time, these particular wars are being fought in the post–Cold War era in the guise of humanitarian, moral, or economic action. These three buzzwords define foreign and domestic interventions even as the term "war" continues to be used. The word *war* is used in much the same way that Lyndon B. Johnson used it in his "War on Poverty" and suggests surgical (that is, selected, individual) application as well as benign and humanitarian (that is, nonpolitical) motives. In this way, the expansion of power in these areas is depoliticized and intervention is variously portrayed as individual (in the case of workfare, as recipients are ostensibly left to face the market alone); as humanitarian or police action (in the case of foreign intervention, including the War on Iraq); and as a penal issue (and therefore not political, economic, or racial, but rather sociological or psychological, in the case of the War on Drugs).

60. See Garland, *The Culture of Control*, 131–35. I would like to thank Chris Sturr, editor of *Dollars 'n Sense*, for suggesting this text.

61. Ibid., 98.

62. As Garland notes in his book.

63. Note: "Responding to Terrorism: Crime, Punishment, and War," *Harvard Law Review* 115 (February 2002): 1225.

Both Carl Schmitt and Giorgio Agamben warn about the consequences of a politics that is thoroughly infused with economic and thus biological concerns, and about the dangerous effects of contemporary humanitarian politics. These trends depoliticize politics by removing any substance beyond material well-being and existence; at the same time, they extend authoritative and arbitrary power. Agamben argues that we have largely depoliticized power so that *oikos* has become the means and ends of our politics. Politics is increasingly concerned with bare life; that is, it has become thoroughly entangled with economic globalization in the form of neoliberalism: "In our culture, the decisive political conflict, which governs every other conflict, is that between the animality and the humanity of man. That is to say, in its origin Western politics is also biopolitics."[64] According to Agamben, the sovereign exception then becomes the rule and the inhumanity of sovereignty is revealed. This power is by no means total or even uniform; even so, its role in contemporary politics has become decisive.

Because power can never be said to be total (except in slavery), there is always room for agency or resistance, as Foucault would have argued.[65] There have been many instances throughout the world of agency, and of resistance to neoliberalism, ethnocentrism, sexism, xenophobia, and globalization, and they are all over the political spectrum. But this agency is often conceptualized as a question of human rights or economic empowerment in the global economy. Agamben shows that very often these efforts are framed in the same biopolitical terms as sovereignty and thus affirm the inhuman aspects of our political economy instead of challenging them.[66] What can be concluded is not that biopower is inevitable but rather that growing concerns about morality and humanitarianism are obscuring political aims and treating subjects as bare life. Resistance to the predominance of biopower should not stay mired in the very same binary oppositions that lead to bare life's radical exclusion.

Resistance?

Agamben has been accused of nihilism and determinism in his analyses of prerogative and bare life.[67] This interpretation ignores his work on

64. Agamben, *The Open*, trans. Kevin Attell (Stanford: Stanford University Press, 2004), 80.

65. This argument obviously goes against more conventional readings of Foucault. See Turner and Rojek, for example.

66. And can explain why there is racial, ethnic, and gender antagonism and why workers appropriate biopolitical categories to relate to one another.

67. For discussions of this point, see Colin McQuillan, "The Political Life in Giorgio Agamben," *Kritikos* 2 (July 2005); Antonio Negri, "The Ripe Fruit of Redemption," trans. Arianna

potentiality, extraterritoriality and the politics of the refugee, and forms of life. However, he seems to be awaiting a future in which sovereign violence, the nation-state, and genocidal exclusion are banished so that a "coming community" can truly act democratically. Similarly, Simone de Beauvoir awaits a future of greater democratic agency and sees complicity and domination in the current circumstances. In contrast, Foucault has a more active notion of resistance, one that is less binary than that of Agamben and Beauvoir.[68] Bonnie Honig has commented that when confronting major obstacles to democratic action, theorists often engage in their own binary splits—not just Right versus Left but "good" Left versus "bad" Left, for example. In certain respects, Agamben and Beauvoir's call to delay democracy until a future time is similar in its binary splitting: both of them presume that political action today continues to be co-opted, that it is operating within the framework of bare life (or immanence) instead of trying to bring about a new politics that would eschew both the bare life/citizen binary and the deep division that Beauvoir correctly intuits between immanence and transcendence. What is assumed is that there is some political field *outside* current power structures and that acts of political agency manifesting elements of current undemocratic political structures must be dismissed as wellsprings of revolution.

For example, in the growth of human rights and humanitarian organizations after World War II, Agamben sees a separation between the rights of man and those of citizens such that the former can only replicate sovereign power structures and cannot be a true alternative to them: "Humanitarian organizations . . . can only grasp human life in the figure of bare or sacred life, and therefore, despite themselves, maintain a secret solidarity with the very powers they ought to fight." In actuality, these organizations are "in perfect symmetry with state power."[69] In other writings he has compared refugee camps to concentration camps in that both treat individuals as bare life and are characterized by legal undecidability.[70] His critique makes it adamantly clear that "humanitarian" action is often inhumane and that the actions of NGOs often reflect state power instead of actively resisting it; however, he ignores the complexities of transnational

---

Bove, http://www.generation-online.org/t/negriagamben.html; Antonio Vázquez-Arroyo, "Agamben [. . .]," *Theory and Event* 8, no. 1 (2005).

68. Again, this goes against more conventional (and incomplete, in my mind) interpretations of Foucault.

69. Agamben, *Homo Sacer*, 133.

70. See, for example, Agamben, "The Camp as the *Nomos* of the Modern," in *Violence, Identity, and Self-Determination*, ed. Hent de Vries and Samuel Weber (Stanford: Stanford University Press, 1997); Agamben, *Homo Sacer*, chap. 7.

organizations and their power to produce new subjectivities. Similarly, Beauvoir views many women's efforts to resist gender divisions as participating in those very divisions. In this way, women's acts of rebellion are more an effect of *ressentiment,* replicating the male power structure and reproducing the splits between immanence and transcendence rather than creating something new. For example, she argues that "feminism itself was never an autonomous movement: it was in part an instrument in the hands of politicians, in part an epiphenomenon reflecting a deeper social drama. Never have women constituted a separate caste, nor in truth have they ever as a sex sought to play a historic role." Indeed, "the majority of women resign themselves to their lot without attempting to take any action."[71] Like Agamben, resistance is an either/or proposition—if there are elements of the existing power structure, then action is not really transcendent (in the Heideggerean or existential sense).

Foucault also recognizes that acts of resistance and attempts to break away from the past (for example, the sexual revolution of the 1960s) often reproduce the very power structures they aim to challenge. Unlike Agamben and Beauvoir, though, he argues that one can be complicit with power at many levels yet still make oneself a subject and be an agent of one's own possibilities. He maintains that power is not an article that is possessed by one person while another is deprived of it. Rather, it is *relational* so that even in situations of inequality or hierarchy, all actors have some power: "Power must be analysed as something that circulates . . . it is never localised here or there, never in anybody's hands, never appropriated as a commodity or piece of wealth. Power is employed and exercised through a net-like organization." Accordingly, individuals "are always in the position of simultaneously undergoing and exercising this power . . . [they] are the vehicles of power, not its points of application."[72] Thus Foucault sees possibilities—constitutive, emancipatory—in all acts of resistance as well as remnants and residues of current power structures. He envisions struggles against disciplinary power, for example, but he does not hold out for a domination-free future. His perspective is analogous to—if not perfectly congruous with—Patchen Markell's analysis of Hannah Arendt.[73] Markell's Arendt does not split democracy into *either*

71. Beauvoir, *The Second Sex,* trans. and ed. H. M. Parshley (New York: Vintage Books, 1989); 129; on complicity, see, for example, 64, 188, 263, 615, 698, 699, and 721.

72. Foucault, "Two Lectures," in Colin Gordon, ed., *Power/Knowledge: Selected Interviews and Other Writings, 1972–1977,* trans. Colin Gordon, Leo Marshall, John Mepham, and Kate Soper (New York: Pantheon Books, 1980), 98.

73. Patchen Markell, "The Rule of the People: Arendt, *Archê,* and Democracy," *American Political Science Review* 100 (February 2006).

institutional, static, repressive *or* constantly revolutionary, agonistic, temporary. In fact, such a division would hark back to the hierarchical distinctions
noted by Agamben and Beauvoir. For Arendt, democratic agency is not the
opposite of established political power or somehow "outside the system";
in this regard, she focuses on "'beginning' [which] picks out . . . the
sense in which action, whether disruptive or not, involves attention and
responsiveness to worldly events; and what threatens 'beginning' thus
understood is not the enforcement of regularity, but the erosion of the
contexts in which events call for responses and, thus, in which it makes
sense to act at all."[74] Arendt and Foucault's analyses of resistance have in
common the idea that action does not have to be entirely destabilizing in
order to count as something new or innovative. At the same time,
though, neither theorist accepts the idea that actors are always already
realized—performance and action do in fact count, and this common
thread unites these two thinkers with Beauvoir and Agamben.

At issue here is the idea that life is always already determined by or
fated in current matrices of power. Both Agamben and Beauvoir suggest
that instead of rising above the binaries of zoë/bios or immanence/
transcendence, that we hold them in suspension or tension. In *The Open*,[75]
Agamben analyzes the idea that we need somehow to reconcile human
with nonhuman or animal, *oikos* with *polis*, immanence with transcendence, and so on. These splits have made possible the either/or logic that
has enabled biological life to increasingly dominate raison d'état in late
modernity. He suggests that in order to combat the inhumanity of neoliberal policies and deployments of sovereignty, we embrace the moments
when humans are animalized, as in sexual relations or boredom (boredom
not being a deactivation of our animality but a sort of captivation, a suspension between man and animal).[76] Added to the notion of suspension or
captivation, consider his notion of potentiality (or possibility) in the essay
"Form of Life":

> By the term *form-of-life* . . . I mean a life that can never be
> separated from its form, a life in which it is never possible to
> isolate something such as naked life. A life that cannot be sepa-
> rated from its form is a life for which what is at stake in its way
> of living is living itself. What does this formulation mean? It
> defines a life—human life—in which the single ways, acts, and

74. Ibid., 2.
75. See Agamben, *The Open*.
76. See Joshua Dienstag's review of *The Open*, in *Political Theory* 34 (2006): 148–52.

processes of living are never simply *facts* but always and above all *possibilities* of life, always and above all power. Each behavior and each form of human living is never prescribed by a specific biological vocation, nor is it assigned by whatever necessity; instead, no matter how customary, repeated, and socially compulsory, it always retains the character of a possibility; that is, it always puts at stake living itself. That is why human beings—as beings of power who can do or not do, succeed or fail, lose themselves or find themselves—are the only beings for whom happiness is always at stake in their living, the only beings whose life is irremediably and painfully assigned to happiness. But this immediately constitutes the form-of-life as political life. . . . Political power, as we know it, on the other hand, always founds itself in the last instance on the separation of a sphere of naked life from the context of the forms of life.[77]

According to Agamben, contemporary power configurations do not allow for human potentiality; rather, they split "life" in ways that are increasingly inhuman. Similarly, according to Beauvoir, the key is not to deny animality but to cease designating one group as chained to biology and the other as capable of transcending this animality. Life itself is no longer divided, it is no longer the determination of political status. Rather, Beauvoir contends:

Man, like woman, is flesh, therefore passive, the plaything of his hormones and of the species, the restless prey of his desires. . . . They [man and woman] live out in their several fashions the strange ambiguity of existence made body. In those combats where they think they confront one another, it is really against the self that each one struggles, projecting into the partner that part of the self which is repudiated; instead of living out the ambiguities of their situation, each tries to make the other bear the abjection and tries to reserve the honor for the self. If, however, both should assume the ambiguity with a clear-sighted modesty, correlative of an authentic pride, they would see each other as equals and would live out their erotic drama in amity. . . . In both sexes is played out the same drama of the flesh and the spirit, of finitude and transcendence; both are gnawed away by

---

77. Agamben, "Form of Life," trans. Vincenzo Binetti and Cesare Casarino, *International Journal of Baudrillard Studies* 2 (July 2005): 9.

time and laid in wait for by death, they have the same essential end for one another; and they can gain from their liberty the same glory.[78]

Here we have both Beauvoir's diagnosis and her prescription: authentic love rather than the unequal, exploitative relations that have characterized intimate relations throughout history. Although she appears to participate in affirming the hierarchies she critiques (by constantly valuing transcendence over immanence), she holds that all beings are capable of transcendence. Thus far, whenever man has acted transcendently, "he created; he burst out of the present, he opened the future. . . . He has worked not merely to conserve the world as given; he has broken through its frontiers, he has laid down the foundations of a new future."[79] Transcendence for all beings involves "the freedom to engage in projects of ever widening scope that marks the untrammeled existent."[80]

All of these thinkers suggest that power is productive, not merely repressive or juridical. However, context matters—the context of openness to democratic possibilities that are not terminated once enacted but suggest a future of democratic action, as Markell suggests. In investigating possible solutions, I begin with Beauvoir's call for authentic relations (that is, love) between free existents; I then tie this to Agamben's appeal for refugees to be at the center of any future politics, supplemented by Foucault's analysis of power as (again) relational and capable of producing rather than just repressing.

Agency?

Genuine love ought to be founded on the mutual recognition of two liberties; the lovers would then experience themselves both as self and as other: neither would give up transcendence, neither would be mutilated; together they would manifest values and aims in the world. For the one and the other, love would be revelation of self by the gift of self and enrichment of the world.[81]

—SIMONE DE BEAUVOIR

78. Beauvoir, *The Second Sex*, 728.
79. Ibid., 63.
80. H. M. Parshley, translator's note in ibid., 63n.
81. Ibid., 667.

There are, I think, two types of "love" that are dangerous, given the cases I have described. The first is the demand for an unconditional giving of oneself in exchange for mere living. This first type mirrors the love expected of women in a sexist society, as analyzed by Beauvoir. The second, what could be called brotherly or fraternal love, might ensure equality and reciprocity between citizens but is deficient in a number of ways toward outsiders, both foreign and domestic. This second type has perhaps been structurally weakened by the global economy and by sites of power that undermine state sovereignty, but it continues to exist in its rhetorical and therefore nationalist form; this is especially true since the events of 9/11. I will briefly explore the first type of love and then examine Beauvoir's analysis of authentic love as an alternative to current relations.

Beauvoir's investigation of the exploitative type of love pertains to my discussion of low-tier workers, *maquiladora* employees, and others who cross the border and are subject to our wars. With this love—as opposed to friendship—one can be asked to sacrifice all for another. This is particularly true in situations of political inequality. The love expected of women in the context of profound inequalities is similar to ascetic values in low-tier work: both require self-sacrifice, self-abnegation, thrift (in feelings or money), and mastery over physical or psychic pain. This type of love calls for an unconditional giving over of the self in return for piecemeal, arbitrary, and even violent actions and feelings on the part of the more powerful. For this reason, in the context of neoliberal political economic policies and the demands made on low-tier workers, love is a more appropriate analogy than friendship. Free-market policies demand the total self-abandonment of low-tier workers. Assimilation—cultural, linguistic, and in attitudes toward work—is required and coerced, not only from immigrants but also from welfare recipients and minorities. Low-tier workers must work long hours with no job security; they are charged with not assimilating, yet they face discrimination in loans, housing, education, and employment, which practically forces groups to act in separatist ways; their political apathy is decried, yet when they do organize themselves, such activities are branded treasonous, a public nuisance, and signs of the failure to assimilate. Neoliberals argue that jobs with no benefits are better for the economy, and on that basis, workplaces have been deregulated, thus guaranteeing that individuals will suffer sickness or injury.

In the same way that Beauvoir explains the total giving over of a woman to a man in an unequal society, political and business elites want to appropriate these workers' lives while treating them as disposable. As Beauvoir points out, in unhealthy love, a man retains his sovereignty, never giving himself over entirely to the woman; similarly, "we" demand abdication of these workers' sovereignty while retaining our own. "We" get angry when they resist naturalization (marriage); "we" accuse them of exploiting us, sending money back to their home country, taking our jobs, and destroying our language and cultural values. And perhaps because they toil the hardest, work two jobs, and undergo great stress, we are daily reminded of their hard work. This in turn evokes an implacable guilt and general irritability, a feeling of unresolved debt even as we believe that they owe us (i.e., Schuld).

Agamben's approach to these existential categories reveals ambivalence as well as a more difficult resolution to exploitation and power inequalities. The fact that bare life[82] and life are constantly being defined and redefined, even while organized hierarchically and presented as a unity (whether as *oikos* and polity or as man's lower functions and his soul), shows that there is an "incongruity of these two elements."[83] One is reminded of Marx's arguments in "The Meaning of Human Requirements,"[84] and of his footnotes in *Capital, Vol. 1*, in which he cites various government studies as well as debates among political economists, politicians, and religious figures regarding just how low income, nutritional intake, work conditions, and housing conditions can be pushed and still ensure bare survival. The result, Marx says, is to reduce "the workers' need to the barest and most miserable level of physical subsistence."[85] In this way, "even the existence of men is a pure luxury."[86] With the advent of predominantly neoliberal economic and political policies, human needs have once again shifted (and reshifted) so that what was once considered unacceptable has again become acceptable. This demonstrates that "human" is by no means a stable concept and that the inhuman—the politically denigrated or abandoned other—constantly informs the human. In the same way that household labor and those associated with the household have come to be detached from the economic and political spheres, love has been conceived of as an irrational emotion that interferes with the political friendship that civilized individuals share in the civil and public spheres. I believe that this opposition can be reconciled—not, however,

82. Animality or vegetative life, which are not equivalent.
83. Agamben, *Homo Sacer*, 16.
84. In Karl Marx, "The Economic and Philosophic Manuscripts of 1844." Friedrich Engels and Karl Marx, *The Marx–Engels Reader*, 2nd ed., ed. Robert C. Tucker (New York: W. W. Norton, 1978).
85. Ibid., 95.
86. Ibid., 97.

by calling for transcendence of the two, but rather by conceiving of a particular kind of love as including these binaries and holding them in healthy tension.

Beauvoir's notion of authentic love is informed by (Heideggerean) existentialist notions and remains true to Agamben's framework. Her vision of authentic love embraces the two sides of animal and human—immanence (which pertains to *oikos*, the natural) and transcendence (which involves political and economic action)—in a dialectical relation that is neither hierarchical nor transcendent (in the Hegelian sense) and that remains in active tension.[87] To Beauvoir, one must be free to love authentically. Unlike friendship, romantic love as she elucidates it allows for dissent, tension, and otherness. As Sigmund Freud contends, true love involves the dropping of ego boundaries in a healthy—that is, non-narcissistic—way.[88] A notion of democracy that proceeds from this existentialist perspective challenges any unitary conception of sovereignty and necessarily demands responsibility and accountability in the use of prerogative power.

First, Beauvoir believes that authentic love can only be between two individuals who recognize each other as distinct and autonomous. The relationship cannot involve coercion or undue obligations.[89] Men have constructed women as emotional and financial burdens; in just the same way, poor immigrants are constructed as draining the welfare system, as undermining cultural and family values, and as taking away "our" jobs. In both cases, the contributions of the exploited Other go unrecognized. Second, authentic love must be oriented toward the past and the future, not just the present. This does not mean that authentic love cannot be exited; it does mean that commitments need to be serious and responsible while they do last.[90] For truly democratic politics to flourish and for the poorest workers to have a voice that is recognized as legitimate and worthy of citizenship, long-term commitments must replace the various emphases on "flexibility," the free movement of capital, a nonunionized workforce, and guest-worker programs. Authentic love cannot involve either exploitation or viewing the other merely in terms of the self: "The

87. I realize that this is not the reading that critics of Beauvoir have of her work. It is often contended that Beauvoir implicitly establishes a hierarchy of transcendence over immanence, but I believe that her discussion of love in the future—found in the conclusion of *The Second Sex*—does not entail this hierarchy.

88. See Sigmund Freud, *Civilization and Its Discontents*, ed. and trans. James Strachey (New York: W. W. Norton, Standard Edition, 1961), chap. iv.

89. Beauvoir, *The Second Sex*, 472.

90. Ibid., 473.

union of two human beings is doomed to frustration if it is an attempt at a mutual completion which supposes an original mutilation; marriage should be a combining of two whole, independent existences, not a retreat, an annexation, a flight, a remedy."[91] The present-day exploitation of *maquiladora* workers, immigrants, and women, who are viewed simultaneously as models of the work ethic and as destroyers of all political, cultural, and economic values, reflects an unhealthy view of the Other in terms of self.

Third, while total freedom may not appear to foster strong commitments, it is the only ground on which commitments can truly flourish. Dissent is a crucial measure of both freedom and authentic love: "An individual who is loved as a free being, in his humanity, is regarded with that critical, demanding severity which is the other side of genuine esteem."[92] Fourth and finally, authentic love in the form of political liberation must involve a collective effort.[93] Solutions will not be achieved solely through the protests and revolts of unauthorized immigrants or low-tier workers; these people's political efforts are not really the point—the *suspension of law* is the point. Put another way, these groups are already building their own communities, acting spontaneously in political ways, and organizing themselves democratically to bring about change; the problem is that these activities are being cordoned off in "free speech zones,"[94] actively discouraged or criminalized in the case of unions, or viewed as treasonous, separatist, or ungrateful. As an example of this denigration, the mass demonstrations against punitive immigration proposals of April and May 2006 were portrayed variously as an "invasion," treason, or mass rioting.[95] Even so, as the largest mass demonstrations in recent U.S. history, those same events offer hope for future collective action. We must rethink not only our inclusionary status but also what political exclusion means. It must never be based on humanitarian criteria—that is biological, mere-life criteria. Authentic love connotes something more fragmented than brotherly love or selfless love. It is contingent but necessarily interpersonal. Its power rests not on human need but on something beyond human need.

Of course, it is argued back that if things were to change, economic growth and innovation would be lost. Also, that some degree of economic

91. Ibid., 478.
92. Ibid., 618.
93. Ibid., 627.
94. On this subject, see Paul Passavant's work, for example, "Policing Protest in the Post-Fordist City," paper presented at the annual meeting of Law and Society, Las Vegas, October 2006.
95. For such portrayals, see, for example, the *National Review* or FAIR's website.

inequality is necessary as a spur to creativity and growth. It is pointed out over and over that workers who belong to exploited groups are not revolting—that in fact they are lining up to take low-tier jobs—and that their lives have improved overall.[96] Beauvoir calls this the "happy slave" argument; her rebuttal is that when inequalities are profound, no justice can be done and no responsibility taken: "Justice can never be done in the midst of injustice. A colonial administrator has no possibility of acting rightly toward the natives, nor a general toward his soldiers; the only solution is to be neither colonist nor military chief."[97] In the current economic and political context, there is always a reason why *maquiladora*, free-zone, and guest-worker employees must be discouraged from unionizing or outright prohibited from doing so; why they must work in conditions that will potentially harm them, with no legal recourse or affordable health care; why some of those workers are enslaved (or have their passports and wages withheld by employers); why their mobility is limited; why they can be more easily deported; and why they are subject to greater surveillance than the average citizen. These conditions in their totality are inhuman, and no individual would freely choose them for any extended time.

Authentic love as the holding of immanence and transcendence in healthy tension challenges the inhumanity of sovereignty based on bare life. It does not resolve the animal–human dichotomy; rather, it eschews it. Authentic love as a political program does not place faith in the unbroken sovereignty of the people any more than it does in the unbroken unity of political and economic elites deploying prerogative power. Its contingency and its interactiveness preclude fixed asymmetries of power. It also challenges the economic ethos that guides political decision making, how we view political others (be they formal citizens or not), and the exercise of prerogative power on behalf of global capital. When mere life or preservation is construed as the baseline of a political project, that project inevitably exploits dehumanized others (through their exclusion, even their work) and later on justifies their disposal when their utility has ended. If Agamben is right, the politics of bare life has ensured that certain individuals are subject to the state of war. In the United States, the

96. See Friedrich Hayek, *The Essence of Hayek*, ed. Chiaki Nishiyama and Kurt R. Leube (San Francisco: Hoover Institution Press); Paul Krugman, "In Praise of Cheap Labour: Bad Jobs at Bad Wages Are Better Than No Jobs at All," Slate/The Dismal Science, March 20, 1997, <http://slate.msn.com/id/1918>; Arvind Panagariya, "The Miracles of Globalization: A Review of *Why Globalization Works*," *Foreign Affairs*, September–October 2004, http://www.glboalpolicy.org/globali/define/2004/10review.htm, among others.

97. Beauvoir, *The Second Sex*, 723.

paradox is that the groups filling low-tier positions are also the "enemy combatants" in the War on Terror, the War on Drugs, and the related "shadow wars."

De Beauvoir offers insights into the particular mechanisms and discourses of exploitation and inequality, as Foucault later called for. Perhaps, though, she does not see the political elements of this inequality as clearly as Agamben does. Individuals on the border, refugess, and the stateless are all emblematic of the political indeterminacy that he analyzes. Importantly, we should recognize that these groups "throw into crisis the original fiction of sovereignty . . . [they] unhinge the old trinity of state/nation/territory."[98] The refugee should be recognized as "nothing less than a border concept that radically calls into question the principles of the nation-state. . . . In the meantime, the phenomenon of so-called illegal immigration into the countries of the European Community has assumed (and will increasingly assume in coming years, with a foreseen 20 million immigrants from the countries of central Europe) features and proportions such as to fully justify this revolution in perspective. What the industrialized states are faced with today is a *permanently resident mass of noncitizens,* who neither can be nor want to be naturalized or repatriated."[99] What Agamben provocatively suggests is that holes be opened in nation-states so as to permanently allow regions to be in exodus to one another—"divided from each other by a series of reciprocal extraterritorialities" in a politics that rejects the bare life inscribed in political belonging based on *ius soli* or *ius sanguinis.* In this new politics, the refugee would be at the center. Instead of being defined by territory, this new polity would be marked by "holes," like a "Moebius strip, where exterior and interior are indeterminate."[100]

Thus, like de Beauvoir, Agamben suggests challenging the current order by creating something new by taking old binaries and holding them in tension. For example, in *State of Exception,* he tells us that he does not want to tame the state of exception or return it to something contained within the rule of law. Rather, he wants to call into question contemporary notions of the state and law.[101] His hope is that

> one day humanity will play with law just as children play with disused objects, not in order to restore them to their canonical

98. Agamben, "We Refugees," paragraph 5.
99. Refugees, paragraph 6; see Agamben, *Homo Sacer,* 134.
100. Ibid.
101. Agamben, *State of Exception,* 87.

use but to free them from it for good. What is found after the
law is not a more proper and original use value that precedes
the law, but a new use that is born only after it. And use, which
has been contaminated by law, must also be freed from its own
value. This liberation is the task of study, or of play. And this
studious play is the passage that allows us to arrive at that justice
that one of Benjamin's posthumous fragments defines as a state
of the world in which the world appears as a good that absolutely
cannot be appropriated or made juridical.[102]

Agamben's work on potentiality is also suggestive of a politics held in
tension or suspension.[103] When politics is directed at a form of life, life
is not already designated or assigned a fate; rather, it is defined by its
possibilities, which are never exhausted, even after actions occur.[104] Hence
if he is trying to create a new ontology,[105] that ontology is marked by
potentiality and endless possibility, not by fixity.[106]

Like de Beauvoir, he wants to make the marginal less exceptional—to
heal an ancient fracture in a new way. Bare life can be recognized as
having a form of life,[107] just as immanence can become part of all existents'
lives rather than just women's. This is only possible when political life is
directed at "happiness and cohesive with a form-of-life is thinkable only
starting from the emancipation from such a division, with the irrevocable
exodus from any sovereignty,"[108] and when thought, action, and political
belonging are conceived of interrelationally.[109] It is in this sense that Antonio
Negri sees in Agamben's work the possibility of a "multitude."[110]

Agamben's work highlights for us the linkages among seemingly
various aims—in particular the linkages between the War on Terror (and
its associated wars) and the neoliberal project, whose great project is
economic globalization. Foucault, for his part, demonstrates that as traditional "borders"—be they political, economic, territorial, or juridical—break
down and authority becomes more dispersed, acts of resistance can occur
daily in the forms of microresistance and collective action. De Beauvoir's

102. Ibid., 64.
103. See Brian Dillon, "Potentialities" (review), SubStance 30, nos. 1 and 2 (2001): 254–58.
104. Mcquillan, "The Political Life," 3.
105. And I think this is less clear than other interpreters of Agamben's work do.
106. See Agamben, Homo Sacer, 44; Mcquillan, "The Political Life," 7.
107. See Mcquillan, "The Political Life"; Agamben, "Form of Life," 10.
108. Agamben, "Form of Life," 11.
109. Ibid., 12.
110. Antonio Negri, "The Ripe Fruit of Redemption."

analysis of exploitative love investigates acts of resistance and mechanisms of power, and her ideas about love and authentic relations point to a new politics based on innovation, action, and freedom. I would argue that acts of resistance—from illegally crossing borders, to microresistance in *maquiladoras*,[111] to unionization efforts—are truly "revolutionary" and mark the beginning of the "holes" that Agamben calls for to be made.

There is a great deal of evidence that even when individuals are stripped of their rights—be it temporarily or for longer periods—they can still resist. At a micro level, Leslie Salzinger has shown how women workers are forced into hyperfeminine roles in some factories but at the same time use their femininity as a means to control their male supervisors and coworkers.[112] What is more, she notes: "Although women workers generally enter the arena of sexual play on the terms set by their male coworkers, they resist their denigration as workers. . . . Locating themselves at the intersection of two discourses of domination, women workers elaborate a femininity marked both by a ritualistically receptive sexuality and a highly capable work persona."[113] Other authors, such as Saskia Sassen and Pierrette Hondagneu-Sotelo, argue that work itself, and the modicum of economic independence it brings, can allow women to transform gender roles and challenge traditional norms. In other words, wage work can empower women even while it is exploiting them.[114] Alternatively, migrant work—which is generally viewed as exploitative and oppressive—can be a means of empowerment if the family is leaving an area where, for whatever reason, it has been facing intolerance.[115] And despite the outcry against day laborers in various communities, this sort of work does give marginalized men a way to work and control their environment. Unlike in guest-worker programs, these workers can say no if they choose, and that power should not be underestimated.[116] All of these acts of resistance must be viewed in a context of profound inequalities; even so, they remind us that agency is still possible.

111. See, for example, Salzinger, "From High Heels to Swathed Bodies."

112. I am not particularly fond of this argument; see Susan Bordo's discussion of this form of "power" in *Unbearable Weight* (Berkeley and Los Angeles: University of California Press, 1993).

113. Salzinger, "From High Heels to Swathed Bodies," 562.

114. See Sassen, *Globalization and Its Discontents*"; Pierrette Hondagneu-Sotelo, "Overcoming Patriarchal Constraints: The Reconstruction of Gender Relations Among Mexican Immigrant Women and Men," *Gender and Society* 6 (September 1992): 393–415.

115. See Peter Skerry, *Mexican Americans: the Ambivalent Minority* (Cambridge, Mass.: Harvard University Press, 1993).

116. See Valenzuela, "Working on the Margins."

The film *Bread and Roses* illustrates the difficulties arising from the dynamics of a more flexible labor market. A key moment in this movie occurs when the youthful organizer is confronted by an "old school" union man, who accuses him of not playing by the rules. Indeed, it would appear that he, like the group he is trying to unionize, needs to act outside the system in ways that the older unionists did not. The central theme in this part of the movie is the cooption of unions by the state, but I think the more important points are about tactics—that is, they illustrate the political and economic difficulties that the disenfranchised face when they try to organize. The struggle by AIWA (Asian Immigrant Women Advocates) against the designer Jessica McClintock shows how workers can organize despite being disenfranchised (literally in this case), being subject to harsh work conditions, facing domestic and other abuses, and not speaking English well. Their status as bare life did not stop them from beating all the odds. And their tactics were not conventional in the liberal sense. They did not sue their direct employer, a subcontractor for McClintock who refused them their last few paychecks before laying them off; instead, they staged a media campaign against the designer herself (this tactic is mirrored in *Bread and Roses*). After gaining national attention, they were able to sue for back wages.[117]

Nathan Newman's analysis of the potential of the Internet as a form of civic association, a means of grassroots communication, and a forum for public discourse also indicates that very real acts of resistance, protest, and dissent have been launched since the 1980s.[118] The Internet can help the oppressed as much as the oppressors; quite possibly, it is the "ether" that Hardt and Negri believe will bring about revolutionary change. The Internet, after all, can be instrumental in "growing" political awareness and organizing mass protests (for example, environmental protests).[119] More broadly, efforts to unionize among all types of workers—failed or not—demonstrate that political precariousness does not preclude democratic activity or increased personal autonomy. But it cannot be said that these efforts lead to a broad overturning of power asymmetries. Furthermore, that people can resist and sometimes succeed does not prove that they are being treated democratically or according to any rule of law. As Markell has already told us, what may be at stake in this sort of situation

117. See Miriam Ching Louie, "Breaking the Cycle," in *Dragon Ladies: Asian American Feminists Breathe Fire*, ed. Sonia Shah (Boston: South End Press, 1997).
118. Nathan Newman, *Net Loss: Internet Prophets, Private Profits, and the Costs to Community* (University Park: Penn State University Press, 2002), Conclusion.
119. Hardt and Negri, *Empire*, 346–47.

is "the erosion of the contexts in which events call for responses and, thus, in which it makes sense to act all."[120]

Transnational subjectivities can increase individual well-being through gains made in gray areas *at the same time* that sovereign power is asserted, ensuring further political precariousness. Biopolitical discourse and policies, combined with "grassroots activism," reinforce binary modes of operation and allow for a contradictory situation: these workers sustain the low-tier workforce even while they are treated as potential threats to national security. We must question any "war" that punishes status more than criminal acts and that enables a subject to gain something even while denigrating that subject. The combination of low-tier work conditions in a more global economy with the War on Drugs and the War on Terror can only lead to more ambivalence and to the strengthening of sovereignty over and above democratic activity.

As Agamben has argued, the stateless and refugees must become the model for a new citizenship that is without borders and that challenges the logic of biopower.[121] Resistance is always possible, but it will only be meaningful once politics is no longer defined by bare life. Once we begin to treat individuals who occupy politically ambivalent spaces not as deviants or criminals but as the center of a new politics, we may begin to envision a postnational citizenship and create new spaces for *sustained* democratic action.

Protest

Consider the implications were a broad, popular political movement to press for welfare policy to include a guaranteed social income to all adults, which would provide adequately for subsistence and also participation in social life. For such a demand to be made, the old dichotomies must already have started to break down—the opposition between paid and unpaid work [. . .] between full- and part-time work, between public and private work, between independence and dependence, between work and welfare.[122]
—CAROLE PATEMAN

Protest and nongovernmental activism, including union activity, are absolutely essential to respond to the problems I have posed in this book.

120. Markell, "The Rule of the People," 2.
121. Agamben, "We Refugees."
122. Pateman, *The Disorder of Women*, 202–3.

Nevertheless, institutional solutions are necessary for several reasons. First, the democratic context of protest always matters—the reception to protest, organizing, and community and civic group activities always shapes the behavior of actors and the outcomes of these efforts. It is unrealistic to think that democratic power can have any stability or longevity without some sort of institutional support.

Second, the social safety net is best administered by a mix of governmental institutions and self-help groups rather than faith-based groups or other types of charity. When individuals must rely on "compassion" or "tolerance," their moral worth is then used as the basis on which judgments about their survival depend.[123] Nevertheless, a social safety net need not be administered solely at the nation-state level. As authors like Sassen, Hardt and Negri, and Schwartz have argued, centers of power and authority operate at the urban *and* transnational levels. Only after political and financial powers are redistributed in this manner will *maquiladora* workers, service workers brought in through regional trade agreements, and other transnational groups be politically equal to native-born individuals. The hierarchies of reproductive and productive work, gendered wage systems, racial wage differentials, legal versus illegal immigrants, and so on, should all be rejected so that all labor is recognized as productive. Once this comes about, a minimum income will be able to replace welfare and indicate the contributions that all individuals make. Job creation through public works, as was initiated during the Depression, would provide work under less coercive circumstances than the current workfare program.

Third, a crucial factor in creating more democratic contexts for action is recognition of the importance of collective bargaining and representation. Transnational groups like the International Labor Organization (ILO) should have equal weight with national groups, and unionization should be permitted for groups formerly considered bound labor: workfare recipients, prisoners, and guest workers, among others. Furthermore, democratic international groups should have consultative and voting rights both in national governments and at the United Nations.

Fourth, essential to creating more openness to democratic activity is the recognition that civil disobedience and group organizing are time-honored, democratic ways of fostering debate, educating the public, and

---

123. On compassion, see Karen Zivi, "Contesting Motherhood in the Age of AIDS: Maternal Ideology in the Debate over Mandatory HIV Testing," *Feminist Studies* 31, no. 2 (2005): 347–74.; on tolerance, see Wendy Brown, *Regulating Aversion: Tolerance in the Age of Identity and Empire* (Princeton: Princeton University Press, 2006).

expressing dissent. The unprecedented use of free speech zones and exclusion zones by President George W. Bush is a reflection of the zeitgeist—the idea that we are in an endless war with no clear enemy. It must be recognized that national security measures are not securing democracy and in fact are significantly detracting from it.

Institutional openness to civil disobedience, civic groups, and mass protest should be matched by the public recognition that all forms of extra-institutional protest are vital, given the shifting boundaries of political power and citizenship. First and most obviously, protest is always a necessary corrective to the black/white, either/or questions on a ballot. Protesters set their own agenda, one that always goes beyond any bounds the government might set. Second, too many issues are now regional or transnational in nature to rely on nation-state politics alone. Some examples are Shell Oil's collusion with the Nigerian government at the expense of that country's citizens. A lawsuit filed in an international court awarded residents what they thought they were due. Because local communities affected by multinational corporations do not often have any formal way of influencing a company's decisions, protest is absolutely necessary, and it has been found to be effective.[124] Workers in free zones (for example, in the Mariana Islands and Jamaica) and in the Border Industrial Program are also in a legal and economic gray area that is inadequately represented by the nation-state. What is more, the nation-state is often cooperating with corporations at the expense of workers. This is increasingly true now that corporations are being given more rights as "individuals"—that is, as superindividuals whose rights somehow trump those of other individuals.[125] Also, environmental degradation, workers' rights and protections, and trade practices are most often regional issues and therefore cannot be dealt with at the domestic level.

A third reason for protest is that it encourages groups that are clinging to their "authentic" identities to loosen their grip and recognize that protest should revolve around common interests, common grievances, and common goals. It may seem idealistic to talk about the educative aspects of protest and organizing, but examples abound of groups forming coalitions and recognizing common issues. In one case, in the Pacific Northwest, mostly white Boeing workers who had been demoted or laid off actively sought the cooperation of workers generally perceived as new to the workforce: immigrants, minorities, and women.[126] In another case,

124. For example, the Brent Spar case.
125. See Newman, *Net Loss,* Introduction.
126. I thank Paul Gomberg, Chicago State University, for this insight.

highly disparate groups have accepted the broad and artificial label of "Asian" in order to organize on common issues; as a consequence, the Asian Immigrants Workers Association (AIWA) has been exerting enormous influence in the garment industry. Other groups have been banding together under the label "Latino" (or "Hispanic") in spite of the broad disparities among these groups. In this context, it is obviously not just a matter of the government opening itself to dissent. But workers' recognize that the problem is their work conditions and labor relations; it is not scabs, strikebreakers, or those who may undercut wages. The successful partnership between United Auto Workers organizers and the leaders of Justice for Janitors indicates that new approaches—speaking more than one language, showing familiarity with workers' cultural backgrounds, knowing their specific issues—and new tactics—working the media, going after those who may be only indirectly implicated in a case—can work when given a chance. These organizers are in a unique position to educate workers and foster cooperation, and their importance here should be acknowledged. Similarly, NGO protesters have been educating the public through debates, provocations, and various forms of "street theater." The alternative media have been doing vital work in opening debates and challenging the "manufactured consent" that is an increasing problem in today's mainstream media.

The Internet—the "ether," as Hardt and Negri call it[127]—is ensuring that even the most remote or marginal groups can communicate with other groups as well as with policymakers to air their demands. Access to the Internet may still be limited in many areas; even so, it has revolutionary potential to create holes not only in national exclusiveness and territorial boundedness but also in capitalist domination. Now classic examples include the Zapatista movement, the Seattle protesters, and protests at meetings of the G-7.[128] The uses to which the Internet is being put are already demonstrating what Hardt and Negri have posited—that capital is "parasitical" on workers rather than the reverse. Using the tools of capitalism *against* capitalism amounts to a recognition that there is no "outside" to power; it also demonstrates that resistance today must confront repressive institutionalized power by reflecting its dispersion and nonterritoriality as well as its local character. The Internet enables groups with varied agendas to work in solidarity without homogenizing their differences.[129]

127. Hardt and Negri, *Empire*, 346.
128. See Newman's conclusion in *Net Loss*.
129. See, for example, Naomi Klein's "Does Protest Need a Vision?" *New Statesman*, July 2000, http://www.newstatesman.com.

To put it differently, protest and extra-institutional activity should be made the centerpiece of democratic politics instead of a mere supplement to voting. "Freedom is never voluntarily given by the oppressor," and those who want equality should not wait: these two ideas should be central to democratic politics, as Martin Luther King once argued. This is not to discount the role that institutions and the law should play; rather, it is to acknowledge that the most significant advances in equality have been made through war (the Civil War), dissent (the Civil Rights Movement), and unions (the International Brotherhood of Sleeping Car Porters). Today, protest is the only way to address adequately the transnational character of those individuals, groups, and institutions that wield the most power.

One example of this involves the homeless. They group together for companionship and survival; but in addition, in nearly every major city they run and sell newspapers. As Len Doucette (the editor of *Hard Times,* a homeless newspaper) has stated, this is deliberately political activity. Efforts to ban such activity undercut political agency; they also make it more difficult to keep the issue of homelessness "in people's faces," in that members of this group are not allowed to occupy public space.[130] Another example is groups such as MECHA to La Raza and recent efforts to unionize Latino and Asian workers, which remind us (if we have forgotten) that immigrants have been organizing ever since they began entering the United States. These activities should not be interpreted as separatist; rather, they should be seen on their own terms and for what they really are, which is avenues of dissent and political activism. The too common perception is that immigrants do not assimilate and that these groups prove it; but that view ignores that they represent what is truly the test of any society's democracy—whether dissent is not merely tolerated but respected on its own terms.[131] The WTO protests in Seattle in 1999 are one example of how contemporary dissent has been depicted as anarchical, empty of meaning, and the work of childish societal outcasts with incongruent goals.[132] Even urban violence and gang activity—rather, activities labeled as these by the mainstream media—can be viewed politically. Despite what the media say, inner-city violence (and gang violence in particular) is not necessarily meaningless, nihilistic, or mindlessly

---

130. Antonio Olivo, "City Without a Porpoise: A Santa Monica Solution to Panhandling," *LA Weekly,* July 1–7, 1994, 15.

131. On this subject, see Alejandro Portes and Rubén Rumbaut, *Immigrant America* (Berkeley and Los Angeles: University of California Press, 1996), Conclusion.

132. See Klein's Web discussions of these portrayals.

destructive. It can also signal political frustration and outrage.[133] These
groups and activities are absolutely outside the realm of the juridical, but
it does not necessarily follow that they are treasonous and threatening;
from another angle, they are just as easily the essence of the political *because*
they are spontaneous, collective, and contingent. The forms of dissent as
just described should be viewed as alternative paths—as concrete efforts
at political organizing that challenge unitary sovereignty and that hold
acts of prerogative accountable.

Power, Agency, and the Future

The question is this: How can authentic love—instead of recasting the
political as a transcendence of the biological—bring about the second
meaning of the political as agonistic democratic action and effectively
challenge the growing predominance of the first as prerogative power?
Instead of giving a blanket answer, I will focus on three concrete examples.

To institutionalize a more open context of reception, the legal exploitation of workers must end. For example, the category of guest worker
must be abolished. Essentially, it is a form of legal indentured servitude.
A glance at the government's H-2 website does not even deny this; instead,
it explains that the nature of the work justifies it. Apparently, child labor
is vindicated for the same reasons. As of this writing, eighteen states
lack a minimum age for guest workers; in other states, the minimum
age is nine or ten. We must ask ourselves why it is acceptable for these
workers to face dangerous and debilitating conditions (the loss of limbs,
the inhaling of dangerous chemicals) when those same conditions are not
acceptable for middle-class, American-born citizens. Similar dynamics
face workers in the meatpacking and garment industries.

Deregulation has opened a space for the exercise of prerogative power
and the sharply unequal treatment of foreign employees. To reinstitute
worker protections, ranging from safe work conditions to the right of free
agency, would not only lengthen these workers' lives but also challenge
the current limits of our citizenship. A more global world must be matched
by a more global politics as well as by work conditions that ensure that
illiteracy, injury, and death (not to mention conditions that are arguably a
form of indentured servitude) cannot be part of "low-wage strategies" or

---

133. With regard to the political meaning of urban violence, see Wolin, "Democracy and
the Welfare State"; Sassen, *Civilization and Its Discontents*.

deregulation. It is a joke to argue that the total control of these workers and the coercion involved—including forcing workers to ignore illnesses and to be on call for twenty-four hours in remote regions of the Southwest—is part of a "free market." In this regard, corporations and agribusiness should not receive the same protections as true individuals. Note well here the irony of our own protectionist policies in the agriculture industry, which shut down agribusiness elsewhere and which have practically forced workers from the Caribbean and Central America to leave their countries and accept conditions such as these.

A politics of authentic love would involve "risks," including allowing workers to demonstrate, bargain, and possibly "infiltrate" society. A politics of authentic love would recognize that self-help groups, ethnic communities, and bilingualism allow a healthy transition into society and do not demonstrate anti-assimilationist behavior.[134] And a politics of love would preclude sinking into bare life, which is what has certainly happened in this country (despite hard-won gains). Pragmatically, it must be recognized that the underlying assumption of guest-worker programs—that workers will eventually leave—has been flawed,[135] and that regardless, they are not merely factors of production whose existence and desires can be defined economically. Provision must be made for this reality and the boundaries of citizenship made more hospitable. European countries that have extended foreign workers political rights, safe workplaces, and the right to organize have effectively dismantled traditional modern citizenship and are modeling the political inclusion that will be necessary in order to bring about a more integrated world.[136] This is true de jure, even though, admittedly, recent riots and uprisings demonstrate that inclusion and integration have not been achieved de facto as well. More broadly, U.S. immigration policies are now based on a binary of legal versus criminal; as a consequence, immigrants are being policed but nothing is being done to help them integrate. Host countries such as Sweden foster positive sorts of incorporation by helping immigrants in a multitude of ways; respect is shown for their cultures and languages, and immigrant councils are allowed to take part in policymaking.[137]

In the matter of welfare to workfare, coercive efforts to control poor women's reproduction, marriage rates, abortions, work attitudes, and so

134. See Honig, *Democracy and the Foreigner;* Portes and Rumbaut, *Immigrant America.*
135. See Sassen, *Civilization and Its Discontents;* Portes and Rumbaut, *Immigrant America.*
136. See Yasemin Soysal, *Limits of Citizenship: Migrants and Postnational Membership in Europe* (Chicago: University of Chicago Press, 1994).
137. See ibid.

on must end. Authors ranging from T. H. Marshall to Carole Pateman to William Julius Wilson have argued that a universally available basic income would destigmatize welfare relief and delink racist and sexist associations from aid. Alternatives to welfare could include a Japanese model of "welfare" that provides long-term jobs to individuals,[138] or a public works model of work placement and training, such as was established during the Depression of the 1930s. In any case, the coercive and highly irrational elements of workfare must be terminated. Workfare, as it is, is clearly aimed at low-tier, dead-end jobs that further impoverish recipients. The ascetic elements of the welfare state have not achieved their purported goal; they have succeeded only in coercing recipients and forcing assimilation. Moreover, they are rooted in the control of biological life, evidenced by racist and sexist policies and by rhetoric associated with welfare/workfare. Finally, domestic work ranging from industrial homework to au pair positions to maid services must be valued equally with other jobs. If it were, then unequal pay, sexual abuse,[139] and the complete subsumption of the costs of health care and management would no longer be acceptable. The recognition of the domestic sphere as a worksite and thus the end of the private/public distinction once and for all would ensure that workers' very existence is not illegal or subject to violent or arbitrary actions on the part of employers. Allowing all workers—regardless of their status—to unionize and have basic safety standards that are applied equally to all would facilitate these changes.

A third area of the utmost importance in workers' lives is the revival of unions. As a precondition for this, the government must recognize that democratic organizing includes union activity. Furthermore, it must establish a National Labor Relations Board with elected members who will represent workers instead of corporate interests. Also, employers who are antiunion must be pressured by citizens, workers, and NGOs to accept union activity in workplaces as valid. Unions themselves must move away from the 1950s and 1960s style of organizing. Most major unions that have survived today have in fact adjusted their recruitment practices and are signing up racial minorities, women, and immigrants. Smaller groups fighting for unionization have also emerged, with varying success.[140] These

138. See Dani Rodrik, "Feasible Globalizations," http://ksghome.harvard.edu/~.drodrik.academic.ksg/Feasglob.pdf.

139. See Human Rights Watch, "Migrant Domestic Workers Face Abuse in the U.S.," June 14, 2001, http://hrw.org/English/docs/2001/06/14/usdom176_txt.htm.

140. See Paul Apostolidis's ongoing work in this regard, for example, "La Lucha y La Casa: Neopolitics of the Labor Movement," conference paper presented at the meeting of the Western Political Science Association, Oakland, March 2005.

groups will be truly effective and democratic when they reach beyond their own "racial" or "ethnic" identities and include all workers. A number of critics have argued that a politics of deconstruction is unrealistic or leads to cultural relativism; others, such as Iris Marion Young, Judith Butler, Chantal Mouffe, and Kirstie McClure, have replied forcefully that coalitions can be formed based on action, goals, and democratic ideals rather than essentialized identities. Historically, the best coalitions have reflected this spirit.

Finally, political theorists must disabuse themselves of the notion that the poor are apathetic. Many examples exist of efforts to unionize, form community self-help groups, and protest working conditions; beyond this are examples of daily microresistance. Antisweatshop movements and the organizing efforts of Justice for Janitors and are evidence of this. In fact, Hardt and Negri are quite optimistic about what these activities mean. However, as Gopal Balakrishnan puts it: "Decades later, Empire offers by contrast an optimism of the will that can only be sustained by a millenarian erasure of the distinction between the armed and the unarmed, the powerful and the abjectly powerless."[141] So the issue is not the apathy of the poor—there are many instances that contradict this image—but power asymmetries that limit spaces (dialogical, geographical, and so on) in which to exercise dissent, disagreement, and political mobilization. The difficulty is that the meanings of the political—the notions that inform our sovereignty—have been laid out in terms of bare life and prerogative power (two sides of the same coin), while politics as democracy and grass-roots organizing is increasingly devalued or criminalized. Flexible labor, guest-worker programs, and low-wage strategies have subsumed transcendence in favor of immanence. This would not be a problem if immanence were not historically devalued and a site of arbitrary power. Authentic love as respecting and not merely tolerating difference is a model of holding immanence and transcendence in healthy tension rather than placing them hierarchically. In this respect, the War on Drugs, the War on Terror, and our endless wars against the poor must be critically examined and ultimately stopped.

The issue, however, does not lie simply with poor workers and their need to rise up—it lies with all of us and what we find acceptable as a political community. Everyone is implicated in the problems of the poor— not in terms of charity or some abstract appeal to a common humanity,

141. Gopal Balakrishnan, "Virgilian Visions," *New Left Review* 5 (September–October 2000): 147. See Fredric Jameson, "Globalization and Political Strategy," *New Left Review*

but because elites and the middle classes profit from their labor, demand the policing of their neighborhoods, are relieved when walls are built, and tolerate abominable conditions because we have a religious faith in trickle-down economics. Everyone is implicated in low-tier working conditions, not just in the United States but abroad. But most importantly, as a civilization, we have reached the point where the stateless are not simply second-class citizens or noncitizens but treated as subhumans. No amount of organizing of the poor can change that—collectively we must act.

INDEX